Enhancing Teaching Practice in Higher Education

HILDESHEIM STUDIES
IN INTERCULTURAL COMMUNICATION

Herausgegeben von / Edited by
Friedrich Lenz, Stephan Schlickau und / and Beatrix Kreß

VOLUME 11

*Zu Qualitätssicherung und Peer Review
der vorliegenden Publikation*

Die Qualität der in dieser Reihe
erscheinenden Arbeiten wird vor der
Publikation durch einen Herausgeber der
Reihe geprüft.

*Notes on the quality assurance and peer
review of this publication*

Prior to publication, the quality of the
works published in this
series is reviewed by one of the editors
of the series.

Beatrix Kress / Holger Kusse (eds.)

Enhancing Teaching Practice in Higher Education

International Perspectives on Academic Teaching and Learning

PETER LANG

Bibliographic Information published by the Deutsche Nationalbibliothek
The Deutsche Nationalbibliothek lists this publication in the Deutsche
Nationalbibliografie; detailed bibliographic data is available in the internet at
http://dnb.d-nb.de.

Library of Congress Cataloging-in-Publication Data
A CIP catalog record for this book has been applied for
at the Library of Congress.

Printed with support of the Erasmus + Programme of the European Union:
PROJECT N°: 586225-EPP-1-2017-1-DE-EPPKA2-CBHE-JP ENTEP
The European Commission's support for the production of this
publication does not constitute an endorsement of the contents, which
reflect the views only of the authors, and the Commission cannot be
held responsible for any use which may be made of the information
contained therein.

ISSN 1686-372X
ISBN 978-3-631-86097-7 (Print)
E ISSN 2750-8048
E-ISBN 978-3-631-88554-3 (E-PDF)
E-ISBN 978-3-631-88555-0 (EPUB)
DOI 10.3726/b20153
© Peter Lang GmbH
International Academic Publishers
Berlin 2023
All rights reserved.

Peter Lang – Berlin · Bruxelles · Lausanne · New York · Oxford

This publication has been peer reviewed.

www.peterlang.com

TABLE OF CONTENTS

Beatrix Kress, Holger Kusse

Enhancing Teaching Practices in Higher Education – Introduction

With the eponymous project for this book – ENTEP: Enhancing Teaching Practices in Higher Education in Russia and China – a highly interesting, sometimes rough, always exciting journey began in 2018. The focus of the project, on improving education and teaching in higher education, implies two prerequisites: That there are special teaching practices in higher education, which differ from other institutional settings, and that there are different ways of teaching and learning in higher education, depending on the cultural setting of the institution. What we have seen and learned through this project is the importance of a reciprocal understanding of the notions, assumptions and methods not only of higher education, but of science as a whole. Only a holistic approach is able to improve teaching practices, as they are embedded into a social, cultural and institutional handling of science, learning and teaching. Furthermore, a project like this one can only work on the basis of reciprocity: Improving practices means also learning from existing practices, bearing in mind not only the aforementioned differences, but also the common and uniting aspects of academia.

The present book represents this approach and the journey we made through this project. It documents strategies and policies in science, as well as political and scientific understandings of higher education and specific associated measures. Over the project's lifetime, it became apparent that the expectations with regard to higher education didactics in the various traditions and in the higher education policy contexts of the project partners are in some ways quite different. This pertains to methodological questions, but the social and moral tasks assigned to didactics, independent of a specific subject, are of concern as well. We have seen that the cultural (and therefore the normative, ideational and political) background interferes with the general concept and comprehension of education and science. A crucial event during the project, however, was the outbreak of the Covid-19 pandemic, which led to a shift in the project's research interests towards questions of digital teaching and learning. This is also reflected in the present volume through four contributions devoted to this subject, though we have decided to structure the present volume not by topic. We still see the local and cultural aspects as the unifying factor and have therefore arranged the contributions by area.

We begin with different inputs from Germany, Great Britain, Italy and Portugal. The contribution from Kathrin Schweiger and Beatrix Kress, *Written and Oral Communication as a Didactical Tool and the Relevance of Academic Genres in the Digital Space*, combines an overview of the two different forms of communication – the written and the spoken word – with the didactical expectations and the influence of all the changes caused by the digitalization of higher education during the pandemic.

In Holger Kusse's contribution, *Intercultural Teaching and Learning in Foreign Language Education. Using the Example of Teaching Russian*, language learning is considered from an intercultural point of view. The different factors, influences and challenges of intercultural didactics in foreign language teaching are discussed. At the end, Kusse reflects on these considerations against the background of this specific project, which makes theoretical assumptions applicable.

Maureen Royce, Madeleine Stevens, Joshi Jariwala and David Soehren discuss in their contribution, *Perspectives of Authentic Assessment and Professional Practice Interventions in Teaching and Learning in UK Higher Education*, the general principles of curriculum development and assessment, considering the requirements of professional practice. Their observations are then aligned with a specific module in human resource management and the authors show how the principles are implemented in this case.

Whereas Royce, Stevens, Jariwala and Soehren provided an example from their home university, Liverpool John Moores University, Aurora Ricci takes the University of Bologna as a model. She returns to the pandemic as a call for renewal in *The Innovation of Learning and Teaching Practices in Higher Education: A Methodological Focus on the University of Bologna's Model*. Here, she presents learner- and teacher-focused activities to face the challenge of remote learning and illustrates them with a case study and quantitative, evaluative data.

Olga Mennecke returns the focus to language learning, but the situation caused by Covid-19 is also a key factor in her considerations. As language learning is associated with a face-to-face arrangement, she discusses the factors influencing students' motivation in her contribution, *Contentualizing Students' Motivation in Online Language Courses*, and gives examples of how to deal with distance language learning.

In her contribution, *New Prospects in Higher Education: Hybrid Learning Environments and Creative Teaching*, Susana Gonçalves takes general reflections on societal change and the changes caused by the pandemic as a starting point to reflect on the factor of creativity in higher education and hybrid teaching.

The changes and challenges brought about by Covid-19 also play a major role in the chapters from Russia, starting with the contribution from Irina

Pervukhina, Marina Vidrevich and Natalia Vlasova. Under the title *Impact of the COVID-19 Pandemic on Modern Management Technologies in Higher Education as Knowledge-Intensive Activity*, the authors give a general and statistical overview of the progression of the pandemic in higher education from both the international and the Russian perspective, highlighting the impact of this situation on management, teaching and learning in universities.

Tatiana Tregubova, Irina Ainoutdinova and Vadim Kozlov present a deep insight into foreign language learning and teaching. After introducing the history and variety of methods, they pursue the *Transformation from Conventional Methods to Web-based Technologies: Enhancing FLT/FLL Practices in Russian Universities*, again seeing Covid-19 as an impetus. The authors discuss methods and influencing factors, and also introduce the necessary first steps for establishing efficient digital methods in foreign language teaching and learning.

The perspective in the contribution from Sergei Vasin, Konstantin Korolev, Tatiana Razuvaeva is, on the one hand, broader, as they look into general teaching and learning strategies and the systematic transformation needed to change those. But *Enhancing Teaching Practice in HEIs through the Development of University Learning and Teaching Strategy* is, on the other hand, a microscopic view, as the authors examine the case of Penza State University, one of the project universities.

Three contributions from China complete the volume. In *Improving Teaching Practice in Higher Education from the Perspective of Learning Science*, Juan Fu develops a teaching system in higher education against the background of higher education policy in China in accordance with the findings of learning psychology. New technologies in teaching, such as massive open online courses (MOOCs), are also taken into account.

Starting from the concept of respect, Tang Xueming describes the requirements for English teachers who should also provide moral education at the same time. *Effective Ways of Integrating Moral Education into College English Teaching* focuses on this practice at the college level.

The last contribution in the volume, *The Present Situation, Dilemma and Path of Internationalization of Higher Education in the Central Region of China – Taking S University as an Example*, by Qin Yuan and Yigang Peng, can be seen as a kind of project summary from a Chinese perspective. It deals with the internationalization of universities, one of the major goals of the project. The authors describe the internationalization strategies of one university against the background of regional differences in internationalization at Chinese universities.

In the end, the projects summary is differentiated. The journey changed through the course of the pandemic and the ensuing situation in still-surprising ways. Project meetings and conferences could not be held in person, but were organized through video conferences. This book, standing at the end of the project, reflects this in many ways. However, this book and the project behind it are unique in another and – at least for many of us – unexpected and sad way. The world is always changing, but in February 2022, we find it in a state in which a project like this would no longer be possible. So looking back, we cherish the experiences we had through the ENTEP journey, and we still hope that the world will change again – for the better.

Kathrin Schweiger, Beatrix Kress

Written and Oral Communication as a Didactical Tool and the Relevance of Academic Genres in the Digital Space

Abstract: The aim of this paper is to discuss the role of different forms of communication in teaching in higher education and their functions in face-to-face teaching and learning and in the digital surrounding. At the same time, the question is asked to what extent oral and written communication and academic text genres have changed due to the pandemic and/or which text genres have emerged newly through digital tools.

Keywords: Teaching and learning discourse, genre, oral and written communication, digitalization

Introduction

The pandemic-related changeover to online teaching led to a series of further training measures for university didactics. At the beginning, the question was: Which video conferencing system is best suited or, to put it more bluntly: Which system is the quickest to get to grips with and the most cost-effective and technically least susceptible to faults? In a second phase, the focus was on getting to know and using so-called tools; didactic added value was then to be derived from their applicability. At the Hildesheim University, it is primarily the department of teaching development and university didactics that deals with (digital) university continuing education programs in teaching. In the course of short presentations, the following digital tools or similar were presented in the period between 2020 and 2021: Mahara: The e-portfolio software, Powtoon animated, Sciflow: Collaborative scientific work, Digital Kanban boards, Digital pinboards Digital notebooks, Etherpad, Rocket.Chat (etc.).

During the hectic discussion about instruments, which might function under the given circumstances, actual purposes and functions of communication in higher education got somewhat out of sight. When we talk about communication we have in mind that this means more than the sheer transfer of information. Communication and especially the formed or shaped communication – shaped through the mediated transmission – is functional in itself, it is purposive through its form (cf. Ehlich 2017, p. 22). This counts even more for the communication in higher education, which is formed even more strictly. The task of information transfer is accompanied by educational goals, which contributes to the expectations on the right form. Teacher in higher education have a very certain concept of a term paper, an oral presentation, a seminar paper or even a discussion in class. Against this background, it is the more surprising that even now, after almost 20 months of online teaching, communication and its different forms play no or just a minor role in higher education didactic training. If we look at the plan and the titles of an online course on "new e-learning" at the University of Hildesheim as an example, we find a lot of lectures on tools, but almost nothing on communication:

1. Combined visualization! Application examples of tool linking from (political) teacher: inside education – Padlet, Mangatar and Co.
2. HilChat: A Campus App at Hildesheim University
3. Development of a digital platform for innovative teaching
4. Learning in three-dimensional rooms
5. etc.

Academic Communication: Written and Oral Text Genres

Looking deeper into these lectures and presentations we actually find discussions on communication – often hidden behind other terms such as "establish and maintain social presence in digital surroundings" and so on; however, the challenges and problems are not directly linked to communication itself by the speakers and participants.

As already mentioned above, teachers in higher education do have a very distinct concept of communicative forms in their teaching, especially when it comes to examination and assessment. So academic teaching and learning takes place within the framework of academic text genres. Text genres are usually defined as conventionally valid patterns for complex linguistic actions. They exhibit typical combinations of contextual (situational), communicative-functional and structural (grammatical and thematic) features. Furthermore, they developed historically in the language community and therefore belong to the everyday knowledge of language participants. They have a standardizing effect, but at the same time they facilitate communicative interaction by providing communicators with more or less fixed orientations for the production and reception of texts (Brinker 2010, p. 135).

Usually text genres as results of a longer process are immediate or primary categories. Academic genres however are instruments to process knowledge and scientific findings and therefore they are highly taken over by different expectations. Students at the university have to deal with very different academic genres, as "for the student, genres serve as keys to understanding how to participate in the actions of the community." (Miller 1984, p. 165) Students have to write term papers, final papers, exams, minutes of seminar meetings, write excerpts and thesis papers and take notes in lectures. In university teaching, it is above all the persecutive text genres that are central to process knowledge/in learning, i.e. such text genres that have a high degree of processing. Here it is not a matter of generating new knowledge, as in the case of generative text types (scientific articles), but rather of retaining, reproducing, and processing the knowledge that has been absorbed. The lecture, for example, a central oral text genre, is flanked by note taking, a processing text genre, fulfilled by students. It has an informal character, i. e. it is usually not made public and its purpose is to record the contents of the lecture.

Certain aspects can be pointed out using the example of the lecture and the corresponding notes. The academic genres range between orality and writing. In addition – and also depending on its written and/or oral character – these text genres place different cognitive demands on the students. For example, Ehlich (2003, p. 18) defined the different cognitive processing of individual text genres in terms of their degree of orality and writing and against the background of "whether they are more discursive or more textual in nature." The written/spoken paradigm can be understood as a continuum between a written text form, that has to meet the demand for scientific linguistic precision, and the oral form, that has to correspond especially with the social expectation to interpersonal interaction, while it is still scientific in nature. So, the expectations related to the persecutive genres in higher education are also linked to the expectations we have concerning orality and writing. To sum it up: Text genres in the academic world and in higher education are not just historically grown and conventionalized solutions for complex linguistic challenges, but they are on the one hand places where certain educational/cognitive goals are to be achieved, and on the other hand there form/patterns (written, oral) are part of a social expectation: Knowing how is the prerequisite to play in science.

However, historically evolved solutions can also be seen as historically changeable solutions that have grown in a cultural and linguistic community. It can therefore be assumed that the linguistic community's preferred solution paths have changed under the influence of extra-linguistic factors, precisely due to technological innovations, and medial changes etc. To put it more abstract: Form has not only an impact on function, form and function are interrelated (cf. Ehlich 2017). So, it can be assumed that the digital changes of the past 20 months effected the text genres itself and therefore also the inherent character (orality vs. writing) as well as the possible cognitive outcomes for the students and the related expectations of teachers.

Example 1: Communication in Videoconference-Based Seminars

We would like to demonstrate this on the example of the discussions taking place in the classroom. Classroom debates have been in the times of face-to-face learning clearly oral, and therefore linked to certain expectations and learning outcomes. Here, not only the transfer of knowledge plays a key role, but also the capability of taking a stand, of argumentation and evaluation. An acceleration of knowledge and the creation of new insights is expected through that (cf. Lemke 1990, pp. 87–124; Redder 2014, pp. 32–33; Ehlich 2014, pp. 45–48; Kreß 2021). This is accompanied by social goals: Although argumentation, debate and scientific dispute are paramount, the standpoints should be carried out in a socially acceptable way. Relational work and also finding compromises are at work. So, the expectation is an oral, scientifically appropriately phrased contribution.

Looking at digital synchronous teaching via video conferencing, we have to do with certain limitations and/or changes. Due to the missing physical presence the social presence is also limited, especially as the participants have the opportunity (and quite often do so due to technical reasons) to switch of the camera. The participants can be identified by names, but their facial expression is missed. Moreover, as Coman et al. (2020, p. 14) also points out, the "vast majority of students prefer to interact more with teachers in writing, on chat/ forum (52.4 %)". This creates a situation, where the usual communication in the classroom is transferred partially or completely into the written form.

Against this background certain observations can be made, concerning the teaching and learning discourse. First of all, the usual setting of a seminar (as distinguished from a lecture) changes, as it is way more teacher centered than before. The teacher might feel like tight up in a long monologue. However, as some kind of a side effect, a pattern develops that could be called "the comment section", comparable to social media, where we can find the main contribution of some identifiable author, and then remarks of a confirming or criticizing or just associative kind by so called followers. In the videoconference-based seminar the chat function is used for this kind of side communication. In the following section an illustrative and prototypical authentic example from a seminar on "Language and Migration":

ai
00:20:16
man passt sich automatisch an die kultur an
one automatically adapts to the culture

ai
00:30:45
unmut
resentment

am
00:31:08
Ausgrenzung
marginalization

ai
00:31:11
viel sich fremd an. ein nicht akzeptabler mensch
much strange. a not acceptable person

ai
00:31:31
*fühlt
**feel (strange)*

gm
00:32:39
im pflichtpraktikum in tokio, begenete mir der begrif gaijin auch noch :/
during the mandatory internship in tokio i meat also the notio gaijin :/

mh
00:36:29
Mittlerweile ist doch "Gaikokujin" im öffentlichen Raum üblich, oder? Also ist es zumindest unhöflich, wenn es z.B. von einem Polizisten verwendet wird.
Meanwhile "Gaikokujin" is costumary in public space, isn't it? Hence it is at least impolite used e. g. by a policeman.

This "side communication" is triggered by a remark of the lecturer "Apart from migration, you for sure now the feeling of being a stranger in a new cultural surrounding." The statement is not intonationally marked as an interrogative form, the only hint to some kind of – then rather rhetorical – question is the adverbial expression "for sure". In any case, it leads to the thread shown above, which is characterized by certain remarkable features. It has traces of orality and of written communication, merged in an interesting way: Whereas spelling is suspended by some participants concerning capitalization, which is of some importance in the orthography of German (cf. "kultur"/Kultur, "unmut"/Unmut, "mensch"/

Mensch, "tokio"), punctuation as one of the key features of textual communication, is used quite consequently (although wrong in some cases). Typos are
not corrected ("begenete"/begegnete, "begrif"/Begriff), a lexical mistake/mix-up
(interestingly based on phonetical likeness, but this might also be the result of
speech recognition at the device used there) "viel"/"fühlt", that might lead to a
misunderstanding, is updated. Elliptic one word expressions ("Ausgrenzung")
and tag questions ("oder?") could count as a signal of orality, whereas the lexical
items themselves are clearly not everyday language, but rather from the common
scientific vocabulary (e. g. "öffentlicher Raum"/public space). The past tense is
not compound, which is also typical for the written language. And then the use
of emojis (:/) can be observed, although the chat function does not offer them
automatically and they have to be produced using signs. In sum, this rather special language use – written orality, oral text with the special features of social
media – is typical for social applications such as Instagram, Youtube etc., so we
might see this phenomenon as a sign for social presence and the emerging of
some text patterns (not yet genre maybe) that is rather new for the academic
paradigm and higher education.

Despite the expectation concerning certain limitations and the observation
above that a chat accompanying video conferencing is rather a place for side
comments, short remarks and the social part of communication, it is possible
that shorter dialogical sequences and even some kind of discussions arise. This
can be seen even in the example above, where the remark of **gm** is questioned/
doubted by **mh**. In the next example from a seminar on political communication students were asked to position themselves towards the use of political talk-
shows in TV for informational purposes.

ls
00:43:14
Ich glaube, dass Talkshows dazu dienen, dass die Politiker das Publikum informieren
und dann natürlich die eigene Partei hervorzuheben, also eigentlich eine Mischung
aus beidem
I believe that talk-shows serve politicians to inform the audience, and of course to highlight
their own party, so it is a mixture of both

me
00:46:09
Also ich denke, es dient eher der Selbstinszenierung, aber das finde ich auch verständlich,
weil es glaube ich schon hilft, eine "Persönlichkeit" hinter der politischen Meinung
zu sehen
So I think, it serves rather self dramaturgical purposes, but I find this understandable, as it
is – I think – useful to see a personality behind the political opinion

ml
00:46:59
Ich finds schwer , wenn man ab und an mal Lanz schaut dann merkt man dass wenn der
sich auf jemanden eingedchossen hat dann ist das schon sehr jemanden zu torpedieren
*I find it difficult to decide. Watching from time to time "Lanz", one can see that when he
zeros in on somebody than it is difficult to jeopardize*

The statement of **me** relates to **ls**. It restricts the first statement and reinterprets it: it is "rather" something else. However, not only the opposition is important here, all participants are cautious with their opinion, they "think" and "believe", it is "rather" different or "difficult to decide". One might assume that the social side plays a role in this debate session despite the social distance. It can also be seen though, that technical limitations influence this kind of communication as well. The written communication in the chat is not to the same extent synchronous as the video conferencing itself, and so the last statement has been contributed only 50 seconds after the previous one, but it is full of typos and even syntactical mistakes, a part of the statement seems to be missing, so the whole contribution is hard to understand. Here, time and the affordances of the written medium clearly limit or impede the debate.

In sum, what can be seen here is that in these surroundings new patterns arise (which have models in other media settings), old patterns might be transferred also, but they show to some extent a different shape. Besides that, even new academic genres might develop, which will be discussed in the second part of this contribution.

Example 2: Changing Genres – From Oral Presentation to Screencast

Basically, one has to ask what the change of a text genre consists of and how much change it tolerates or needs before one can speak of the transition to a new text genre. To do this, one must know how one can recognize whether a series of text copies belong to one text genre. (Fix 2014). Fix suggests looking for propositional, functional, and formal correspondences. In addition, she notes the following tendencies/trends in text genre change (cf. Fix 2014, p. 21 et seq.):

1. **Mixedness:** genres are intertwined in one text genre (e. g. media-induced mixing of varieties/speech-slang; media-induced blending of orality and writing – e. g., email, chat, Twitter, advertising; mixing of genres).

2. **Interconnectedness** means that individual texts are related to each other in intentional, text genre-dependent relationships. Texts are used in functionally

and/or thematically bound text type networks. (e. g. hypertext in the electronic medium, the abstract placed in front of the scientific article).

3. **Fragmentation** means texts are interrupted or accompanied by other texts, which need not have any connection with the former. As a consequence, other modes of reception are necessary. The reception proceeds partly in succession, but partly also in cooperation (e. g. commercials in a TV movie: reception takes place one after the other).

4. **Non-finalization** means that texts can always be continued and also changed retroactively.

5. **Openness** to reception means that the direction and method of reception are not or that the content transfer is not completed (e. g. hyperlinks).

6. **Authorship diversity**: The fact that a text can have more than one author is related to the fact that texts are not closed and open to reception (e. g. blog, Wikipedia).

7. **Standardization**: The execution of texts is to a large extent predetermined. The reason for this is the economization of text production. This is especially true for institutional texts, e. g., text patterns with little leeway (official texts, diploma texts), text modules (official texts).

In Kreß/Schweiger (2021), we showed that the "screencast" has in part replaced the "live" student oral presentation or is used as an alternative and is possibly a variant/modification of the "student oral presentation" text genre. After all, the presentation is digitally preserved and it can affect the character of the text, whether it is stored digitally and read in a specific arrangement on the screen or whether it is written on paper or performed live. As indicated above, we assume a modification, since functional and propositional functions do not differ from the conventional student presentation, but there are just deviations of a formal nature. The following differences were found between Student oral presentation and Screencast.

In any case, it can be stated that the possibility to re-record the speech as often as necessary, thus eliminating the volatility of speech, virtually eliminates typical characteristics of oral language use (sentence breaks, for example). But also, the probability of plagiarism increases, if sentences and thoughts are taken over word for word without naming the source. Thus, the orally recorded text will increasingly approach the conceptual written form.

In the digital seminar room there is indeed an increased mixing of the written and the spoken – as Fix generally states in the case of changes in the genre of text (see *mixedness* (a)). Furthermore, the medially written commentary bar just described is then also repeatedly interrupted by the (re)playing of the lecturer's

Table 1 Student oral presentation vs. screencast

Student oral presentation	Screencast
facial expressions and gestures support understanding	no gesture and facial expression support
syntax lexical error discontinuation of syntax	error prevention by re-recording
hastiness of the spoken word makes it impossible to listen again	watching again and again if one has not understood something correctly
"feels more personal"	impersonal
space for intermediate questions and interaction -> spontaneous	no for intermediate questions and interaction
PDf or Powerpoint easier for storage	screencasts rather impractical as a storage option

PowerPoint slides (see *fragmentation* (c)), a genre of text that is in any case situated between orality and writing.

Example 3: Forum in a Digital Learning Surrounding

The screencast in example 2 demonstrates the shift from synchronous to asynchronous communication and towards the written pole of communication. The seminar discourse from example 1, already slightly asynchronous in an intermediate form of "oral writing", can also be shifted towards asynchronicity. The virtual space also makes it possible, for example, to outsource the entire seminar discourse to so-called forums. The word forum, from Latin, literally means a place surrounded by a board fence or an area divided off (with planks) (forus) and was then in ancient Roman cities a place for the administration of justice and the people's assembly. Today, according to the dictionary Duden, forum is understood to mean a suitable group of people, which guarantees an expert discussion of problems or issues, but also a public discussion, debate in general. As a further meaning is indicated: Platform, suitable place for something.

In the following teaching example, it is a seminar platform via moodle, in which students discuss the content of the presentation and exchange their opinions about it. In advance, the students have uploaded their presentation in the form of a screencast, time-independent it can be viewed. There are questions that should be discussed in the forum. Afterwards, the answers and reflections are summarized in short notes by the speaker and thus take over the function of another genre of text, namely the scientific protocol. The scientific protocol in its function of recording the seminar discourse seems to be "threatened

Fig. 1: Discussion forum

with extinction" in the digital teaching-learning context – video recordings or photographing the slides or the question whether a discourse arises at all seem to make the scientific protocol in its traditional way superfluous.

The following figure illustrates the digital course of the seminar unit and at the same time exhibits another "text genre trend" noted by Fix (2014), and that is that all texts (forum texts, screencast) are interdependent (*interconnectedness b))*: to participate in the discussion forum, the screencast must be seen beforehand.

Here, under "discussion forum" we actually have the reference to a type of discourse that we would absolutely assign to orality. A discussion, in fact, is a conversation between at least two people who are working on a particular topic, with each side presenting its arguments to support its point of view. In this case, the discussion shifts to a medially written environment. The question is, of course, to what extent the contributions are shaped. In contrast to the comment bar/chat mentioned above (Example 1), the participants have time to formulate their contribution to the discussion due to the extension of the speech situation. And in contrast to Internet forums, which are strongly conceptualized orally, the seminar forum shows that the contributions are strongly shaped and conceptually written.

Von xxx - Montag, 14. Juni 2021, 10:47

Das erste Bild lässt viel Raum für Interpretation, hätte bei mir aber ohne das Wissen über das Präsentationsthema nicht in die gewollte Richtung gelenkt. Das zweite Bild lässt kaum Spekulation zu, da es sich eindeutig um eine antirechtsradikale Kampagne handelt. Der diskursive Ansatz scheint bei solchen Aufgaben passend zu sein, setzt aber auch voraus, dass die Lernenden diese kulturellen Muster "ich bin stolz Deutscher zu sein" und "nicht jeder Deutsche ist blond und blauäugig" auch erkennen. Andernfalls ist es wichtig, sich damit im selben Zuge auseinanderzusetzen, um eine Position beziehen zu können und an dem Diskurs teilhaben zu können.

By xxx - Monday, 14 June 2021, 10:47

The first image leaves a lot of room for interpretation, but would not have steered me in the intended direction without knowledge of the presentation theme. The second image leaves little room for speculation, as it is clearly an anti-right-wing campaign. The discursive approach seems to be appropriate for such tasks, but also requires that the learners also recognize these cultural patterns "I am proud to be German" and "not every German is blond and blue-eyed". Otherwise, it is important to deal with them in the same course in order to be able to take a position and to participate in the discourse.

Sonntag, 20. Juni 2021, 11:12

Danke für deinen Beitrag. Hat der vorausgegangene Vortrag von Frau Steinke deine Interpretation der Bilder gelenkt bzw. hat dieser deine Assoziationen beeinflusst? Uns interessiert außerdem, woher dein Wissen, welches zu deinen Interpretationen und Vermutungen geführt hat, stammt. Ist dir das Thema Rechtsradikalismus in der Schule, in den Medien oder sogar im alltäglichen Leben schon begegnet?

Sunday, 20. June 2021, 11:12

Re: D Thank you for your contribution. Did the preceding lecture by Ms. Steinke guide your interpretation of the images or did it influence your associations? We are also interested in where your knowledge, which led to your interpretations and assumptions, came from. Have you encountered the topic of right-wing radicalism at school, in the media, or even in everyday life?

von YY - Dienstag, 15. Juni 2021, 11:20

Durch fehlende Wortelemente kann Bild 1 auf ganz verschiedene Weisen interpretiert werden, wohingegen Bild 2 deutlich eindeutiger ist. Dennoch liegt auch bei Bild 1 die Assoziation einer Anti-Rassismus-/Anti-Rechts-Kampagne nahe. Dies könnte daran liegen, dass solche Kampagnen häufig auf ähnliche Weise gestaltet werden. Das setzt wiederum voraus, dass Wissen darüber und über den Diskurs zum Thema vorhanden ist. Außerdem wird hier betont, dass nicht alle Deutschen einen bestimmten "Typ" entsprechen, sondern sehr unterschiedlich sind. Dieses Wissen ist entweder bereits vorhanden und wird aktiviert oder muss im Rahmen der Interpretation neu erlernt und eingeordnet werden. In diesem Fall kann die Kampagne einen guten Anhaltspunkt geben, um Stereotype herauszuarbeiten und zu widerlegen.

by YY - Tuesday, June 15, 2021, 11:20

Due to missing word elements, image 1 can be interpreted in quite different ways, whereas image 2 is much clearer. Nevertheless, the association of an anti-racism/

anti-rights campaign is also obvious in image 1. This could be due to the fact that such campaigns are often designed in a similar way. This, in turn, assumes knowledge about it and about the discourse on the topic. Furthermore, it is emphasized here that not all Germans correspond to a certain "type", but are very different. This knowledge is either already available and is activated or must be newly learned and classified in the context of the interpretation. In this case, the campaign can provide a good point of reference for elaborating and refuting stereotypes.

Sonntag, 20. Juni 2021, 11:31

Danke für deinen Kommentar! Interessant, dass du das vorangegangene Thema "Stereotypen" einbringst. Die Erläuterung, die wir dazu in dem Vortrag gehört haben, sind hier ebenfalls sehr gut einzubringen.

Sunday, 20 June 2021, 11:31

Thanks for your comment! Interesting that you bring in the previous topic of "stereotypes". The explanation we heard about this in the lecture are also very good to bring in here.

The degree of orality is quite low. The extended turn-taking and the address by means of the speaker deixis "your" as well as the speaker deixis in "we agree" reveal aspects of orality. Otherwise, the contributions are linguistically formulated in elaborated scientific language. We can see this from the use of terminology such as "cultural patterns", "the discursive approach" or "stereotypes". The authors not only adhere to orthography and write grammatically correct, but use rather complex syntactic structures and forms of de-personalization through passive constructions ore the use of indefinite pronouns ("man"/"one"). Also, when using connectors, care is taken to use them alternately.

The use of such a teaching-learning scenario allows to practice the connection between reception and production and to come to an active, critical reception attitude. Lecturers can support this process by providing structured feedback. Moreover, the forum "qualifies" here as a place to transform discursive orality into textual writtenness, whereby orality also approaches conceptual writtenness here, and it is thus only "a leap" to the elaborated, formed written text.

Conclusion

The Science community has different genres of texts to communicate its knowledge, which originate in different ways, e. g. primarily written (e. g. scientific article, protocols) or primarily oral (such as contributions to discussions at conferences or classroom/seminar discussions (cf. Foschi 2014). Further forms result from the combination of written and oral forms (Powerpoint). However, the prototypical medium for conveying and imparting knowledge is the written form, seen as the prototypical medium of knowledge transfer and mediation. Traditionally, knowledge must be "writable" and "printable" as Polenz notes (1981, p. 85), so that it can be cited.

According to our "digital experiences", writing is expanding in virtual communication, be it in the form of "comment lines" or in fully formed written contributions that are submitted in a time-delayed manner. Oral scientific communication, discussion and debate in the seminar room seem to be restricted by the virtual environment, but at the same time the possibility of expanding written scientific communication opens up within the framework of forums.

The medial change affects the modes of writtenness and orality. In this regard, Ehlich notes (2018), even before the pandemic caesura, that virtual environments lead to a shift of discursive orality to writtenness. However, he formulates it even more drastically, that orality is being forfeited and changed into a mediation-methodical finished product. Through this, discursivity is even pushed to the margins of university processes (2018, p. 18). The decline of discursivity through a decline of orality has direct consequences for the competencies we can build in higher education, but might also lead to changes in the way academics debate their findings in general, as the expectations to the way new findings are introduced and argued, might change. Which channels are adequate to talk about new findings for the first time? And do they have to described and argued in a discursive or textual way? When we think of new forms of scientific communication through e. g. social media, the observations of this paper might be interrelated also with these forms of scientific communication.

Literature

Brinker, Klaus: *Linguistische Textanalyse. Eine Einführung in Grundbegriffe und Methoden* (= Grundlagen der Germanistik; Bd. 29), Schmidt: Berlin, 2010 (7th edition).

Coman, Claudiu / Tiru, Laurentiu Gabriel / Mesesan-Schmitz, Luzia / Stanciu, Carmen / Bularca, Maria Cristina: "Online Teaching and Learning in Higher Education during the Coronavirus Pandemic: Students' Perspective". *Sustainability*, 2020 (12, 24), pp. 1–24, Doi: 10.3390/su122410367.

Ehlich, Konrad: "Universitäre Textarten, universitäre Struktur". In: Ehlich, Konrad / Steets, Angelika (eds.): *Wissenschaftlich schreiben – lehren und lernen*. Walter de Gruyter: Berlin / New York, 2003, pp. 13–28.

Ehlich, Konrad: "Argumentieren als sprachliche Ressource des diskursiven Lernens". In: Hornung, Antonie / Carrobio, Gabriella / Sorrentino, Daniella (eds.): *Diskursive und textuelle Strukturen in der Hochschuldidaktik: Deutsch und Italienisch im Vergleich*. Waxmann: Münster, 2014, pp. 41–54.

Ehlich, Konrad: "Zur Funktionalität von Form – Versuch". In: Krause, Arne / Lehmann, Gesa / Thielmann, Winfried / Trautmann, Caroline (eds.): *Form und Funktion. Festschrift für Angelika Redder zum 65. Geburtstag*. Stauffenburg Verlag: Tübingen, 2017, pp. 17–31.

Ehlich, Konrad: "Wissenschaftlich schreiben lernen – von diskursiver Mündlichkeit zu textueller Schriftlichkeit". In: Schmölzer-Eibinger, Sabine / Bushati, Bora / Ebner, Christopher / Niederdorfer, Lisa (eds.): *Wissenschaftliches lehren und lernen. Diagnose und Förderung wissenschaftlicher Textkompetenz in Schule und Universität*. Waxmann: Münster / New York, 2018, pp. 15–32.

Fix, Ulla: "Aktuelle Tendenzen des Textsortenwandels – Thesen". In: Hauser, Stefan / Kleinberger, Ulla / Roth, Kersten Sven (eds.): *Musterwandel – Sortenwandel. Aktuelle Tendenzen der diachronen Text(sorten)linguistik*. Peter Lang: Bern, 2014, pp. 15–48.

Foschi Albert, Marina: "Informale" Wissenschaftssprache: eine kontrastive (deutsch-italienische) Untersuchung der Beziehungen zwischen Mündlichkeit und Schriftlichkeit am Beispiel argumentativer Texte des akademischen DaF-Bereichs". In: Fandrych, Christian / Meißner, Cordula / Slavcheva, Adriana (eds.): *Gesprochene Wissenschaftssprache. Korpusmethodische Fragen und empirische Analysen*. Synchron: Heidelberg, 2014, pp. 207–224.

Kress, Beatrix / Schweiger, Kathrin: "Video Presentations, Video Conferences, Seminar Discourse or Oral Student Presentation? – Are "Traditional" Academic Genres Changing or even Disappearing?" SHS Web of Conferences 99, 01047 (2021), International Research Conference Proceedings, Jekaterinenburg, 2021. Doi:10.1051/shsconf/20219901047

Lemke, Jay L.: *Talking Science: Language, Learning, and Values*. Ablex Publishing Corporation: Greenwood, Norwood, NJ, 1990.

Miller, Carolyn R.: "Genre as Social Action". *Quarterly Journal of Speech*, 1984, pp. 151–167.

von Polenz, Peter: "Über die Jargonisierung von Wissenschaftssprache und wider die Deagentivierung". In: Bungarten, Theo (eds.): *Wissenschaftssprache. Beiträge zur Methodologie, theoretischen Fundierung und Deskription*. Fink: München, 1981, pp. 85–110.

Redder, Angelika: "Wissenschaftssprache – Bildungssprache – Lehr-Lerndiskurs". In: Hornung, Antonie / Carrobio, Gabriella / Sorrentino, Daniella (eds.). *Diskursive und textuelle Strukturen in der Hochschuldidaktik: Deutsch und Italienisch im Vergleich*. Waxmann: Münster, 2014, pp. 25–40.

Holger Kusse

Intercultural Teaching and Learning in Foreign Language Education. Using the Example of Teaching Russian

Abstract: In foreign language teaching cultural heterogeneity is one of the challenges of higher education. Instead of seeing this as a barrier, the task is to use inter- and transculturality as a resource for effective learning. The paper deals with intercultural didactics, develops models of heterogeneous learner groups and presents concrete methods of teaching and learning in culturally mixed classes. The article refers primarily to the teaching of Russian as a foreign language in Germany, where beginners with L1 in German or another language and heritage speakers of Russian usually learn together. It includes the following topics: An introduction into the problem of mixed classes in foreign language education (1), Challenges of interculturality and transculturality in foreign language teaching (2), Russian as a Foreign Language in Germany (3), Modeling effective foreign language teaching in culturally mixed classes (4).

Keywords: Intercultural communication, foreign language teaching, intercultural learning

Introduction: Mixed Classes and Interculturality in Foreign Language Teaching

In today's foreign language classroom, two cultural challenges come together. First, foreign language teaching is intrinsically intercultural. Learning a language means coming into contact with a culture of which the language is a part. If the language is truly foreign, i.e., completely new to the learner, he or she will find him or herself in an intercultural learning situation, even if he or she does not meet a native speaker and does not have the opportunity to visit countries where the language is primarily spoken. While this in the past used to be the norm for most learners and also for foreign language teachers, today learners not only have the opportunity to meet native speakers and visit the target countries or even live there for a while, but native speakers often come to their classes and learn together with them. From this follows the second challenge. The learning group itself becomes a place of intercultural encounter, which is not always harmonious, but can be full of conflict and is characterized at least by different learning prerequisites and language skills among its members.

This paper addresses some issues related to foreign language teaching in mixed classes at schools and universities. The focus is on Russian language teaching in Germany where, due to immigration from the Soviet Union and post-Soviet successor states, mixed learner groups are the rule rather than the exception in both universities and schools.

The example of Russian language teaching also shows that the requirements for foreign language teaching in culturally mixed classes go beyond issues of interculturality, which have been associated with the terms such as intercultural pedagogy or intercultural foreign language teaching since the late 1960s. Already the word *mixed* refers to a broad spectrum of diversity and encompasses more than just classes in which native and non-native speakers learn together, since even the concept of a native speaker today has to be considered in a very differentiated way. The competencies and cultural background of a so-called heritage speaker, for example, is not the same as that of a short-term exchange student from the target country or one of the target countries addressed in class.

Including the introduction the paper has four parts. The second part addresses basic issues of diversity and interculturality relevant to the effective teaching and learning management in foreign language teaching in mixed classes. The third part focuses on the Russian language teaching in Germany. Here, the history and current challenges of foreign language teaching are addressed. In the fourth part, a model for effective teaching in culturally mixed classes is developed, emphasizing diversity as a motivation for learning. Various topics and methods, such as commercial advertising, learning games and the formation of tandem groups are presented in this part.

Challenges of Interculturality and Transculturality in Foreign Language Teaching

In the Federal Republic of Germany, migration since the 1960s, beginning with the so-called guest workers and their families to the immigration of late repatriates from the Soviet Union and the post-Soviet successor states after 1991, has led to the emergence of Intercultural pedagogy, which is aimed primarily at schools and develops concepts, designed to respond to the cultural heterogeneity of students in the classroom. Already in 2010, pedagogue Georg Auernheimer could state that Intercultural pedagogy "after more than twenty years is now established as an educational science discipline" (Auernheimer 2010, p. 9 – translated from German: H.K.).

Migration, which was the main motivation for the development of Intercultural pedagogy, is not in itself a new phenomenon. Gogolin/Krüger-Potratz (2010,

p. 32–34), for example, pointed to the large migration movements, among other places, to Prussia at the time of religious persecutions in the 17th and 18th centuries. Migration takes place through flight, expulsion and deportation, but largely also for economic and family reasons as labor migration or family reunification. Motives can be mixed. The migration of ethnic Germans from the Soviet Union was political (escape from the communist regime), economic (in the hope of better working and living conditions) and also culturally motivated (due to a sense of belonging to German culture). Above a certain level of migration, family reunification again plays an important role.

These different reasons for migration have to be considered in intercultural pedagogy, as well as cultural backgrounds that are traditionally distinguished nationally and lead to sometimes stereotypical classifications such as "the Russians", "the Turks", "the Germans". This is not only true for the beginnings of intercultural pedagogy and general interculturality research in the German context. Definitions of diversity in schools are often reductionist, for example "A diverse multicultural classroom is an environment where both students and teachers belong to different ethnic backgrounds, accepting all races, cultures, and religions" (Hoosein 2014) or "A multicultural classroom has been defined as one in which there is a blend of students from various cultures, and it forms a diverse learning environment [Nadda 2017]" (Jabeen 2019, p. 128).

In Hoosein's definition, which is already more complex than Nadda's somewhat later one, ethnic groups; cultures and religions are distinguished, but, for example, no social or linguistic differences and no differences in the length of stay in a country, which can be of great importance for students. How complex multiculturalism can actually be, and often is, in the process of learning and teaching results from the many influences that contribute to the formation of each individual personality. Banks (2001) and Banks and McGee Banks (2019, p. 12) include, for example, nationality, race/ ethnicity, religion, gender, social class, and exceptionality/nonexceptionality. Auernheimer (2010, p. 108) speaks in abstract terms of five dimensions of interculturality that are essential to interpersonal relations: Power asymmetries, collective experiences, images of others (stereotypes, prejudices), difference of codes (scripts, cultural standards).

The diversity or heterogeneity of students in a class raises an ethical and a didactic challenge (cf. Grant/Tate 1995; Bennett et al. 2003; Janakiraman et al. 2019). It is about fairness, on the one hand, and effective learning, on the other. Banks and McGee Banks (2019, p. 3) state: "Multicultural education incorporates the idea that all students – regardless of their gender, sexual orientation, social class, and ethnic, racial, or cultural characteristics – should have an equal opportunity to learn in school."

Teachers therefore have a unique responsibility. They need, as Alsimail (2016) suggests "to understand multiculturalism in detail to provide equal education for all the students" (Jabeen 2019, p. 128).

Didactically, the great challenge is to pursue and achieve common learning goals with students who have different backgrounds, and at the same time not to see differences, otherness and different preconditions as deficiencies. The danger that must be overcome is: "Confusing diversity with disability" (Gay 2002, p. 616).

Both the ethical and the didactic challenge are already well reflected in different approaches such as intercultural pedagogy, multicultural education, culturally responsive pedagogy, immigration pedagogy and others (Gromova/ Khairutdunova 2019, p. 978). Diversity thereby appears more and more as a possibility and an opportunity and not only as a difficulty to be overcome. Even the claim "today's classroom must celebrate diversity" (Moore/Hansen 2012, p. 4; Jabeen 2019, p. 132) has its justification, since cultural identities and cultural homogeneity, while seemingly facilitating schooling, actually also limit it, since every culture draws boundaries that are often difficult to overcome and not rarely even recognized.

Culture simultaneously anchors and blinds us. It forms our center in the dynamics of living and interacting with others while leading us to assume that our own ways of being and behaving are the only right way (Gay 2002, p. 617).

The direct confrontation with cultural diversity, the need to adjust to others, not only to accept otherness but also to recognize it in its value, and the ability to learn from the other is an essential competence in the globalized world. And this competence can be acquired more easily in culturally mixed classes than in homogeneous class communities. For this reason intercultural teaching and learning has to be seen as a practice in which otherness is not a barrier, but an aim of the learning process (see Kusse 2019, pp. 81–89).

"Teaching otherness" (Kusse 2019), however, is not only a task of schools, but equally, and perhaps even to a much greater extent, a task of universities (Reiff 1997), where an open view and curiosity about the other and the different must be the fundament for teaching and learning. In the globalized world, universities as places of free thinking and research in all subjects, not only in the social sciences and humanities, should train students to deal successfully with cultural otherness, differences in values, norms and life environments (cf. Mennecke 2021). Heterogeneous groups of learners are a great and quite natural help for this. It can therefore only be considered fortunate that in recent decades, university teaching has become increasingly international and students complete their studies in more than one country. A significant number of students study abroad for at least one semester, and many have both a domestic and an international degree. For the sake of the entire global community, it is very much to be hoped that this development will continue and that more and more students worldwide will be able to benefit from it.

A precondition for this is knowledge of foreign languages. The teaching and learning of otherness necessarily include the teaching and learning of foreign languages. Foreign language teaching is therefore of outstanding importance for the process of learning on and with the other. Today it is no longer only about formal language competence, but in a very special way also about learning otherness. Already in 1989, Michael Byram wrote in his monograph "Cultural Studies in Foreign Language Education": "One of the contributions of foreign language teaching to pupils' education is to introduce learners to and help them understand 'otherness'" (Byram 1989, p. 25).

In German didactic studies, the term *intercultural didactics in foreign language teaching* was introduced in the 1980s for methods that expand the goals of communicative language teaching within the context of the internationalization of business, higher education and everyday life (cf. Müller-Jacquier 2013, p. 352).

For a long time, however, the rapid development of intercultural pedagogy and intercultural didactics did not refer to the phenomenon of multilingualism, in which students with different cultural backgrounds live. This phenomenon of multilingualism among students has only recently received attention (cf. Krüger-Potratz 2011, p. 51). In fact, however, multilingualism is an essential factor of otherness as a "feature of any society, which contains more than one ethnic group and, usually as a consequence, more than one natively spoken language" (Byram 1989, p. 25).

This multilingualism is largely, but not only, due to migration. Globalized social forms such as social media have made multilingualism a matter of course that is hardly noticed (cf. Sarter 2013, p. 8). Foremost among these is English, but classes with students who bring very different family and heritage languages are now taken for granted in many schools, and the school as well as the university cannot ignore this natural multilingualism (cf. ibid., pp. 9–10). Rather, the task is to regard it as a resource and to integrate it into the teaching and learning process.

Already in the 1980s, Ingrid Gogolin called for the productive use of the bilingualism of children from migrant families in the classroom, i.e., not to understand multilingualism as a deficit due to monolingual competence claims, but as a value even if the competencies in the dominant language of the environment and school are not fully developed in the students. At that time she demanded to use "meta-linguistic abilities and the linguistic strategies of distinguishing languages, of switching, choosing, transferring between languages, of playing with languages", in teaching (Gogolin 1988, p. 45; quoted by Auernheimer 2010, p. 149). This demand, which sounded utopian to fantastic at the time, should be standard in foreign language teaching in mixed classes today.

The multilingualism we are here talking about is only partly, sometimes not at all, due to school or university teaching. It is a kind of partial linguistic knowledge (occasionally only of individual expressions, phrasemes and idioms) that youths and young adults acquire through pop culture, social media and mixed peer groups, especially in the metropoles. They belong to forms of identity that are better described by the term transculturality than interculturality (Welsch 1995; Földes 2003, pp. 52–54; Kuße 2012, pp. 258–259).

Transcultural does not only mean the coexistence or encounter of people from different cultures. Transculturality means the manifold connections and mixtures of cultures that are culture-shaping phenomena in modern societies through globalization, migration and cultural transfer. Cultural diversity and cultural mixing enable the choice and variation of cultural roles and identities, which also includes the conscious use of languages and the variation of languages in certain contexts (cf. Fought 2006 on the worldwide varieties of English).

The phenomenon of the mixed class also becomes more complex due to the participation of pupils in different languages and cultures, to which both the didactics and the ethics of multicultural education and teaching otherness must react, because the transcultural mixture is not automatically more conflict-free than the intercultural encounter or confrontation.

I would like to illustrate this with a brief review of the cultural philosophy and dialogics of the Russian philosopher Vladimir Bibler, who developed a remarkable model of the dialogue of cultures as early as the 1970s under the difficult conditions of the Soviet Union. The first major work, "Thinking as Creativity" (Bibler 1975), was still historically based and dealt primarily with the origins of European dialogical thinking in the Antiquity and Renaissance. On this basis, however, Bibler developed the pedagogical and didactic concept of a school of dialogue between cultures (Bibler 2009).

Culture is understood by Bibler as a dialogue in which cultures enter into an exchange and ultimately lead to a synthesis of cultures. However, the adoption of objects, linguistic peculiarities or even behavior from another culture into one's own is not automatically associated with 'understanding', 'comprehension' or 'respect' for the other. Cultural transfer and hostility are unfortunately not opposites. A critic of Bibler's ideal conception of the dialogue of cultures has made this clear with a simple example: people with an aggressive hatred of America, for example, have no problem wearing jeans (Chernyak 2009, pp. 54–55).

The following challenges arise for the didactics and ethics of foreign language teaching in mixed classes, in which students not only belong to different language and cultural areas, but each individual participates in different languages and cultures: Didactically, differences in linguistic and cultural competences have to be balanced. An understanding of differences between linguistic varieties (group languages, language mixture, popular culture, social media language, slang) and the standard linguistic norms must be created without axiologically valuing these differences (as bad and good language, etc.). Ethically, conflicts must be recognized and the disintegration of groups separated by language and culture must be prevented in order to ensure a productive learning and teaching atmosphere.

Russian as a Foreign Language in Germany

The beginnings of regular Russian teaching in Germany date back to the time before the First World War (Kusse / Vardits 2020, pp. 242–257). Especially in Bavaria and Prussia, Russian was already occasionally taught at secondary schools. In 1917, Prussia introduced the possibility of an additional examination in Russian in the teacher training examination. In the Weimar Republic, there were attempts to establish Russian as a regular school subject, which was then implemented in the GDR and the Federal Republic of Germany after the Second World War. In the GDR, Russian was introduced as a compulsory subject at all secondary schools. In the Federal Republic, Russian had been an optional subject since the 1960s, offered at many but not all High schools, occasionally as a second, usually as a third foreign language. The number of learners was therefore small in the Federal Republic compared to English and French.

Furthermore, the teaching materials differed. While in the Federal Republic of Germany until the mid-1980s almost exclusively the international textbook "Russian for Everybody" was used, which was published by the Soviet publishing house "Russkij yazyk", various teaching materials were developed in the GDR. Particularly widespread was the radio course "My govorim po-russki" ("We speak Russian"), which was also implemented in schools – as a thoroughly innovative attempt at intermedia learning for the time. The textbooks differed considerably both in terms of content and lexis.

"Russian for Everybody" showed a self-contained Russian world with pleasures such as chess, ballet and train journeys to the Caspian Sea – without political implications. There are no encounters between Russians and foreigners in the textbook texts, i.e. the visitor from abroad is not introduced. In contrast, "My govorim po-russki" explicitly introduces the Soviet Union with its institutions, especially the Komsomol, kolkhozes and sovkhozes, and sends pioneers from the GDR to meet young Soviet citizens in the Soviet Union. However, the actual encounter with another culture was hardly made possible by these teaching materials in either case. And real encounters with people from the cultural sphere were rare even in the GDR.

However, this situation changed after reunification. In the 1990s there was firstly a significant influx of Russian Jews and of late repatriates, i.e. persons of German origin from the Soviet Union and its successor states, and secondly significant labor and study migration. The group of ethnic German repatriates is the largest in terms of numbers. It has been over 3 million since the end of the 2010s (Bundeszentrale 2018). Russian is the first language for all migrants in many cases, but it can also be the second or third language, i.e. not only the cultural background, but also the actual language competence in Russian sometimes varies greatly depending on the origin. Due to its use as a lingua franca in the Soviet Union and to some extent also in the post-Soviet states, however, Russian is an important language of communication in all migration groups from the post-Soviet region.

Academic interest in Russian in Germany is very high and has developed into extensive research, especially in the last 10 years. Conferences on the topic are held, such as the conference "Russian-speaking Diaspora in Germany & Israel" (2019) organized by the German Society for Eastern European Studies (DGO). A comprehensive handbook of Russian in Germany was published in 2017 (Witzlack-Makarevich/Wulff 2017; see also Hamann et al. 2020). There are studies on Russian-German (Berend 1998; Meng 2001) and German-Russian interference (Goldbach 2005; Levkovych 2012; Pabst 2007; Rethage 2012; Kusse / Vardits 2020, pp. 257–265) among Russian-Germans and other migration groups with a Russian-speaking background.

Research questions target the relationship between language and cultural identity (Meng 2001; Hinnenkamp / Meng 2005) and the mutual influence of languages on language acquisition and development (Anstatt 2007; Senyildiz 2010; Mehlhorn / Brehmer 2018). At the University of Bochum, there is a special Master's program on "Empirical Multilingualism Research", and a number of dissertations have been defended on bilingual lexis (Karl 2012) and on the development of the aspectual category in Russian among children with a Russian language of origin growing up in Germany (Dieser 2009; Clasmeier 2015). Large research projects are dedicated to multilingualism, including especially Russian-German bilingualism. At the University of Hamburg, the project "Multilingual development: A longitudinal perspective", funded by the Federal Ministry of Research and Education (BMBF), is ongoing. Also funded by the BMBF is the project "Russian and Polish Language of Origin as a Resource in School

Teaching?", based at the Universities of Greifswald and Leipzig (cf. Mehlhorn / Brehmer 2018). At the University of Hildesheim, a project funded by the VW Foundation is underway entitled "Language of origin and multilingual identities", in which Russian in Germany also plays a central role (cf. Kreß/da Silva / Grigorieva 2018).

There are now also specific studies on Russian language teaching and its challenges (Mehlhorn / Heyer 2011; Kurz 2015), which are devoted, among other things, to questions of multilingualism and different levels of language competence among students in the same teaching context. How native speakers who have come to Germany with their parents only recently and possibly for a limited period of time, speakers of origin who have different levels of proficiency in Russian and beginners in Russian can be taught together is one of the topics in the modern subject didactics of Russian published in 2014 (Bergmann 2014).

In this volume, the Leipzig professor for didactics of Slavic languages, Grit Mehlhorn, mentions possibilities of transferring expert tasks such as telling one's own experiences, reciting new texts, pronunciation demonstrations or vocabulary explanations in the target language (ibid., p. 248) and gives hints and exercises for interpersonal intercultural encounters in class or outside. Key methods are the comparison of images or situations and the creative implementation of cultural content (e. g. theater scenes) (ibid., p. 222) and exercises on social action, e. g. along guiding questions for class discussion such as "Is it okay to ask about age when getting to know someone?" (ibid., p. 220).

Textbooks published by various publishers with titles such as "Konechno!" ("Of course!"), "Dialog" ("Dialogue"), "Vmeste" ("Together"), etc., meet the needs of communicative and interculturally oriented teaching today. The beginners' textbook "Konechno!", for example, contains a page with a large-format photo of a family at the kitchen table, on which not only the family members are labeled with their first and father's names, but above all, various elements such as a certain design of the teacups and the interior decoration can be observed and easily translated into a class discussion, especially if there are pupils in the class who have their own memories of Russia (Kusse 2019, p. 88; Kusse / Vardits 2020, p. 255).

In the sophisticated textbook "Vmeste", a change of perspective is also introduced in one chapter, where the experiences of a Russian woman in Germany are reported under the heading "My year in Germany as an au pair". The textbooks teach the standard language, but also common colloquial expressions and constructions that are necessary for active competence in Russian casual communications.

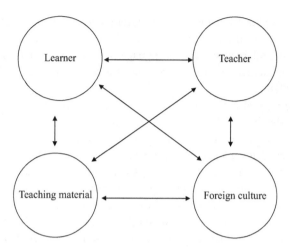

Fig. 1: J. Roche: Interkulturelle Sprachdidaktik 2001, p. 49

Modeling Effective Foreign Language Teaching in Culturally Mixed Classes

In Kusse (2019, p. 85) I already suggested, that foreign language teaching can be described as a complex role play with at least four roles: teacher, learners, learning material and the foreign language and culture. These four roles and their relations between each other are described by Jörg Roche about 20 years ago in his introduction into intercultural language didactics "Interkulturelle Sprachdidaktik" (Roche 2001; Figure 1). Four configurations of the four roles are distinguished by him: a) Teacher and learners share the same cultural code, but the teacher knows the code of the foreign culture and of the learning materials, whereas the learners don't know the foreign code or do not know it fully; b) Teacher and learners don't share the same cultural code. The teacher is a member of the foreign culture and a native speaker of the foreign language he or she teaches, whereas the learners have other cultural backgrounds; c) the teacher is neither a member of the culture he or she teaches nor the culture of the learners; d) all factors involve different cultures (Roche 2001, p. 49; Kusse 2019, p. 85).

In Roche's model the complexity of the interaction grows from the first to the fourth configuration, but, as I already mentioned in Kusse (2019, p. 85), the learner group is seen as rather homogenous. In case of nowadays widespread heterogeneity of learner groups, the model has to be expanded to two or more learner groups with different language skills, cultural knowledge and cultural backgrounds. In Germany, in elementary courses of Russian as a foreign language in schools as well as in courses which are included in Russian philological studies at universities, non-native speakers are learning with heritage language speakers as well as native speakers. Furthermore, non-native speakers are not necessarily members of the German linguistic and cultural community, and to teach Russian to a native speaker of another Indo-European language like German or French is not the same as teaching it to a native speaker of Turkish, i.e. an agglutinative language, or to a speaker of an isolated language like, for instance, Chinese. Heritage language speakers have very different language skills (cf. Raecke 2007), and a different connection to the related, i.e. Russian culture, and native speakers can be very close to the (German) surrounding learning culture, but can be also very unfamiliar with it.

All these groups should be led to an adequate level of linguistic competence, which ideally enables them to communicate freely about cultural differences or other topics in the target language. With regard to Russian as a Foreign Language at Russian Universities, Sadygova / Yusupova / Agababaev (2021, p. 3) state:

It should be noted that the main component of the development of creative intercultural and communicative competence at the lessons of Russian as a Foreign Language is the foreign students' participation in intercultural communication with a full understanding of the speech and social behavior of native speakers of the Russian language.

This goal of linguistic and communicative competence also applies to mixed learner groups outside Russia, but is more difficult to achieve here than in the target country. However, even there, learners are not simply non-native speakers, but come from different linguistic and cultural backgrounds and thus also have different learning requirements.

In certain phases, especially at the beginning of foreign language teaching, it would be useful to form groups of learners according to their prerequisites, in order to bring the groups together again once they have reached a certain level of language competence. At an advanced stage of linguistic competence and communication skills, diversity can be used specifically to develop intercultural competence and to discuss one's own and others' transcultural identities.

Due to practical reasons, normally it's not possible to divide the groups into specialized courses like Russian for heritage speakers, Russian for non-native speakers, Russian for German native speakers, Russian for Chinese native speakers and so on.

Furthermore, differences not only lay in competence of language skills and cultural knowledge. In schools and sometimes even in universities teachers have to be aware of the possibility that some groups separate themselves from others, so that the class splitters into the "Russians", the "Germans", the "Turkish" who rather don't communicate to each other. In the worst case hostility arises between these groups. Therefore, the teacher has to handle negative occurrences of heterogeneity in order to build a productive and pleasant learning environment.

In Kusse (2019) I already presented a scheme for prototype diverse setting that includes three groups: learners from the surrounding culture, where the teaching and learning process is located (for example in Germany a German school or Universities or another German institution of higher education), learners who are directly or (as heritage speakers) indirectly connected to the target culture, and learners who don't belong either to the surrounding or the target culture (see Figure 2).

The scheme illustrates the complexity of the learning process in mixed classes, although it does not present all the varieties of learner groups or all relations between learners, teachers, cultures and teaching material. Transcultural identities can only be concluded indirectly as an outcome from the different interactional roles and the relations between them that are shown in the scheme.

It is important, however, that on the basis of the scheme the roles of teachers, the different learner groups and the teaching materials used can be discussed. The scheme highlights that teaching material must meet specific requirements, as very different groups with very different linguistic and cultural learning prerequisites access it. Modern textbooks, which were briefly mentioned in the previous chapter, already attempt not only to consider this diversity through numerous illustrations, lively dialogues and multi-perspectivity (e. g. the description of Germany from the point of view of Russians), but also to make use of it for foreign language teaching. Interactive and better adapted to current learning situations, especially digital learning and teaching materials, will be able to meet the requirements even better in the future.

A particularly important role in the different mixed learning situations is that of the teacher. The role of the teacher, however, can no longer be merely that of a transmitter of knowledge. Rather, the teacher must act as a mediator for communication and learning in the heterogeneous group of learners. The demand that the teacher does not teach 'his' material frontally, but interactively strengthens competences of independent and joint learning in the group, is not new, or related just to foreign language teaching. It has not risen from the experience of heterogeneous learner groups either. Even before the First World War, and especially in the 1920s, this modern role of the teacher was discussed within the framework of reform pedagogy and tested in practice at reform schools (cf. Kusse 2019, pp. 84–85). The important reform pedagogue Martin Wagenschein (1896–1988) saw the role of the teacher not so much in imparting knowledge

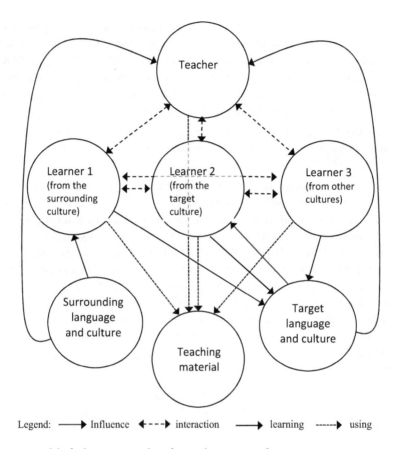

Fig. 2: Model of relations in modern foreign language teaching

as in teaching understanding. His art-of-teaching-didactics was to be Genetic, Socratic and Exemplary. Genetic means that all teaching and learning has to do with becoming: "with the becoming human being and – in teaching, as didactics – with the becoming of knowledge in him" (Wagenschein 1968, p. 55 – translated from German: H.K.).

Socratic is the knowledge acquisition in a dialogical process, that should be a complex interaction of the whole learning group, and exemplary means to recognize the best examples for understanding the discussed phenomena and dealing with them (see Kusse 2019, pp. 84–85).

Current reflections on the role of the teacher closely resemble Wagenschein's art-of-teaching-didactics, even though they rarely refer to it directly. I will give only two examples. Many others could be added: Jabeen (2019, p. 135) for instance suggests, "teachers should play the role of researchers, always planning, investigating the needs of a diverse classroom, and sharing their experiences with their peers." Mukhametzyanova (2021, p. 9) defines:

> Cognitive dialogue between the teacher and students […] as a factor of enhancing the quality of higher education in the conditions of international cooperation in the sphere of higher education […].

Especially in foreign language teaching, this dialogue should particularly include issues of trans- and interculturality and not ignore conflicts. "The teacher should encourage the students to speak freely and discuss their culture, ethnicity, and traditions with the teacher as well as the fellow students, to make others aware of their culture." (Jabeen 2019, p. 128 with reference Friswell et al. 2013).

The facilitator role of the teacher in Socratic (dialogical) intercultural teaching is successful when it comes to a productive dialogue among the learner groups, in which each group and each individual contributes their respective special knowledge and competences. The goal is always a learning togetherness. Whether and how this can succeed depends very much on the differences in competence and the interpersonal relationships between the learner groups. Several prototypical constellations related to the scheme above are conceivable.

1. There are only minor differences in language competence between learner groups 1–3. All have a good communicative language level. In this case, intercultural dialogue is a good way to promote the development of language competence.
2. The language competence between learner group 2 and learner groups 1 and 3 differs considerably. Here too, intercultural dialogue can be didactically useful, but learners in learner group 2 partly fulfill the tasks of instructors. In dialogue together with the teacher, they convey not only cultural knowledge, but also all language skills.
3. The language competence between the learner groups differs, but also the feeling of unfamiliarity up to non-acceptance. In this case too, language competences have to be overcome in order to be able to enter into a productive dialogue in the target language, but the facilitator role of the teacher becomes incomparably more important than in case 2. The first task now is to create a common learner group and an atmosphere of understanding.
4. There is a hostile atmosphere between the learner groups. In this case, the goal of building language competence may take a back seat at times. Intercultural

dialogue is not the result of good language competence, nor is it necessarily the means by which this language competence can be achieved. It serves first of all to overcome animosities so that a learning group can emerge in which the individuals do not hinder each other but support each other.

Different methods are available for the various constellations in order to increase language skills, stimulate intercultural dialogue and form productive learner groups.

For instance, project work such as the development of city marketing in the target language is particularly suitable for constellation 1. The different learner groups with their different cultural backgrounds develop advertising materials for different cultural target groups and enter into an intercultural dialogue.

For constellations 1 and 2, for example, commercial advertising for the same products (for example sweets or fashion) or social advertising, memes, humor etc. within societal issues (the COVID 19-pandemic for instance; cf. Kusse 2021) in the target culture and the surrounding culture and also other cultures can be used to convey elementary everyday lexis and certain idioms and to enter into a dialogue about different aesthetics, values, perhaps also historical allusions.

In constellations 3 and 4, it is possible to tackle common tasks in which cultural differences become visible and have to be overcome in order to solve the task. Such intercultural role plays, which I have already briefly presented in Kusse (2019, p. 87), were originally developed for intercultural working groups in business. In foreign language teaching the participants have to recognize linguistic misunderstanding, and to discuss cultural differences and peculiarities in behavior in order to develop effective strategies of collaborating.

A method that is already well established today and is particularly suitable for constellations 2 and 3 is the formation of tandems from learner groups 2 and 1 or 2 and 3. On the starting page of its website, the ENTEP project shows a European and an Asian girl looking at a tablet together (Figure 3). This can be a tandem learning situation. The picture symbolizes the linguistic and cultural exchange between two people, which can later be reflected back to the entire learner group.

At the Institute of Slavic Studies at the TU Dresden, tandem teaching in Russian is also offered internationally within the framework of digital teaching, among others with the University of Calgary in Canda and the Kazan Federal University in the Russian Federation. Finally, I would like to quote feedback from a tandem, from which both the intercultural and the linguistic significance of this form of learning can be seen.

"This project has taught me a lot about my ability to communicate in Russian, and also shown me just how far I have come so far in my overall learning. The

Fig. 3: Website of the ENTEP-Project [https://entep-tudresden.de/]

ability to communicate with someone who speaks another language while communicating in a language we are both learning was a great experience, and I am glad to have been able to be a part of it. The project has really highlighted where my strengths and weaknesses lay, and it gives me a basis of how I would like to strengthen my language learning in the future" (Feedback on the Tandem between Learner groups of the University of Calgary and TU Dresden in Winter term 2020 / 2021).

Literature

Alismail, Halah Ahmed: "Multicultural Education: Teacher's Perceptions and Preparation". *Journal of Education and Practice*, 11(7), 2016, pp. 139–146, retrieved 4.7.2021, from https://pdfs.semanticscholar.org/bb81/309e93ef1084583a3a298f91a4a8ffad4d48.pdf.

Anstatt, Tanja (ed.): *Mehrsprachigkeit bei Kindern und Erwachsenen. Erwerb, Formen,* Förderung. Attempto Verlag: Tübingen, 2007.

Auernheimer, Georg: *Einführung in die interkulturelle Pädagogik.* Wissenschaftliche Buchgesellschaft: Darmstadt, 2010 (6th Edition).

Banks, James A.: *Cultural Diversity and Education.* Allyn & Bacon: Boston, 2001.

Banks, James A. / McGee Banks, Cherry A.: *Multicultural Education: Issues and Perspectives.* University of Washington: Brothel, 2019 (10th Edition).

Bennett, Janet M. / Bennett, Milton J / Allen, Wendy.: "Developing Intercultural Competence in the Language Classroom". In: Lange, Dale L. / Paige, R. Michael (eds.): *Culture as the Core: Perspectives on Culture in Second Language Learning. A Volume in Research in Second Language Learning*. Information Age Publishing: Greenwich, CT, 2003.

Bergmann, Anka (ed.): *Fachdidaktik Russisch. Eine Einführung*. Narr Francke-Attempto Verlag: Tübingen, 2014.

Berend, Nina: Sprachliche Anpassung. Eine soziolinguistisch-dialektologische Untersuchung. Gunter Narr: Tübingen, 1998.

Bibler, Vladimir S.: *Myshlenie kak tvorchestvo. Vvedenie v logiku myslennogo dialoga* [*Thinking as Creativity. Introduction to the Logic of Thought Dialogue*]. Politizdat: Moskva, 1975.

Bibler, Vladimir S.: "The Foundations of the School of the Dialogue of Cultures Program". *Journal of Russian & East European Psychology*, 47(1), 2009, pp. 34–60.

Bundeszentrale für politische Bildung: Zuzug von (Spät-)Aussiedlern und ihren Familienangehörigen. *In absoluten Zahlen, nach Herkunftsgebieten, 1950 bis 2016*, retrieved 1.4.2018, from https://www.bpb.de/nachschlagen/zahlen-und-fakten/soziale-situation-in-deutschland/61643/spaet-aussiedler.

Byram, Michael: *Cultural Studies in Foreign Language Education*. Multilingual Matters: Clevedon / Philadelphia, 1989.

Byram, Michael: *From Foreign Language Education to Education for Intercultural Citizenship. Essays and Reflections*. Multilingual Matters: Clevedon et al. 2008.

Chernyak, Lion S.: "Vnenahodimost' v dialogike: samodeterminacija mysli i determinacii vnemyslenie [Inclusion in Dialogics: Self-Determination of Thought and Determination of Out-of-Thinking]". In: Ahutin, A. V. / Berljand, I. E. (eds.): *Vladimir Solomonovich Bibler*. ROSSPĖN: Moskva, 2009, pp. 10–128.

Clasmeier, Christina: *Die mentale Repräsentation von Aspektpartnerschaften russischer Verben*. Otto Sagner: München et al. 2015.

Dieser, Elena: *Genuserwerb im Russischen und Deutschen. Korpusgestützte Studie zu ein- und zweisprachigen Kindern und Erwachsenen*. Otto Sagner: München / Berlin, 2009.

Földes, Csaba: *Interkulturelle Linguistik. Vorüberlegungen zu Konzepten, Problemen und Desiderata*. Universitätsverlag/Edition Praesens: Veszprém / Wien, 2003.

Fought, Carmen: *Language and Ethnicity*. Cambridge University Press: Cambridge, 2006.

Friswell, T. et al.: "Teaching Bilingual Education and English Language Learner (ELL) Students: Recommendations for Teachers" (1), 2013, pp. 1–5, retrieved 4.7.2021, from https://www.education.udel.edu/wp-content/uploads/2013/01/BilingualEdPrograms.pdf.

Gay, Geneva: "Culturally Responsive Teaching in Special Education for Ethnically Diverse Students: Setting the Stage". International Journal of Qualitative Studies in Education, 15(6), 2002, pp. 613–629.

Gogolin, Ingrid: *Erziehungsziel Zweisprachigkeit. Konturen eines sprachpädagogischen Konzepts für die multikulturelle Schule*. Bergmann und Helbig: Hamburg, 1988.

Gogolin, Ingrid / Marianne, Krüger-Potratz: *Einführung in die interkulturelle Pädagogik*. Verlag Barbara Budrich: Opladen / Farmington Hills, MI, 2010 (2nd. Edition).

Goldbach, Alexandra: *Deutsch-russischer Sprachkontakt: deutsche Transferenzen und Code-switching in der Rede Russischsprachiger in Berlin*. Peter Lang: Frankfurt a.M. et al. 2005.

Grant, C. A. / Tate, W. F.: "Multicultural Education through the Lens of the Multicultural Education Research Literature". In: Banks, James / McGee Banks, Cherry A. (eds.): *Handbook of Research on Multicultural Education*. Macmillan: New York, 1995, pp. 145–166.

Gromova, Chulpan / Khairutdunova, Rezeda: "Cultural Diversity in Russian School: Results of Research of Elementary School Teachers' Experience with the Immigrant Children". In: V International Forum on Teacher Education. Proceedings IFTE. ARPHA Proceedings: Kazan, 2019, pp. 977–987.

Hamann, Katharina / Witzlack-Makarevich, Kai / Wulff, Nadja: "Russian in Germany". In: Mustajoki, Arto / Protassova, Ekaterina / Yelenevskaya, Maria (eds.): *The Soft Power of the Russian Language: Pluricentricity, Politics and Policies*. Routledge: London et al. 2020, pp. 163–174.

Hinnenkamp, Volker / Meng, Katharina (eds.): *Sprachgrenzen überspringen: sprachliche Hybridität und polykulturelles Selbstverständnis*. Gunter Narr: Tübingen, 2005.

Hoosein, S: Teacher's Perspectives and Instructional Strategies in Multicultural Diverse Classrooms. Ontario Institute for Studies in Education of the University of Toronto, 2014. Retrieved 4.7.2021, from https://tspace.library.utoronto.ca/bitstream/1807/68671/1/Hoosein_Sabah_2015506_MT_MT.pdf.

Jabeen, Rakhshinda: "Multicultural Diverse Classroom. Addressing the Instructional Challenges and Reflections, from a Teacher's Perspective". *Arab*

World English Journal, Special Issue: The Dynamics of EFL in Saudi Arabia, 2019, pp. 127–136. DOI: https://dx.doi.org/10.24093/awej/efl1.10

Janakiraman, Shamilla et al.: "Instructional Design and Strategies for Multicultural Education: A Qualitative Case Study". Journal of Educational Research and Practice, 9(1), 2019, pp. 300–315.

Karl, Katrin B.: Bilinguale Lexik. Nicht materieller lexikalischer Transfer als Folge der aktuellen russisch-deutschen Zweisprachigkeit. Otto Sagner: Berlin / München, 2012.

Kreß, Beatrix / da Silva, Vasco / Grigorieva, Ioulia (eds.): Mehrsprachigkeit, Sprachkontakt und Bildungsbiografie. Peter Lang: Frankfurt a.M. et al. 2018.

Krüger-Potratz, Marianne: Mehrsprachigkeit: "Konfliktfelder in der Schulgeschichte". In: Fürstenau, Sara / Gomolla, Mechtild (eds.): Migration und schulischer Wandel: Mehrsprachigkeit. VS Verlag für Sozialwissenschaften/ Springer Fachmedien: Wiesbaden, 2011, pp. 51–68.

Kurz, Natalia: „Muttersprachler ist kein Beruf!" Eine Interviewstudie zu subjektiven Sichtweisen von (angehenden) Russischlehrenden mit russischsprachiger Zuwanderungsgeschichte. Stauffenberg Verlag: Tübingen, 2015.

Kuße, Holger: Kulturwissenschaftliche Linguistik. Eine Einführung. Vandenhoeck und Ruprecht: Göttingen, 2012.

Kusse, Holger: "Teaching Otherness: Intercultural Didactics in Foreign Language Teaching". In: Tregubova, Tat'jana M. (ed.): Issledovanija v praktike prepodavanija i obučenija v sisteme vysšego obrazovanija [Research in teaching and learning practices in higher education]. Kazan, 2019, pp. 81–89.

Kusse, Holger: "The Linguistic Landscape of the Coronavirus Crisis in Foreign Language Didactics by Using the Example of German". In: Vidrevich, Marina (ed.): International Scientific Conference "Delivering Impact in Higher Education Learning and Teaching: Enhancing Cross-Border Collaborations" (DIHELT 2021) = SHS Web of Conferences 99, 01001, 2021, retrieved 4.7.2021, from https://www.shs-conferences.org/articles/shsconf/pdf/2021/10/shsconf_dihelt2021_01001.pdf.

Kusse, Holger / Vladislava, Vardits: "Russkij jazyk v Germanii [Russian in Germany]". In: Norman, Boris Y. / Kusse, Holger (eds.): Russkij jazyk za predelami Rossii [Russian Outside of Rusia]. Armchair Scientist: Moskav / Yekaterinburg, 2020, pp. 235–269.

Levkovych, Nataliya: Po-russki in Deutschland. Russisch und Deutsch als Konkurrenten in der Kommunikation mehrsprachiger Gruppen von Personen mit postsowjetischem Hintergrund in Deutschland. Universitätsverlag Brockmeyer: Bochum, 2012.

Mehlhorn, Grit / Brehmer, Bernhard: *Potenziale von Herkunftssprachen. Sprachliche und außersprachliche Einflussfaktoren.* Staufenberg Verlag: Tübingen, 2018.

Mehlhorn, Grit / Heyer, Christine (eds.): *Russisch und Mehrsprachigkeit. Lehren und Lernen von Russisch an deutschen Schulen in einem vereinten Europa.* Stauffenburg Verlag: Tübingen, 2011.

Meng, Katharina: *Russlanddeutsche Sprachbiografien. Untersuchungen zur sprachlichen Integration von Aussiedlerfamilien.* Gunter Narr: Tübingen, 2001.

Mennecke, Olga: "Intercultural Competence in Practice: Internship Abroad in the B.A. Program "International Information Management" at the Hildesheim University Foundation". In: Vidrevich, Marina (ed.): *International Scientific Conference "Delivering Impact in Higher Education Learning and Teaching: Enhancing Cross-Border Collaborations" (DIHELT 2021) = SHS Web of Conferences 99, 01001,* 2021, retrieved 4.7.2021, from https://www.shs-conferences.org/articles/shsconf/pdf/2021/10/shsconf_dihelt2021_01027.pdf.

Moore, Kenneth D. / Hansen, Jaqueline: *Effective Strategies for Teaching in K-8: Teaching Diverse Students.* SAGE Publications Inc.: Thousand Oaks, CA, 2012.

Müller-Jacquier, Bernd: "Interkulturelle Didaktik (Intercultural Didactics)". In: Byram, Michael / Hu, Adelheid (eds.): *Routledge Encyclopedia of Language Teaching and Learning.* Routledge: London / New York, 2013, pp. 352–356 (2nd Edition).

Mukhametzyanova, Larisa: "Cognitive Dialogue as a Factor of Enhancing the Quality of Education in the Conditions of International Cooperation in the Sphere of Higher Education". In: Vidrevich, Marina (ed.): *International Scientific Conference "Delivering Impact in Higher Education Learning and Teaching: Enhancing Cross-Border Collaborations" (DIHELT 2021) = SHS Web of Conferences 99, 01001,* 2021, retrieved 4.7.2021, from https://www.shs-conferences.org/articles/shsconf/pdf/2021/10/shsconf_dihelt2021_01009.pdf.

Nadda, P: "Teaching Strategies in a Multicultural Classroom." *Imperial Journal of Interdisciplinary Research (IJIR),* 2(3), 2017, pp. 741–743.

Pabst, Birte: *Russisch-deutsche Zweisprachigkeit als Phänomen der multikulturellen Gesellschaft in Deutschland.* Peter Lang: Frankfurt a.M. et al. 2007.

Raecke, Jochen: "Wenn Migrantenkinder als Studierende die Sprache ihrer Eltern sprechen – was können sie dann?" *Zeitschrift für Slawistik,* 52(4), 2007, pp. 375–398.

Reiff, Judith C.: Teaching and Learning Styles from a Multicultural Perspective. In: *Multicultural Prism: Voices from the Field.* (Ed 414585), 1997, pp. 67–78, retrieved 4.7.2021, from https://files.eric.ed.gov/fulltext/ED414585.pdf.

Rethage, Wilma: *Strukturelle Besonderheiten des Russischen in Deutschland. Kontaktlinguistische und soziolinguistische Aspekte.* Otto Sagner: München et al. 2012.

Roche, Jörg: *Interkulturelle Sprachdidaktik. Eine Einführung.* Gunter Narr: Tübingen, 2001.

Sadygova, Arzu / Yusupova, Lyalya / Agababaev, Mushfig: "Development of Creative Intercultural and Communicative Competence of USMU International Students at the Lessons of Russian as a Foreign Language". In: Vidrevich, Marina (ed.): *International Scientific Conference "Delivering Impact in Higher Education Learning and Teaching: Enhancing Cross-Border Collaborations" (DIHELT 2021) = SHS Web of Conferences 99, 01001,* 2021, retrieved 4.7.2021, from https://www.shs-conferences.org/articles/shsconf/pdf/2021/10/shsconf_dihelt2021_01013.pdf.

Sarter, Heidemarie: *Mehrsprachigkeit und Schule. Eine Einführung.* Wissenschaftliche Buchgesellschaft: Darmstadt, 2013.

Senyildiz, Anastasia: *Wenn Kinder mit Eltern gemeinsam Deutsch lernen. Soziokulturell orientierte Fallstudien zur Entwicklung erst- und zweitsprachlicher Kompetenzen bei russischsprachigen Vorschulkindern.* Stauffenburg Verlag: Tübingen, 2010.

Wagenschein, Martin: *Verstehen lehren. Genetisch – Sokratisch – Exemplarisch.* Beltz: Weinheim, 1968.

Welsch, Wolfgang: "Transkulturalität. Zur veränderten Verfaßtheit heutiger Kulturen". *Zeitschrift für Kulturaustausch,* 45(1), 1995, pp. 39–44.

Witzlack-Makarevich, Kai / Wulff, Nadja (eds.): *Handbuch des Russischen in Deutschland. Migration, Mehrsprachigkeit, Spracherwerb.* Frank & Timme: Berlin, 2017.

Maureen Royce, Madeleine Stevens, Joshi Jariwala, David Soehren

Perspectives of Authentic Assessment and Professional Practice Interventions in Teaching and Learning in UK Higher Education

Abstract: In supporting student preparation for professional business careers, universities are increasingly developing and designing teaching and learning practice which supports professional practice skills in addition to academic content. Within the UK, universities work alongside professional bodies to reflect changes in practice within an academic setting. In this way, the professional has input into the curriculum and assessment design, and this paper considers the authenticity of curriculum design and assessment in an authentic professional context. The practice elements of the paper reflect work embedded in module development in Liverpool John Moores University in the North West of England. The focus will be situated in the area of authentic assessment and its role within Human Resource Management professional practice.

Keywords : Authentic assessment, professional practice, teaching and learning, professional body partnership, student co-creation.

Understanding the nature of professional practice involves academic in a consideration of the volatility of the business environment as the context or practice and skills have been subject to rapid and consistent change (Kemmis 2009; Lester 1995). Such changes are technological and social but also reflect changes in the value systems of organizations. In England, higher education is regulated by the Office for Students (OfS) and their belief that students are experts in their own experience has encouraged English institutions to broaden student involvement in curriculum and assessment design and to explore the nature of co-created content involving students and academics. Advance HE is a British professional membership organization promoting excellence in higher education who have advocated for a sector-wide reappraisal of assessment. This is, in part, a reflection on market-driven metrics relating to value for money education in respect of student fees but also acknowledges the changes in technology and the importance of knowledge contextualization. Increasingly, a desire for authentic assessment which incorporates preparation for future learning and employment is influencing the culture of assessment in higher education.

In periods of rapid change, such as traditional environmental changes in Higher Education and the political impact, new technologies or as recently experienced globally, the Covid pandemic, decisions on the knowledge content require constant review and reinterpretation. A more significant area of change is around teaching delivery and interaction with students. The authors believe that the design of teaching sessions has become more complex as guidance from external and internal stakeholders continues to focus on students as consumers and their real-life ability to gain employment upon graduation. This complexity reflects the ambition for authenticity and the integration of technology but also involves an appreciation of student involvement in the process of learning and assessment and the subsequent acquisition of skills. Lester (1995) argues that professionals, responding to change, have needed to become far more reflective, to embody principles, ethics and morals and these areas then also feed into the teaching and assessment environment. Teaching then moves from a description of the practice to a deeper understanding of the practice through co-created content which challenges students to apply knowledge, yet also to be aware of ethical judgment and awareness of alternative approaches. In taking this broader perspective, students learn to reflect and respond to change while developing skills which support their competence in delivering learning outcomes yet aligned within a professional environment. Within this paper, we explore practice-based teaching and learning within the Human Resource Management (HRM) profession and understanding how the relationship with the professional body, the Chartered Institute for Personnel and Development (CIPD) supports the framework for authentic assessment, that which reflect real-life situations. The European University Association in 2019 in discussing active learning supports this approach to teaching and learning believing in the importance of testing the application of knowledge in new and authentic situations (EUA 2019).

The assessment of competence that delineates the professional from others presents interesting challenges to the more traditional assessment strategies found in Higher Education. Lester (1995) would view application of reflection as an ongoing strategy as part of the assessment process. The questioning self-action provides a critical connection between theory and practice. Illustrating this, the CIPD advocates the importance of analytics. The ability to understand and interpret human resource (HR) metrics to guide policymaking and people practice is a growing essential requirement for HR practitioners (CIPD 2017). The appreciation of metrics enhances problem-solving and decision-making faculties associated with demonstrating acumen (CIPD 2018). This narrative lends itself to integrating employability into both teaching and the way professional skills are assessed. The EUA recognized that for teachers to maximize the impact of both technological competence and professional competencies in designing their programs, teachers themselves needed to be supported by their institutions

(EUA 2019, p. 7). Institutions were encouraged to move forward in small steps and allow time and budget for experimentation as well as a culture of long-term planning. The case study example preparing students to investigate allegations and work within a legal framework provides an opportunity for reflection on the institutional cultural changes supporting the development of practitioner work.

Within the HR programs, practitioner content and assessment started with some simple changes to develop content beyond theory and to engage students in co-creating content through their responses. For example, teaching the components of individual key metrics in HRM, e. g., staff turnover or sickness absence rate, has been integrated into the curriculum, in theory but only recently has a practice dimension been included. To resolve this deficiency, a database simulating a typical HR staff database was developed by students as part of an extra curriculum project. This database would serve many functions including the appreciation of what and how personal data is organized in workplaces, and the multiple uses not limited to sourcing, establishing patterns, benchmarking and predicting future people and organizational performance to guide and optimize business sustenance. In actively manipulating the data, the students were able to construct responses which were authentic and diverse. Additionally, as there was ownership of the data base, the core data could be adapted to reflect changing priorities reflecting a real-world environment.

Cole et al. (2011) explore the cultural gap between the relatively positivistic professional practice and wider theoretical questioning of the academic world. Through the use of real-world co-created data, the students are able to identify for themselves the ethical and organizational dilemmas arising from the creation and interpretation of data. They echo Lester's (1995) model with their call for greater reflexivity or a questioning of assumptions and bias. Such models of working bring students into the co-creation of the curriculum areas and allow for reflexivity which may challenge both teaching and learning and organizational practice models.

In 2018, George Huh provided the keynote address at LJMU's Teaching and Learning conference where he shared his concept of Teaching High Impact Practices (HIPs). Discussion and reflection following this address led academic leaders at LJMU to understand that much of their work in the field of business practice is based on promoting deep learning by promoting student retention, engagement and performance. Beyond that, working within a HIP framework creates parity between students within a large range of social/economic situations. This has been achieved through curriculum design, assessment and facilitation with content co-created by students. A further example of student engagement with content can be seen through the design and deliver of assessment centers testing competencies for recruitment purposes. In this example the students choose a job role and identify and measure key competencies related to the job. Collectively, students design an assessment center using a range of measurements to make a recruitment decision. The students alternatively play the part of assessors and applicants allowing academics to report on both the knowledge and practical application in designing the measurement tasks that identify candidates for employment, but also on the way in which the student responds as an applicant looking for employment. The feedback from both perspectives allows for a rich reflection on knowledge, skills and behaviors and employability readiness. The structure involves students in design influenced by selection theory. The requirement to put their designs into practice increases the performance expectation, encourages students to earn higher grades and retain, integrate and transfer information at higher rates. There is potential for professional practice learning and assessment similar to this case example to build on the individuality of student knowledge and experience and accelerate the development of peer and independent learning. The student view of practice-based learning was captured in a paper to the LJMU Teaching and Learning Conference in 2019 'Student Partners in Designing Professional Content and assessment'. Students reflected on how a blend of practice-based 'modules' within a program enhanced student independence and accelerated the acquisition of skills more usually only learned from employment rather than an academic environment. The importance of behaviors in transforming organizational practice has long been recognized by those theorizing learning and change. The behavioral aspects are complex and rely on the integration of a number of components which might include the acquisition of knowledge, the distribution of information through communication channels, the interpretation of information and finally the collective memory to capitalize on the learning for the future. Huber in 1991, outlines these components and recognizes that individual learning does not translate into collective learning without additional stages and positive behavioral interventions. In moving students into a sphere where their individual learning influences the collective, practice-based learning prepares students to contribute quickly to a rapidly changing work environment.

Professional practice is a contested area. Involvement of students in co-creating materials and operating with real-world models one where new skills, such as reflection and reflexivity are being promoted alongside theoretical perspectives. In the next section, we will discuss authentic assessment and how it might help embed, develop and support practice in business teaching.

Authentic Assessment

Authentic assessment is a summative assessment where the student has a task that mimics a real-world task rather than a traditional assessment such as essay or exam. In Villarroel et al's. (2018) review of authentic assessment, thirteen consistent characteristics are identified and classified into three conceptual dimensions: realism, cognitive challenge and evaluative judgment. Realism relates to the level by which the assessment mimics problems or activities found in practice and replicating the performance standards expected. Cognitive challenges refer to the high-order thinking skills such as creativity, problem-solving, and decision-making. Evaluative judgment proposes how the student should be involved in creating the criteria by which the performance is judged and be more aware of this, in order to self-regulate and improve their behavior such as through self- assessment and reflection. Authentic assessment can be seen as a challenge to traditional assessment practices within education, which fail to provide methods for students to practice their developing skills and knowledge. This in itself can be seen as a challenge to the professionalism of academic practice, as external bodies exert more control. We could however view authentic assessment as a dialogue or exchange around values and skills within professional practice.

Case Study: Strategic HR Competencies – Investigating Complaints and Preparing for Legal Process

Competency is defined as the ability to use the appropriate knowledge, skills and abilities to successfully complete a specific job-related task (Russo 2016). CIPD (2013) states that in order to be able to handle conflict, HR professionals must attain the following competencies: curiosity, decisive thinker, skilled influencer, credibility, collaborative, driven to deliver, courage to challenge and a role modeling. The content was designed to build and practice these competencies, ratified through students' in-class experiences and personal reflection.

This case study example illustrating this can be seen through a CIPD accredited module for final year undergraduate students on the BA (Hons) Human Resource Management program. In the UK these tribunals hear cases relating to breaches of contract and/or Employment Law. During 2020, single employment tribunals and caseloads increased by 13 % and 22 %, respectively, compared to a year ago with 19,000 multiple claims received in the quarter from July to September 2020. (Gov.uk 2020). With this significant number of cases, we cannot ignore the importance of this aspect of an HR practitioner's role.

Due consideration is given to individual student levels of confidence and as a result, all tribunal roles are adopted on a voluntary basis. In taking responsibility for differing roles in the case study, students learn to work collaboratively with each other but also independently of direct academic direction. Students make choices about their approach to the problems presented and the consequences of the decisions they make and are assessed on five reflective elements. A key part of the learning is for HR students to appreciate at their own pace, that it is essential for HR to develop a positive working environment that fosters good teamwork that helps with employee engagement and performance as suggested by Lo et al. (2015) and Sunahwati and Prusak (2018). The module content also aims to allow students to learn practice-based skills and awareness of competencies such as the importance of HR practitioners processing and demonstrating good levels of resilience, curiosity and to be organized as business environments are very complex (Armstrong and Taylor 2020). The students shape the curriculum. The case study is designed to illicit responses from four fictitious groups; Organizational HR Department; aggrieved individuals seeking redress for a breach; the line managers involved in the decisions which have led to the claim for a breach of policy or employment law and the ET panel members.

Each group receives a set of initial notes which differ in context and from this information, students reflect their own perspective and version of truth. In this way the students are involved in the co-creation of the case and have responsibility for shaping the context as they use their own knowledge and judgment. Parallel lecture sessions ensure that key organizational and legal principles and theory have been understood by all four groups, with the exception of the ET panel which has to hear the case and decisions taken by the HR department objectively. The groups do not share this information. The practice-based role play is supported by knowledge-creating short lectures on the legal, policy and theory context relevant to the case. The students then perform in a role play and respond to information as it emerges from the other groups and the academic leader of the module. The module concludes with a mock trial, which is video recorded so that students can use this to reflect on their levels of knowledge, preparation and decision-making. The ET panel members collectively decide on a suitable outcome of the case and calculate an award based on legal knowledge gained through lectures. The assessment is reflexive and relates to the work of Cole et al. (2011) evaluation and critique in the following areas: HR competencies in managing conflict; good practice in investigations; justification of organizational and individual actions; preparation for and delivery of tribunal role play and documentation; reflection on organizational process improvement. Student feedback in this practice-based module is strong, with students reflecting on the extent to which the ability to work with real-time changing scenarios helped prepare them for work in their chosen profession.

The evaluation process for professional practice academic delivery and assessment must respond to flexibility in the choices made by the students during the course of the module and student involvement in understanding the multiple layers of complexity inevitably requires academic time and resources. While the students are independent learners for much of the assessment, the curation and facilitation of the academic lead requires both professional practice knowledge and skill in integrating the two worlds of academic rigor and clinical business practice.

Professional Body Relationship

Professional body involvement ratifies the behavioral and skills aspects of professional practice delivery. The involvement of the professional body allows practitioner expertise into the academic space and enhances authenticity. The CIPD skills and behavioral framework for practitioners is embedded into the academic delivery of modules within accredited programs. The BA (Hons) Human Resource Management used in the case study examples discussed within this paper has been fully accredited to deliver professional standards. CIPD have emphasized the demonstration of business acumen in HR practitioners and recognizes (CIPD 2018) the importance of integrating professional practice into the Higher Education curriculum to prepare students for employment. The close working relationship between the professional body, CIPD and the academic subject leaders created a partnership with the students evident in the development of materials, delivery and assessment of practitioner work involving data base analysis, assessment of competencies for recruitment and the investigation and decision making involved in the tribunal.

Authentic assessment design flows from the case study and requires the students to begin to walk in each other's shoes as they develop their responses. The identification of criteria broad enough to recognize the refinement of the roles each student or group takes plays a critical role in developing trust in the process and ensuring clarity of purpose. While the authentic nature of the delivery requires student interaction and communication, the reflexivity on responses and actions forms the central focus of the assessment. The module design identifies learning outcomes related to knowledge and practice and these learning outcomes are assessed once the case study tribunal and judgment have been reached.

The reflective assessment of the module aligned directly with the learning outcomes as detailed below:

After completing the module the student should be able to:

1. Evaluate key contemporary disciplinary and grievance issues affecting the HR function within private, public and third sector organizations.
2. Analyze the root causes of disciplinary and grievance action.
3. Review key contemporary business methods in preventing and resolving disciplinary and grievance issues.
4. Reflect on the preparation and execution of an Employment Tribunal from an HR perspective.

The students do not then only consider the facts of the case study and make judgments on possible responses, they also consider why the situation developed through the case might have occurred and how it might be possible to create interventions to prevent similar circumstances from arising in the future. Accordingly, students were asked to prepare a 2000 word-report, reflecting on areas of potential process improvement, specific to the in-class presented Employment Tribunal claim. The assignment needs to highlight and apply all relevant areas of policy improvement, relevant legislation and literature. Students were given guidance on content under the following headings:

- Evaluate, critique and reflect on the management of disciplinary and grievance issues.
- Use of literature / academic referencing
- Draws on relevant sources to support the arguments-
- Integrates theory with practice to tease out problems, opportunities and new possibilities. -academic-practitioner and discusses the following areas for reflection:

  - HR competencies in managing conflict
  - Good practice in investigations
  - Justifying action taken
  - Preparing tribunal bundle
  - Reflection on process improvement

The students share locus of control, between themselves, the tutors and the professional bodies but the student also needs to validate their own agency in the space in order to develop their skills, knowledge and begin to embody their practice. Active student learning is the focus, but additionally an opportunity for feedback on in class behaviors and reflections is created. For this to happen, the student needs to be empowered to employ their own skills, knowledge and judgment to complete this assessment. Bovil (2020) suggests that co-creation is a meaningful collaboration between students and tutors and the preparation of a response to a case study where the student's judgment guides the next steps in the process is an example of how this can work in practice. The student is guided and supported in holding the knowledge required but there is independence of decision making which influences the development of the content and suggests genuine engagement in a co-creative process.

The next generation of professionals will no doubt work in more diverse teams and the opportunity to work collaboratively in a safe environment will support the development of skills and competencies supportive of change and diversity. They will need to work and develop relationships in the virtual as well as the physical world and the need for shared community understanding of practice and behaviors will be even more evident than it is today. Their ability to boundary cross will increasingly become an important skill within their practice. The importance of design in content and authentic assessments supports the development of these skills. It is important to note that the learning is not confined to students. In seeking to create authentic delivery and assessments, the role of staff development must be considered crucial. Institutions with long histories of developing research and academic practice may be challenged by the need to engage tutors with a greater understanding of context and practice. For some tutors, time spent outside the institution or linked mentoring arrangements with the professional world may be needed to support the contextual and behavioral elements of authentic delivery and practice. For this to be successful, time and energy would need to be diverted to ensure that tutors can facilitate the diversity of co-created work with confidence. Professional practice experience will need to become part of the academic toolkit if tutors are to successfully embed authentic design into their modules and programs.

Reflexive practice is at the heart of the module Strategic HR Competencies which has been discussed as the main case study in this paper. Given this, it is important to understand the reflection from students post participation and this next section will move on to look at the qualitative student feedback from 2020 and 2021. The first student demonstrates how their learning developed through critiquing the approach adopted by the fictitious HR department:

'The grievance policy states that its purpose is "to produce a quick resolution where genuine problems exist…in an atmosphere of trust and collaboration". Throughout the process of this investigation, the HR team adhered by this statement, investigating the issue, and attempting to work with all employees concerned in the matter, whilst trying to create a resolution quickly and effectively. Despite this, upon reflection, there are some areas which could have been approached alternatively, that may have improved the effectiveness of the investigation and lessened its impact on the organisation.'

Within this statement it can be seen that the student is developing a sense of confidence in their own personal judgment and so have moved beyond a passive understanding of the application of policy to one of understanding impact and consequences. In reviewing this the student has also moved towards generating alternative options in an organizational context so developing authentic professional skills for the future.

The personal benefits of the role-play are expressed by this student who also successfully critically evaluates the processes followed by the fictitious HR department underpinned by UK employment law, which demonstrates her learning:

'The role play was useful to see because if enabled be to understand that from his perspective he felt anxious or nervous during this time as he was worried that his colleagues were talking about his sudden absence. In addition to that, when looking at the suspension letter that Pete was sent, the ACAS code of practice (2015) has helped me understand how the letter was too brief and lacks context. The letter only states that "allegations of gross misconduct" have been made; however, it does not specify exactly what happened. This outcome has taught me that it is important to be specific with the employee especially where suspension is involved as the lack of information could make the employee reluctant to co-operate or not trust that the organisation is treating them fairly (could result in investigation being prolonged). Lastly, in Pete's minutes HR inform him that he will not be on shift with Suzie for a while and that mediation will be offered to resolve the issue.' Student B.

Problems are correctly identified by this student who noticed errors in process and investigation protocols, demonstrating her learning and creative thinking by proposing alternative solutions:

'The mock trial highlighted some problems, and it was observed that the process was not robust, reflecting a lack of documentation and appropriate investigation procedures that HR should have conducted. The set of documents used at times offered mixed views and contradictions with Suzie having a clear profile on one document but then there were some other claims that Suzie allegedly went to work after having consumed alcohol and had been warned about such behaviour. If there was a more explicit way of tracking the paperwork, than management would have been transparent and only talked based on evidence and avoid claims that are not supported by facts. This could be improved by developing a better staff monitoring systems that provides clear guidance as to how to record and store any documents where employees do not company with organisation's working expectations.' Student C.

Evidence of personal learning is included in this student's reflection that highlights the importance of resolving a complaint professionally to avoid time-consuming grievances and legal action through employment tribunals. She also includes suitable recommendations on how to address potential further occurrences:

'For me the most important aspect of the HR managers role is the responsibility and duty of care to employees to prevent, investigate and manage any report of misconduct. Having experienced the mock tribunal, I have realised the importance of trying the resolve the complaint in a serious, professional manner to avoid the potential of creating further distress and potentially resulting in an employment tribunal. I believe that prevention and awareness can mitigate any future misconduct issues in the workplace. As a HR professional to prevent any further occurrences I would set up an anti-harassment campaign to show clarity on organisational tolerance for sexual harassment' Student D.

The value of the practices-based experience from an inclusive perspective is revealed in the following feedback from a neurodivergent student:

'Overall, I thoroughly enjoyed this experience. It gave me an insight of the skills which are needed to investigate and prepare for a tribunal case. I particularly liked how the work was practical as it allowed me to understand how real-life scenarios worked which helped me gain a better understanding of the module'.

Conclusions: Implications for Practice

Significant responsibility lies with the design element of the module and the integration of academic knowledge and practice support the creation of a coherent design which clearly defines the key elements of professional practice being delivered by the module. The defining of the skills, knowledge, values and behaviors are significant and need to blend with the knowledge content to ensure coherence in the learning experience. This paper has presented different visions from the academic literature and practice examples in teaching, learning and assessment but there is more work to be undertaken in developing academic practice. This practice may be informed by professional bodies' discourse and definitions or may be the outcome of collaborative work with expert practitioners and associated organizations. The Business School in LJMU has provided the opportunity for academic and student to come together in shared spaces where theoretical concepts and business practice are explored together. In a world of rapid change, it becomes important that this shared space expands and that developmental work is not considered in isolation but in a culture of collaborative learning.

To achieve this there is a need for shared conceptual language and discourse. The descriptions of professional practice will differ depending on which community is discussing it. A three-way partnership between professional practitioners, academics and students will support a shared understanding. This development in collaborative learning will be beneficial. Cooke Sather (2014) suggests that appreciating variation and diversity in outcomes supports the development of the student in collaboration. The academic development requirements and resourcing needs associated with professional practice literacy will take time to develop and this needs to be recognized by institutions as they move into the culture of professional practice.

Bovil (2016, 2020) points to the need for clarity in the design of assessment for practice-related modules. Assessment practice may be narrowly defined within institutional culture and the individualistic and diverse approach to practice-based assessment may not fit well with organizational processes designed to provide metrics and standardization. For academics, the need to capture data on student outcomes resulting from practice-based assessments, will form part of the progression route to establishing professional practice design in business modules as standard.

The development of professional practice teaching and assessment requires commonality of purpose between the academic and student but also an appreciative institutional position with regard to preparation time and engagement with external supporting stakeholders. The outcomes as revealed through student confidence engagement and enhanced critical thinking support the effort required to make professional practice a sustainable part of student learning.

Literature

Armstrong, Michael / Taylor, Stephen: *Armstrong's Handbook of Human Resource Management Practice*. Kogan Page: London et al. 2020 (15th Edition).

Bovill, Catherine: "Co-creation in Learning and Teaching: The Case for a Whole – Class Approach in Higher Education". *Higher Education*, 79, 2020, pp. 1023–1037.

Bovill, Catherine / Felton, Peter: "Cultivating Student-Staff Partnerships through Research and Practice". *International Journal for Academic Development*, 21(1), 2016, pp. 1–3.

CIPD 2013: CIPD HR Professional Map, retrieved 10.4.2020, from https://www.cipd.co.uk/cipd-hr-profession/cipd-hr-profession-map/default.html.

CIPD 2017: New CIPD Research Calls for Professionals to Use HR Analytics to Improve Evidence-Based Practice, retrieved 17.12.2020, from https://www.cipd.co.uk/news-views/news-articles/hr-analytics-reserach.

CIPD 2018: New Professional Map, retrieved 17.12.2020 from https://peoplepro fession.cipd.org/profession-map.

Cole, Caroline et al.: "Research Methodologies and Professional Practice: Considerations and Practicalities". *The Electronic Journal of Business Research Methods*, 9(2), 2011, pp. 141–151.

European University Association: *Report on Active Learning 2019*.

Huber, George P.: "Organisational Learning: The Contributing Processes and the Literatures". *Organisational Science*, 2(1), 1991, pp. 88–115.

Kemmis, Stephen: "Understanding Professional Practice: A Synoptic Framework". In: Green, Bill (ed.): *Understanding and Researching Professional Practice*. Brill, 2009, pp. 19–38.

Lester, Stan: "Beyond Knowledge and Competence towards a Framework for Professional Education". *Capability*, 1(3), 1995, pp. 44–52.

Lo, Karen / Macky, Keith / Pio, Edwina: "The HR Competency Requirements for Strategic and Functional HR Practitioners". *The International Journal of Human Resource Management*, 26(18), 2015, pp. 2308–2328.

Russo, Dario: "Competency Measurement Model". *European Conference on Quality in Official Statistics*, Madrid, 2016, pp. 1–22. https://www.ine.es/q2016/docs/q2016Final00276.pdf

Villarroel, Verónica et al.: "Authentic Assessment: Creating a Blueprint for Course Design". *Assessment and Evaluation in Higher Education*, 43(5), 2018, pp. 840–854.

Further Reading

Engeström, Yrjö / Engeström, Ritva / Kärkkäinen, Merja: "Polycontextuality and Boundary Crossing in Expert Cognition: Learning and Problem Solving in Complex Work Activities". *Learning and Instruction*, 5(4), 1995, pp. 319–336.

Jankowski, Natasha A. et al.: "Assessment That Matters: Trending Toward Practices That Document Authentic Student Learning". In: *National Institute for Learning Outcomes Assesment: Occasional Papers 2018*, retrieved 9.12.2020, from http://learningoutcomesassessment.org/occasionalpaperfourteen.htm.

Kuh, George D.: "Beyond Compliance: Making Assessment Matter". *Change: The Magazine of Higher Learning*, 47(5), 2015, pp. 8–17.

Kuh, George D.: *High Impact Educational Practices: A Brief Overview 2008*, retrieved from www.AACU.org.

Ministry of Justice: Tribunal Statistics Quarterly, July to September 2020, retrieved 9.11.2021 from https://www.gov.uk/government/publications/tribunal-statistics-quarterly-july-to-september-2020/tribunal-statistics-quarterly-july-to-september-2020.

Office for Students: Report: Students, Experts In Their Own Experience 2020–2023. OfS Strategy Document, retrieved 9.11.2021 from https://www.officeforstudents.org.uk/media/c1731253-9d84-436f-8b06-8f87f51fd807/student-engagement-strategy-design-web.pdf.

Perkins, David: "From Idea to Action". In: Hetland, L. / Veenema, S. (eds.): *The Project Zero Classroom: Views on Understanding,* Harvard Graduate School of Education, 1999, pp. 17–25.

Segon, Michael: "Managing Organisational Ethics: Professionalism, Duty and HR Practitioners". *Journal of Law and Governance,* 5(4), 2010, retrieved 9.11.2021 from https://doi.org/10.15209/jbsge.v5i4.191.

Soehren, David: "Student Partners in Designing Professional Content and assessment". (Teaching and Learning Conference, Liverpool 2019). (Paper at John Moores University as part of the Teaching and Learning Academy Enhancement Strategy) retrieved 9.11.2021 from https://doi.org/10.15209/jbsge.v5i4.191. www.ljmu.ac.uk/academic-registry/teaching-and-learning-academy/enhancement

Sunahwati, Eka / Maarif, Muhammad S. / Sukmawati, Anggraini: "Human Resources Development Policy as a Strategy for Improving Public Organizational Performance". *JKAP (Jurnal Kebijakan Dan Administrasi Publik),* 23(1), 2019, pp. 50–62.

Aurora Ricci

The Innovation of Learning and Teaching Practices in Higher Education: A Methodological Focus on the University of Bologna's Model.

Abstract: Due to the impact of COVID-19 health emergency on the teaching activities of educational institutions of all levels, higher education had to implement a deep transformation of its organization. University of Bologna's model of intervention is characterized by circular actions of evaluation, analysis, reflection, training, and redesign of teaching activities. The contribution aims to present the main results regarding the processes evaluation and a methodological reflection will be provided to highlight the capacity to transform this unexpected situation into an opportunity.

Keywords: Learner- and teacher-focused activities, remote learning, institution-focused activities, need analysis

Introduction

The national health restrictions caused by the outbreak of the Covid-19 pandemic, which started at the end of February 2020, have forced Italian educational institutions, at each level and grade, to find solutions to ensure quality and fairness in teaching and learning activities. In fact, prevention and risk reduction measures, such as national closures, quarantine, social distancing, and travel restrictions, were implemented (Yanes-Lane et al. 2020), especially for Italy, the first country in Europe to be affected by the spread of COVID-19, and which suffered the greatest losses during the first wave of the pandemic. The interruption of teaching activities requested a sudden change from the traditional face-to-face mode to a brand new emergency full distance mode and this required the deployment of several efforts and resources introduced to cope with the emergency by the University of Bologna.

The emergency occurred within an organization where a previous process of teaching and learning innovation had been implemented since few years; this happened in a sector – University – where innovation is considered to be a central issue all around the world since a few decades. In fact, the change from a teacher-centered to a student-centered perspective, following the Bologna Process (1999), has generated multiple actions for teacher training, in order to support the change itself, but still, there is no standardized curricula for University lecturers and professors and their training and guidance remains at the foremost competence of each University. Another element determining the huge change which has impacted higher education in the last decades is the increase in the demand for University education at an international level (Trow 2007; Stes et al. 2010) with the consequent development of a student population that is more and more heterogeneous in terms of age, origin, socio-cultural background, motivation, basic knowledge, approach to learning and vocational guidance (Mulryan-Kynees 2010). Furthermore, several socio-cultural changes have progressively reshaped the structure of higher education systems and the policies of University institutions are questioning the issue of teaching and learning innovation embodying the urgent need to rethink teaching-learning processes (Coggi 2019). Therefore, as previously briefly retraced the pandemic emergency occurred in a scenario that was already in motion.

After the beginning of the transformation related to the emergency, University institutions have been forced to make decisions on how to cope with a compulsory, sudden innovation. The University of Bologna, following the methodological framework of its teaching and learning innovation model, decided to start from research. From a methodological point of view, in an emergency, it has been considered to be rigorous as well as strategic to adopt an approach based on the systematic collection of information and data, to picture, as reliably as possible student's and teacher's visions and perceptions on the emergency situation. This data collection was aimed to stimulate perspective and open space for reflection and re-design of educational activities for innovation. New activities designed and redesigned, according to new scenarios, were tested for assessment and data collection. Moreover, all of these activities took place in an environment characterized by sharing and collectivism.

In this chapter we are going to reflect on how the innovation process at the University of Bologna has been challenged – as at many other higher education institutions – by the pandemic, and how important it is now to understand which drivers of change deserve to be embedded to move forward and deal with future challenges.

Innovation in Learning and Teaching at the University of Bologna

All activities related to innovation in teaching and learning at the University of Bologna have been designed and implemented in the last few years using a theoretical and methodological framework of Formative Educational Evaluation

The University of Bologna's innovation in learning and teaching

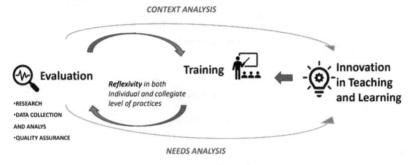

Fig. 1: The University of Bologna's innovation in learning and teaching.

(Kellaghan / Stufflebeam 2003; Bondioli / Ferrari 2004) and Research-Training understood in an evaluative sense (Betti / Vannini 2013; Betti et al. 2015; Asquini 2018). These processes aim to actively involve the stakeholders (students, teachers, and administrative staff) in analysis and the redesign in an improvement perspective (Vertecchi 1976), thereby stimulating the process of analysis and reflection on their own competencies, roles, and teaching beliefs.

Figure 1 (Figure 1) emphasizes the formulation of the three working stages of this approach. Specifically, the first activity concerns the collection and analysis of data, in other words, the stage of systematic collection, with reliable indicators and rigorous procedures of various types of information to study the context and processes. The second stage is to provide data to stakeholders for feedback and to identify the training needs of university teachers. This is, in fact, a central moment since it is focused on the sharing and promotion of the processes of self-evaluation and reflexivity. The third phase is focused on making new hypotheses and redesigning teaching and learning practices, possibly developing new approaches and methods. During this stage, new hypothesis rises collectively and changing direction is always possible. According to the new directions undertaken some specific training interventions addressed to teachers are also designed, in response to the identified needs (Balzaretti et al. 2018; Balzaretti / Vannini 2018; Ciani / Rosa 2020; Luppi 2018; Luppi / Benini 2017).

Based on the previous description, the University of Bologna has developed a plan of strategic activities for innovation based on three levels of intervention (Figure 2):

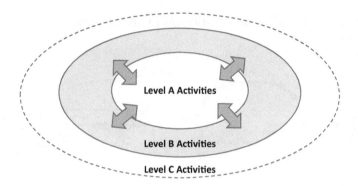

Fig. 2: Synergy between research and training actions for teaching and learning innovation (Source: Guglielmi et al. 2020, p. 139)

- Level A activities: Research-training activities based on the Formative Educational Evaluation model, described in detail above.
- Level B activities: Specific training programs on innovative teaching and learning methodologies. A series of transversal actions, linked to the improvement of University teaching and learning practices, aimed at raising awareness – in a broad way – of the whole teaching staff, on the issues of quality. In addition, the University has developed a comprehensive training program to form students' transversal skills.

Levels A and B are complementary and interrelated, contributing to each other, implement a logic of innovation based on research, reflexivity on teaching professionalism and create opportunities for experiential learning in constructivist contexts (Luppi et al. 2020b).

- *Level C activities*: Design of an organizational model to support innovation and quality in teaching and learning.
- In this activity, synergy is ensured through the Quality Assurance and Innovation in teaching and learning Sector and the Center for Educational Innovation.
- Quality assessment activities are supported by training activities, again following the logic of "formative assessment" (Colurcio / Mele 2008). Thus, from this point of view, quality management is understood as a management approach to the deliberate development of those specific conditions and capabilities that are necessary for the continuous creation and dissemination of knowledge and the subsequent initiation of learning processes (ibidem). In

this regard, the system of quality teaching at the University of Bologna is placed at the service of teaching innovative projects, in order to test its effectiveness in terms of continuous improvement. Therefore, in this system, improving existing good practices plays an important role (Luppi et al. 2020b).

The *Students-Focused* Activities to Face the Emergency

After the suspension of teaching activities to reduce the risk of infection, the University of Bologna transferred 70 % of all lectures online in one week and then100 % in two weeks: it has been decided to adopt a synchronous teaching and learning mode using Microsoft Teams as a platform. In particular: 3.667 lectures, 215.880 examinations and 10.069 graduations have been provided online during the first four months of emergency. Moreover, during distance education, internships were not canceled, thanks to new agreements with host organizations and the provision of alternative activities monitored by academic supervisors. At the same time, during the lockdown, an intense program of activities and events was launched on communication, cultural entertainment, sports, and community networking. By the way, the most valuable efforts of the UNIBO involved innovation in teaching and learning.

Monitoring of Learning Practices for Students

Two weeks after the start of online teaching/learning, the University of Bologna developed an online learning survey for students using a short questionnaire. Almost 10.000 students from all study programs and subject areas answered. Women accounted for 64 %, 98 % of the respondents answered from Italy, of which 66 % from the Emilia-Romagna region, and the remaining 34 % from other regions. The survey was repeated at the end of the semester and the results and needs for improvement inspired the development of a program of training activities proposed to the teaching staff in the second semester.

The data collection technique was based on a self-report questionnaire containing several structured questions aimed at measuring the degree of satisfaction with aspects related to technical difficulties encountered, satisfaction with learning, interaction with the teacher, level of attention, and the overall experience in the very first weeks of online teaching. There were also two open-ended questions asking for three strengths and three areas for improvement in the teaching experience on the online platform. The answers to the open-ended questions were analyzed using the text mining method of Latent Dirichelet Allocation or LDA (Blei et al. 2003) which is used for content analysis, i.e.

identifying the topics contained in a list of texts. Finally, a few questions were designed to obtain information on the place, from which the student was following the lessons, subject areas, and gender.

A total amount of 9,943 students (64 % of which female) from all study courses and subject areas responded. The scores showed a relatively low incidence of technical difficulties (connection and use of the platform) and medium to high levels of satisfaction with learning, interaction with teachers, attention during teaching activities (the average score, in this case, is lower), and overall experience in online classes. The answers to these questions showed high levels of satisfaction for most students; in fact, in the 1–10 range, 75 % of respondents were in the score range of 7 or higher and 50 % were in the score range of 8 or higher.

Concerning the open-ended answers, we are going to briefly present a summary of qualitative results, highlighting several content categories related to the use of the platform, the interactivity, the student-teacher interaction, and the interaction among students. In particular:

- Use of the platform
  The answers highlighted positive aspects of online teaching linked to the experience of a lecture that is not affected by any environmental conditions related to face-to-face teaching (oversized classrooms, distance from the blackboard, acoustics in teaching spaces, background noise, etc.). In addition, students asked teachers to spend time and attention in checking audio and video settings (teachers and students' microphones, cameras, etc.)
- Interactivity
  According to other international research carried out during the COVID-19 pandemic (Lassoued et al. 2020), many students suggested replacing the use of slides with a webcam. In this regard, one respondent stated: "So much quality is missed: the visual contact between teacher and student is fundamental and so it is lost" (Luppi et al. 2020a, p. 52).
- Student-teacher interaction
  According to other international research (Petillion / McNeil 2020), the use of chat as a tool to collect feedback from students, ask questions, respond to solicitations, interact with teachers and the classroom is greatly appreciated. Very much appreciation comes from teachers' attention to the questions that are asked in the chat and to the use of chat as a tool that helps interaction before, during and at the end of the lesson. To this regard, one respondent

stated, "It was much easier to ask questions to the professor directly with ease" (Luppi et al. 2020a, p. 52).

• Interaction among students

Several responses mentioned the limitations of distance, especially in student interaction: "interaction among peers is missing", "Sadness for the absence of socialization" (Luppi et al. 2020a, p. 53). Moreover, it has been said by international students: "It is hard to form groups for a teamwork, especially for international students" (Luppi et al. 2020a, p. 53).

The results were presented in the form of an educational video distributed to the entire community of the University of Bologna, in order to guide teachers in the innovation of their practices, as a response to the emergency[1].

In addition to the survey on online learning (distance and blended learning), a further survey was conducted to investigate students' attitudes towards distance examinations. Data collection was organized through an online questionnaire on Feedback Server platform and was carried out from March to April 2021. Its distribution took place through the official communication channel. The results of this survey have not yet been released.

Case Study: Students of Veterinary Medicine Course

A recent case study (Ricci / Luppi 2021) consisted of 173 observations (375 questionnaires were collected and only questionnaires that could be paired were considered valid, furthermore excluding those that did not fill in one of the two observations at T1 or T2). Participants were mostly female (80,7 %) with an average age of 23.1 (19–45 years old).

Results of research – part of a wider project on the innovation of teaching and learning practices conducted in the School of Veterinary Medicine of UNIBO – are mentioned here. The purpose of this case study was to explore the impact of the pandemic emergency on teaching and learning dimensions, through a short-term longitudinal research design, following the pre-test/post-test logic (Janson 1981; Jöreskon 1981; Fraccaroli 1998). Indeed, comparing the results of the face-to-face learning phase (T1) to the results of emergency distance learning phase (T2), a reflection based on students' beliefs, motivations, skills, and opinions started, and generalizations with the other study programs can be undertaken.

---

1   https://centri.unibo.it/centroinnovazionedidattica/it/docenti/video-innovazione-didattica-nell-emergenza.

The data analyses showed a general pattern of stability in all input variables; indeed, although the levels of motivation (intrinsic and extrinsic), learning self-efficacy, independence, and flexibility increased during the emergency distance learning, the differences between T1 and T2 was not statistically significant. Thus, the emergency change in the learning environment did not influence students' motivations or beliefs concerning their own competence to reach learning goals or their awareness of coping related competencies (Ricci / Luppi 2021).

Concerning process variables, the results of the t-test for paired samples used to detect differences between face-to-face learning (T1) and distance learning (T2), showed that no significant differences are appreciable for most of the items. Indeed, the difference between T1 and T2 was statistically significant only for the item concerning "the evaluation of clearness about how they are assessed". The results could suggest that the shift requires flexibility in adapting teaching practices to the new scenarios and in the way in which professors clarify teaching programs, learning goals and examination modalities (Ricci / Luppi 2021).

Concerning product variables, the results of the t-test for paired samples used to detect differences between face-to-face learning (T1) and distance learning (T2) showed no significant differences appreciable for any items. In fact, although most levels of satisfaction (with the exception of space and equipment) declined during distance learning, the difference between T1 and T2 was not statistically significant. Thus, despite the unexpected change in the learning experience, the satisfaction for teaching and learning remained high. The students' satisfaction detected by the current case study confirmed, in general, outcomes collected from 10.000 students of UNIBO (Luppi et al. 2020a).

The results of the study were shared with the University Course Committee, in order to start a reflection on the improvement of teaching-learning practices in a specific scientific discipline. In addition, the study highlighted the training needs of students and teachers that could be explored in specific workshops.

The *Teachers-Focused* Activities to Face the Emergency

The quality of education and teaching has gained importance in higher education in the recent decades (Gaebel / Zhang 2018; Skelton 2005). Also, during the COVID-19 health emergency, educational innovation actions affected teachers and their professional development. In particular, three activities involved teachers and we would like to highlight here their results: 1) The monitoring and evaluation of teaching and learning 2) The collection of good teaching practices and peer learning community building and 3) video training for teachers.

The Monitoring and Evaluation of Teaching and Learning Practices According to Teachers

A survey involving teachers was initiated by the "interest group" made up of teachers and researchers from the Department of Educational Sciences and the Department of Informatics of the Bologna University; although it was held during the Covid-19 pandemic, it is part of an innovative teaching and learning effort aimed at monitoring teaching and learning processes, offering food for thought and inspiring training activities for teachers. The main question inspiring the questionnaire was: What aspects are related to the methodological and teaching choice of professors during this emergency? In this regard, using the division of the studied variables into context, input, process, and product variables (C.I.P.P. Model), two research objectives were achieved: 1) a descriptive objective aimed at creating a picture of how the teachers found themselves facing the emergency and therefore what difficulties they encountered and what resources were available to them; 2) a correlation objective aimed at describing which factors – input, process, and product – were associated with the methodological choices made by teachers and under what conditions (presence or absence of previous training).

The results of the survey involving 393 professors (31.8 % were 46–55 years old and 48.1 % female) (Ricci 2021) painted a picture of resilient teachers. The analysis of the process variables has highlighted how, while facing a significant workload (albeit with low perceived technological difficulties), teachers' personal resources (such as flexibility and decision-making autonomy) are still identifiable and able to mitigate the impact, by the reference literature on psychosocial risk factors (Xanthopoulou et al. 2007). In parallel, the positive correlation of flexibility with the choice of practical case methodology is in line with Hattie's (2009) findings regarding experienced teachers.

The analysis of the product variables shows that the teachers are overall quite satisfied with distance learning, in line with the answers given by the students, although they are less satisfied with the interaction they had with the latter. Finally, a positive element is represented by the fact that the learning acquired by the teachers during the emergency period is considered by them such as something to be implemented in future teaching. Nevertheless, analyzing the use of teaching methods before and during distance learning it is presumed that many professors had a general perception of the impairment of their teaching practice. Furthermore, it is interesting to observe that the use of active teaching methods (such as problem-solving, group work, and simulation/role-playing) increases, so do teachers' levels of satisfaction and their intention to transfer what has been learned during the pandemic into future practice.

It has been highlighted that those who participated in prior training before the distance learning used less traditional methods and more active practices than the others (Ricci 2021). On the other hand, it was observed that those who received training during distance learning used less transmissive teaching, preferring active forms (e. g. problem-solving, simulations/role-playing) than the other teachers. Finally, it is possible to observe how both targets (trained vs. untrained) implemented "conservative" choices on teaching methodologies, i.e. applying a methodology already tested regardless of the new teaching setting. It was observed that teachers, who found themselves in an emergency and had to adapt their teaching methods in a short time, opted to remain in a teaching comfort zone, adopting small adjustments in the course of the work. Finally, this data, if read from another point of view, shows how teachers who were already using active teaching were still able to experiment during distance teaching, choosing not to retreat to a transmissive mode centered on the teacher (Ricci 2021).

The Teaching Good Practices Collection and the Peer Teaching Community Building

A survey concerning the teaching good practices was conducted to analyze practice and encourage collective comparison. At the Training workshops it was possible to discuss and compare such experiences. The initiative was designed to stimulate the creation of a network for exchange of experiences and to foster initial reflection on innovative strategies and methodologies for online teaching, that will be disseminated to the educational community.

The teaching experiences were described by the teachers themselves using a template and the results have been analyzed and classified into disciplinary areas and 'thematic fields'. In this regard, based on what emerged, 5 training workshops were designed (for Scientific, Technological, Humanistic, Social, and Medical areas), delivered in May and June 2020, and conducted remotely by a teacher expert in teaching and learning in the specific discipline and a facilitator expert in education. The initiative supported the teachers in tackling the following phase characterized by blended synchronous learning. Thus, it can be observed that the project intended to encourage the sharing and dissemination of online teaching experiences, as well as to generate further ideas, to encourage an experimental approach of the methodologies themselves (Luppi et al. 2020a, 2020b).

The workshops highlighted training needs that have been translated into further training actions planned from September 2020 in order to meet the emerging training needs.

Video-Training for Teachers

In addition to the training organized in seminars, in order to guarantee new ways of sharing knowledge, several thematic videos have been produced and made available to UniBo teachers. These videos met the training needs that have emerged and offered teachers hints and ideas to support innovation in emergency teaching.

The videos produced to date included: a video presenting the data coming from students' survey; a video on communication in online teaching and learning, a video on pedagogical implication of online learning and video on peer instruction as a method for promoting participation in distance learning and a video on assessment in online teaching and learning (Luppi et al. 2020b)[2].

The *Institution-Focused* Activities to Face the Emergency

In defining its model for innovation in teaching and learning through the synergy between quality and educational innovation, the University of Bologna has adopted the definition of quality as 'transformation', according to which quality itself is the prerequisite for change (Harvey / Green 1993) and captures its 'dynamic' essence (Pirsig 1991).

The quality of teaching is thus supported by participatory paths and by enhancing a bottom-up approach, which allows the levers and tools adopted and adaptable to act and nurture their role and the quality assurance process itself, in a virtuous way (Luppi et al. 2020b). Examples of activities related to the quality assurance process developed during the pandemic were:

- Training for the role of Program Coordinator. The training course for the role of study program coordinators was held in 2020 to enhance design skills and encourage the sharing of the best experiences of course management identified from the analysis of the annual reviews of study courses.
- Training for the role of the Members of the students and teachers joint Committees. The course was held in 2020 and included a phase of sharing interviews with the peer commission aimed at identifying the role and functions of the commissions both at the national and university level. In addition, video testimonials were provided, in order to share experiences of quality assurance process management.

---

2   https://centri.unibo.it/centroinnovazionedidattica/it/docenti/video-innovazione-didattica-nell-emergenza.

- The paths addressed to the course coordinators and to the members of the students and teachers joint Committees have been also supported through the production of videos and presentations of good practices and experiences already in place and/or proposed to support the quality of teaching in an emergency phase.

The material produced has been organized and the online space "Acting in teaching and learning quality" has been created for learning, sharing, networking, and disseminating good practices, starting from the experiences carried out within the University of Bologna. The space is accessible to the entire academic community, technical-administrative staff, and engaged students, intending to embrace and disseminate a culture of quality, encouraging the exchange of knowledge and the development of process skills, which are useful in achieving the goal of quality assuring in teaching at the University of Bologna (Luppi et al. 2020b).

Final Considerations

Because of the potential "fragilizing" effect that is intrinsic to major emergencies, the spread of the pandemic represents a crucial resilience and integrity test for the values of universities and for their ability to maintain collaborative and excellent teaching and learning community. Regarding this, the unavoidable pandemic spread put universities into a new uncertain and challenging situation. But as Dewey (1933) argued, because the feeling of uncertainty is a necessary condition to experiment and such condition represents the basis for reflective thinking, it could be possible to assume that the pandemic situation could be seen as an opportunity for "learning through and from experience towards gaining new insights of self and practice" (Finlay 2008).

Furthermore, it is possible to argue too that the pandemic emergency has arrived at a time of great reflection and change for university institutions, and the risk that its impact may alter their path is tangible. It will be important for policy decisions to be underpinned by continuous monitoring of contextual data, the training needs of teachers and students, the changes in processes, and their outcomes. Thus, in a changing scenario, universities will have to be particularly adaptive and able to explain to their stakeholders the need for such adaptation, without losing their strive for quality and equitable teaching.

Literature

Asquini, Giorgio: *La Ricerca-Formazione. Temi, esperienze e prospettive.* Franco Angeli: Milano, 2018.

Balzaretti, Nicoletta et al.: "Analizzare i processi di apprendimento degli studenti per innovare la didattica universitaria. Il modello di Formative Educational Evaluation dell'Università di Bologna". *Education Sciences & Society*, 2, 2018, pp. 58–82, retrieved from http://dx.doi.org/10.3280/ess2-2018oa6894.

Balzaretti, Nicoletta / Vannini, Ira: "Promuovere la qualità della didattica universitaria. La Formative Educational Evaluation in uno studio pilota dell'Ateneo bolognese". *Journal of Educational, Cultural and Psychological Studies*, 18, 2018, pp. 187–213, retrieved from http://dx.doi.org/10.7358/ecps-2018-018-balz.

Betti, Maurizio / Vannini, Irina: "Valutare la qualità dei corsi di lifelong learning in America Latina. Alcune riflessioni teoriche e metodologiche sul disegno valutativo utilizzato nel progetto AlfaIII Trall". *Ricerche di Pedagogia e Didattica – Journal of Theories and Research in Education*, 8(2), 2013, pp. 45–61.

Betti, Maurizio et al.: "Una ruta hacia un sistema de aseguramiento de la calidad en Educación Superior: la experiencia del proyecto TRALL". *ECPS – Educational, Cultural and Psychological Studies*, 1, 2018, pp. 77–115, retrieved from http://doi:10.7358/ecps2015-012-bett.

Bettinelli, Annamaria B. / Ferrari, Mónica: *Verso un modello di valutazione formativa. Ragioni, strumenti e percorsi.* Junior: Azzano San Paolo 2004.

Blei, David M. / Ng, Andrew Y. / Jordan, Michael I.: "Latent Dirichlet Allocation". *Journal of Machine Learning Research*, 3, 2003, pp. 993–1022.Ciani, Andrea / Rosa, Alessandra: "Sviluppare le competenze dei docenti universitari nella prospettiva del formative assessment: una ricerca valutativa su un intervento formativo rivolto a docenti delle Università del Myanmar". *Excellence and Innovation in Learning and Teaching-Open Access*, 5(1), 2020.

Coggi, Cristina: *Innovare la didattica e la valutazione in Università. Il progetto IRIDI per la formazione dei docenti.* Franco Angeli: Milano, 2019.

Colurcio, Maria / Mele, Cristina: "Il quality management per il talento e la creatività". *Mercati e competitività*, 2, 2008, pp. 17–44.

Dewey, John: *How We Think: A Restatement of the Relation of Reflective Thinking to the Educative Process.* D.C. Heath & Co Publishers: Boston (MA), 1933.

Finlay, Linda: "Reflecting on 'Reflective Practice'". Practice-based Professional Learning Paper 52, 2018. The Open University, retrieved 7.8.2021 from www.open.ac.uk/pbpl.

Fraccaroli, Franco: *Il cambiamento nelle organizzazioni. Metodi di ricerca longitudinale applicati alla psicologia del lavoro*. Raffaello Cortina Editore: Milano, 1998.

Gaebel, Michael / Zhang, Thérèse: "Trends 2018: Learning and Teaching in the European Higher Education Area". Report of the European University Association, retrieved 7.8.2021 from https://eua.eu/downloads/publicati ons/trends-2018-learning-and-teaching-in-the-european-higher-education-area.pdf.

Guglielmi, Dina et al.: "La ricerca formazione per l'innovazione della didattica universitaria". In: Lotti, Antonella / Lampugnani Paola A. (eds.): *Faculty Development in Italia. Valorizzazione delle competenze didattiche dei docenti universitari*. Genova University Press: Genova, 2020, pp. 133–48.

Harvey, Lee / Green, Diana: "Defining Quality". *Assessment & Evaluation in Higher Education*, 18(1), 2006, pp. 9–34.

Hattie, John: *Visible Learning. A Synthesis of over 800 Meta-Analyses Relating to Achievement*. Routledge: London, 2009.

House Ernest R. / Howe Kenneth R.: "Deliberative Democratic Evaluation". In: Petillion, Riley J. / McNeil, W. Stephen (eds.): *Student Experiences of Emergency Remote Teaching: Impacts of Instructor Practice on Student Learning, Engagement, and Well-Being. Journal of Chemical Education*, 97(9), 2020, pp. 2486–2493.

Janson, Carl-Gunnar: "Some Problems of Longitudinal Research in the Social Sciences". In: Schulsinger, Fini / Mednick, Sarnoff A. / Knop, Joachim (eds.): *Longitudinal Research. Methods and Uses in Behavioral Science*. Springer Netherlands: Amsterdam, 1981, pp. 19–55, retrieved from https://doi.org/10.1037/h0099078.

Jörekson, K.G.: "Statistical Model for Longitudinal Studies". In: Schulsinger, Fini / Mednick, Sarnoff A. / Knop, Joachim (eds.): *Longitudinal Research. Methods and Uses in Behavioral Science*. Springer Netherlands: Amsterdam, 1981, pp. 118–124, retrieved from https://doi.org/10.1037/h0099078.

Kellaghan, Thomas / Stufflebeam, Daniel L. (eds.): *International Handbook* of *Educational Evaluation*. Kluwer: Dordrecht / Boston / London, 2003.

Luppi, Elena: "The University of Bologna During the Covid-19 Pandemic: Protect, Provide and Innovate – Responses from a Resilient Community". In: Bergan, Sjur et al. (eds.): *Higher Education's Response to the Covid-19 Pandemic Building. A More Sustainable and Democratic Future*. Council of Europe Higher Education Series 25, 2021, pp. 155–164.

Luppi, Elena / Benini, Stefano: "Valutare le strategie di apprendimento negli studenti universitari: primi risultati di una ricerca valutativa condotta all'Università di Bologna". *ECPS: Educational Cultural and Psychological Studies*, (16), 2017, pp. 99–127.Luppi, Elena / Neri, Barbara / Vannini, Ira: "Innovare la didattica nell'emergenza. Il percorso dell'Università di Bologna". *Scuola Democratica: Learning for Democracy*, 3, 2020, pp. 591–603, retrieved from https://doi.org/10.12828/99907.

Luppi, Elena et al.: "L'innovazione della didattica all'Università di Bologna durante la pandemia: un percorso basato sulla ricerca valutativa". *Lifelong Lifewide Learning*, 16(36), 2021, pp. 44–57, retrieved from https://doi.org/10.19241/lll.v16i36.557.

Mulryan-Kyne, Catherine: "Teaching Large Classes at College and University Level: Challenges and Opportunities". *Teaching in Higher Education*, 15(2), 2010, pp. 175–185.

Pirsig, Robert M.: *Zen and the art of Motorcycle Maintenance: An Inquiry into Values*. Random House: New York, 1999.

Ricci, Aurora: "L'analisi delle pratiche didattiche dei docenti durante la pandemia. Primi esiti dal modello di Formative Educational Evaluation dell'Università di Bologna". *Lifelong Lifewide Learning*, 17(38), 2021, pp. 431–449, retrieved 8.8. 2021 from http://dx.doi.org/10.19241/lll.v17i38.615.

Ricci, Aurora / Luppi, Elena: "Facing Adversity at the University. A Case Study to Reflect on Pedagogical Challenges in Times of Pandemic Risk". In: Gonçalves, Susana / Majhanovich, Suzanne (eds.): *Pandemic, Disruption* and *Adjustment* in *Higher Education*. Brill: Leiden/Boston.

Scriven, Michael: "Evaluation Theory and Metatheory". In: Kellaghan, Thomas / Stufflebeam Daniel L. (eds.): *International Handbook of Educational Evaluation*. Kluwer: Dordrecht / Boston / London, 2003, pp. 15–30.

Skelton, Alan: *Understanding Teaching Excellence in Higher Education: Towards a Critical Approach*. Routledge: London, 2006.

Stake, Robert: "Responsive Evaluation". In: Kellaghan, Thomas / Stufflebeam Daniel L. (eds.): *International Handbook of Educational Evaluation*. Kluwer: Dordrecht / Boston / London, 2003, pp. 63–68.

Stes, Ann: *Impact of Instructional Development in Higher Education: Effects on Teachers and Students*. Academia Press, 2008.

Stufflebeam, Daniel L.: "The CIPP Model for Evaluation". In: Kellaghan, Thomas / Stufflebeam Daniel L. (eds.): *International Handbook of Education-al Evaluation*. Kluwer: Dordrecht / Boston / London 2003, pp. 31–62.

Trow, Martin: "Reflections on the Transition from Elite to Mass to Universal Access: Forms and Phases of Higher Education in Modern Societies Since WWII". In: Forest, James J.F. / Altbach Philip G. (eds.): *International Handbook of Higher Education*. Springer: Dordrecht, 2007, pp. 243–280.

Vertecchi, Benedetto: *Valutazione formativa*. Loescher: Torino, 1976
  Xanthopoulou, Despoina et al.: "The Role of Personal Resources in the Job
  Demands-Resources Model". *International Journal of Stress Management*,
  14(2) 2007, p. 121.

Yanes-Lane, Mercedes et al.: "Proportion of Asymptomatic Infection Among
  COVID-19 Positive Persons and Their Transmission Potential: A Systematic
  Review and Meta-Analysis". *PLoS ONE*, 15(11), 2021, retrieved from https://
  doi.org/10.1371/journal.pone.0241536.

Olga Mennecke

Contentualizing Students' Motivation in Online Language Courses

Abstract: This article aims to demonstrate the correlation between online language course contents and students' motivational factors and outline possible ways in which the language learning process can be effectively supported even remotely, which has been somewhat uncommon for university language courses before the COVID pandemic. Data is acquired through interviews and qualitative analysis of written questionnaires within the Russian language course lectured at the University of Hildesheim.

Keywords: Motivation, self-determination theory, online language learning, content, course design

Introduction

Since the onset of the pandemic in 2020, the shift to online learning is not just an emerging trend because of many of its benefits but rather inevitable by now. However, the format change brings some challenges, especially when dealing with university language courses. The aim of this article is, on the one hand, to correlate the online language course contents with students' motivation. On the other hand, it is also to point out the possibilities of adequate support within the remote language learning process, as it has been quite a seldom phenomenon in the academic curriculum of the universities till the beginning of the COVID pandemic. The intention behind is not to continue the series of articles devoted to online learning motivation, which has already become very extensive over the past year and a half, but rather to clarify the motivational factors and to trace their connection with the corresponding content of the online language course on the example of the Russian language course lectured within the Bachelor program "International Information Management" at the University of Hildesheim. Firstly, the theoretical framework related to various motivational types and sources will be outlined. It is crucial to understand what sorts of the courses' contents seem most meaningful to each category of students – both the beginners and the advanced ones – based on their motivations and why. Interviews and qualitative analysis of written questionnaires were used to acquire the data. Students' responses reveal their expectations of the course design and what content they favored to maintain their language learning motivation and succeed in learning outcomes during the assessment. Students' self-evaluation of content types and frequency of content access provide essential hints on how the tutor can improve students' motivation through focused support within the online language course to minimize dropout risk.

Learning Environment and Motivation

In order to set specific guidelines for online language courses concerning learning motivation, one might first determine the processes that make people act actively or stay uninvolved. Classic teaching didactics based on the triangle *teacher-student-learning material*[3] assign these three components to be responsible for the quality of the learning process. Compared to this pedagogical model, the constructivist perspective downgrades teachers in their hierarchy, positioning them less dominated in the classroom and rather re-estimating them to companions and mentors of the learning process. By these means, the learning process nature undergoes a significant transformation from static to dynamic, in evolutionary steps by gradually reaching a higher level between experiences and reflections and presenting a continuous alternation process between interaction and concentration phases (Voß 2005, p. 45). Indeed, some external factors impact this process as well. It is not only teachers, students, the material, and the learning topic, but also the learning environment that should possess some activating energy sources (Keller 1995, p. 19). Undoubtedly, motivation is the essential prerequisite for efficient teaching and learning process, especially if we are dealing with unknown terrain and new studying formats such as online language courses that remain underinvestigated. The pandemic-caused uncertainty and transition to online learning affected motivational disorders by students and teachers so that the proceeding teaching and learning process became hampered. In order to analyze motivational factors and give some practical advice on

---

3   This classic scheme, characterized through the reciprocal correlation of its teaching components *teacher-student-learning material* originates from the so-called Herbartianism, a pedagogical approach developed by the German philosopher Johann Friedrich Herbart (1776–1841), who initiated the systematization and the overthinking of the practical teaching process. Although Herbart's idea was to place the student at the top of the triangle and to structure the learning process due to students' needs, so that the teacher's role was one of a supporter or encourager, the teacher-centered view on learning process continued to dominate over two hundred years (Buck 1985, Coriand 2006).

(online) learning in language courses, one needs to understand the theoretical basis of the motivational nature.

Self-Determination Theory as Theoretical Basis

Without exaggerations, motivation can be considered one of the most discussed but still quite confusing and not tangible. Often numerous categories are taken in mind while defining motivation. Instead, it comes out to be a multidimensional phenomenon of various processes affecting someone's behavior in a desirable way to achieve particular goals (Heckhausen 1989; Mook 1996; Rudolph 2003). Accordingly, behavior can be seen as the result of a specific current motivation due to actual interrelation between a person and the environment. However, being a consequence of the current motivation, behavior results from the combination of personal motives and incentive situations. As a result, it is possible for a teacher to affect the situational factor, whether in an online classroom or in an old-fashioned one, and try to impact the personal factor. Since the motivational complexity has become clear, several theories can be called upon (see also the control-value theory (Pekrun et al. 2017), the achievement goal theory (Dweck / Leggett 1988), the expectancy-value theory of achievement motivation (Wigfield / Eccles 2000). For this research, the self-determination theory, SDT (Deci / Ryan 2000), seems to provide a profound theoretical basis concerning both internal and external motivational factors that impact students' engagement in the learning process. Due to the SDT, motivation includes all aspects of activation and intension, i.e., energy, direction, persistence, and equifinality (Deci / Ryan 2000, p. 69). Behavior control is explained through the concept of intentionality, whereby intention stands for both mental and physical actions within goal orientation. Different qualitative manifestations of motivated action are possible, according to the SDT.

Deci & Ryan distinguish several motivational types, influencing the learning and performance process, experiences involved, and personal well-being and frames specific principles of development and sustainability of each of them (ibid.). Motivation types (amotivation, extrinsic, and intrinsic motivation) are parts of the self-determination continuum and differ in how the self initiates the motivations. Amotivation, situated on the one end of the continuum, is characterized as the absent intention to act due to various factors. Extrinsic motivation, put on the continuum's other end, results from a person's need to "satisfy an external demand or reward contingency" (Ryan / Deci 2017). Intrinsic motivation, placed in the middle of the self-determination continuum, is defined by Deci & Ryan as the state of acting out of inner satisfaction and personal interest.

The SDT claims that the transformation of students' motivational attitude because of the internalizing process and initiating to appraise certain activities is possible. In other words, even if a learning motive has been initiated instrumentally and out of some outer reason (to avoid negative consequences at the end of the course), this behavior can gradually change from deceptive approval to active engagement, once the activity value has been integrated into the self. According to Deci & Ryan, the level of self-determination in any behavior differs and ranges from initiated on one's own and out of inner conviction and personal interest to start out of external control or pressure (Deci / Ryan 1994, 2000, 2017).

Pandemic Shift on Motivational Perception and Its Practical Application

Because of the somewhat unexpected pandemic shift to global online learning, the problem of students' motivated participation in online courses has become crucial and not that easy. Therefore, numerous studies on motivation and participation in the online learning environment (De Barba et al. 2016; Dörnyei 2020; Chiu et al. 2021) appeared. Based on the theoretical assumptions of the self-determination theory, possibilities for practical implementation of the motivation-content-correspondence in online language courses will be presented below. Furthermore, it seemed worthwhile to combine the SDT ideas on motivational nature with the online content design and distribution within various student groups due to their motivational factors concerning the language learning process.

Online language learning needs significant instructional and planning changes concerning different motivational factors because of the higher dropout risk. Due to this fact, it seems even more important to look at the online course content and its correlation with various learners' motivations and interests.

Methodology

Research Design and Data

In this qualitative study, the Russian online language course lectured within the "International Information Management" Bachelor program at the University of Hildesheim in the winter term 20/21 is considered as an example. The course deals with the different categories of the Russian language, such as pronunciation, grammar, and vocabulary. Neither prerequisites for participation in the seminar nor the prior knowledge of Russian are necessary. It means that beginners without any knowledge of Russian can be enrolled on the course, as well as students with basic knowledge who had their first previous experience with Russian (at school as a third foreign language) or students who come from families with a Russian-speaking background and sometimes speak Russian only in the family context, and are therefore at least oral Russian native speakers. The latter group often has significant knowledge gaps in the Russian written language. However, there are some exceptions here, where oral and written language comprehension is very high. This study is aimed to determine whether there are some motivational differences between students with a Russian background and those who have a different motivational factor for choosing Russian as a foreign language than origin-defined and family-related one. Since the number of beginners (7) with no previous knowledge and the number of advanced learners (8) with at least good oral and sometimes also written knowledge of the Russian language was roughly equal, it seemed reasonable to divide the course into two groups in order to respond to the personal learning needs and to adapt the seminar content more adequately to each of both. The course consisted of synchronous and asynchronous components: weekly sessions were uploaded as presentations and video recordings of every session done during the class and supplemented with other materials and links to thematically appropriate films and other external materials (podcasts, online videos, and newspapers). Topics discussed included grammatical issues and vocabulary to various themes integrated into oral tasks, discussions, and written assignments. The course consisted of 13 weekly modules with correlated learning objectives for each module, assignments, and materials needed.

It was essential to comprehend what sorts of course content seems most meaningful to each category of students based on their motivations and why. Data is acquired through interviews and qualitative analysis of written questionnaires. Students' responses reveal their expectations of the course and what content they favored to maintain their language learning motivation and succeed in learning outcomes during the assessment (a personal presentation and a written exam).

Findings

The correlation between various motivational factors and the content preferred by students in the beginner and the advanced group was analyzed based on the interviews at the beginning and written questionnaires at the end of the online Russian course. As mentioned above regarding the intrinsic and extrinsic motivation in the SDT, students in both groups differentiated various types of motivation while choosing and participating in the online Russian language course.

Table 1: Motivational categories in the online Russian language course

Beginner group		Advanced group	
Intrinsic Motivation	Extrinsic Motivation	Intrinsic Motivation	Extrinsic Motivation
-Intensive interest in the 3rd foreign language	-External appreciation and admiration	-Enjoyment of being able to read Russian literature	-Ability to communicate more freely
-"Exotic" status of Russian and awareness of personal elitism	-Ability to travel in Russian-speaking countries	-Satisfaction of coming across complex linguistic phenomena	-A chance to weekly discussions with other students and speaking practice
	-Organizational structure (appropriate schedule, time-efforts proportion)	-Personal importance due to family identification	-Writing skills perfection based on teacher comments
			-New possibilities within the job market

Motivational Categories

In the interviews at the beginning of the online course, students defined motives for their enrollment in the course. The table below broadly outlines the two motivational categories in each of the groups derived from a qualitative analysis of the data:

Motivation and Content Preference

The core material consisted of 13 weekly blocks with the related presentation, video recording of the synchronous online class, and assignments for the week. The complete beginner and the advanced group, regardless of the motivational category, retrieved at least the presentation and the files with written assignments every week. Other files most commonly assessed were the grammar tables related to grammar issues (e. g., adjective and pronoun declination, formation of plural forms by nouns, preposition use) and the instructions for writing essays for the advanced group that accompanied the weekly written assignments. Mainly, the rate of the intrinsically motivated advanced learners, who assessed such instructions for their written assignments, was consistently very high. The beginner group with both types of motivation was very active in accomplishing initial reading, writing and lexical tasks, enabling students to read and express themselves in Russian and make their first writing attempts in Cyrillic letters. Unexpectedly, the intrinsically motivated beginners showed significant demand for asynchronous communication beyond the weekly meetings and asked grammar- and lexis-related questions that exceeded the scope of their scheduled tasks. Among the intrinsically motivated advanced learners, this demand was noticeably lower, presumably due to other preferences. This learner group reported being more conscious of getting profoundly commented written assignments with stylistic and lexical recommendations and additional examples after the teacher's revision. Another interesting aspect related to the additional materials and links could be identified in both groups.

All in all, twenty-three various ancillary materials and links to other posted resources (online videos, documentaries, podcasts, radio files, telegram channels) were provided. For the beginner group, many of these materials were documentaries in the German or English language on cultural, sociological, political, or historical topics, giving students without a Russian-speaking family background the first insight into various discourses of the Russian past and present. Both intrinsically and extrinsically motivated beginners reported assessing at least one additional material weekly, although the access rate differed highly depending on the additional resource type. Intense filtering of this kind of materials could be identified, especially by extrinsically motivated beginners. The advanced group got ancillary materials for similar topics, however, in the Russian language. Almost no access rate difference was noted between intrinsically and extrinsically motivated advanced learners. However, the general access rate to additional materials in this group was lower than that of the beginners. Particularly, extrinsically motivated advanced students reported following the additional links once in two or even three weeks. Intrinsically motivated advanced students showed higher interest in ancillary resources and followed at least one of them every week or once in two weeks. Extrinsically motivated advanced learners acted extremely interested within thematically framed discussion panels and preceding tasks. Especially the preference for the latter was observed among the students who see themselves working in the economic segment oriented towards Russia after their graduation. By the beginners, such discussion panels were substituted with simple oral tasks, consisting, on the one hand, of reading practice sessions and, on the other hand, of small conversations at the beginner level. Although the engagement rate in doing these activities was high by both intrinsically and extrinsically motivated beginners, the satisfaction rate of coping with such tasks was considerably lower in both beginner groups. Presumably, it was caused by the time shortage for the detailed pronunciation training of these tasks within the synchronous class. For the future, it seems reasonable to arrange optional reading and pronunciation training blocks within the beginner group for this purpose.

Conclusion

Motivation is the main factor for students' engagement in online language courses, seen from the self-determination theory perspective. The purpose of this research was to get an insight into the motivational categories of students enrolled in the Russian language online class and find out what content they considered to be mostly reasonable due to their motivation. The findings of this research are consistent with other studies (Brown / Voltz 2005; De Barba 2016) related to course content and their correlation with the desired learning outcomes. However, the coherence of these two aspects with motivation within the online terrain has been less researched so far. The qualitative data gained through the interviews and written questionnaires revealed the motivational categories that induced the students to sign up for the course and pointed out the preferences in course content by differently motivated learners. It turned out that the intrinsic and extrinsic motivational factors vary depending on the learners' group. Accordingly, the course content accessed by the intrinsically or extrinsically motivated beginners and advanced learners differed. The beginner group reported generally higher interest and access rate to the contents like reading and pronunciation training blocks, writing and lexical tasks, grammar-related material, and links to additional resources. The advanced group general preferences included the written essays and discussion panels and some selected ancillary materials. Although the data analysis has shown a tendency by extrinsically motivated learners to access the course content they believe was helpful to get satisfying outcomes during the assessment, it does not prevail among the intrinsically motivated learners. Based on the theoretical assumptions of the SDT, the research results make it evident that especially online language courses need to be designed considering learners' self-regulation. The awareness of students' motivational categories can assist the development of an online course in a way that brings students to appreciate the learning process rather than the assessment outcome. The risk of losing initial interest and becoming demotivated is significantly higher within online language courses. The well-designed content with practical assignments and constant feedback instead of excessive pressure and control outlines the advantages of being recognized by learners as worthwhile and encouraging.

Literature

Brown, Andrew / Voltz, Bradley: "Elements of Effective E-Learning Design". *The International Review of Research in Open and Distance Learning* 6(1), 2005, retreived 9.10.2021, from http://www.irrodl.org/index.php/irrodl/article/view/217.

Buck, Günther: *Herbarts Grundlegung der Pädagogik*. Winter: Heidelberg, 1985.

Chiu, Thomas / Lin, Tzung-Jin / Lonka, Kirsti, 2021: "Motivating Online Learning: The Challenges of COVID-19 and Beyond". *The Asia-Pacific Education Researcher*, 30(3), 2021, pp. 187–190, retreived 9.10.2021, from https://doi.org/10.1007/s40299-021-00566-w.

Coriand, Rotraud (ed.): Johann Friedrich Herbart. *Genauere Entwicklung der Hauptbegriffe, welche in die Bestimmung des pädagogischen Zwecks eingehn.* IKS Garamond: Jena, 2006.

De Barba, Paula, G./Kennedy, Gregor, E./Ainley, Mary, D.: "The Role of Students' Motivation and Participation in Predicting Performance in a MOOC". *Journal of Computer Assisted Learning*, 32(3) 2016, pp. 218–231.

Deci, Edward / Ryan, Richard: "Promoting Self-Determined Education". *Scandinavian Journal of Educational Research*, 38(1) 1994, pp. 3–14.

Deci, Edward/ Ryan, Richard: "Self-Determination Theory and the Facilitation of Intrinsic Motivation, Social Development, and Well-Being". *American Psychologist*, 55(1), 2000, pp. 68–78.

Dörnyei, Zoltán: *Innovations and Challenges in Language Learning Motivation*. Routledge: 2020.

Dweck, Carol / Leggett, Ellen: "A Social-Cognitive Approach to Motivation and Personality". *Psychological Review*, 95(2), 1988, pp. 256–273.

Heckhausen, Heinz: *Motivation und Handeln*. Springer: Berlin/Heidelberg, 1989.

Keller, Gustav: *Motivationsstörungen im Schulalter. Formen – Ursachen – Förderung*. Auer: Donauwörth, 1995.

Mook, Douglas: *Motivation*. Norton: New York, 1996.

Pekrun, Reinhard et al.: "Achievement Emotions and Academic Performance: Longitudinal Models of Reciprocal Effects". *Child Development*, 88(5), 2017, pp. 1653–1670.

Rudolph, Udo: *Motivationspsychologie*. Beltz: Weinheim/Basel/Berlin, 2003.

Ryan, Richard/ Deci, Edward: *Self-Determination Theory. Basic Psychological Needs in Motivation, Development and Wellness*. Guilford Press: New York/London, 2017.

Voß, Reinhard: "Unterricht ohne Belehrung". In: Voß, Reinhard (ed.): *Unterricht aus konstruktivistischer Sicht*. Beltz: Weinheim, 2005, pp. 40–62.

Wigfield, Allan/Eccles, Jacquelynne 2000: "Expectancy-Value Theory of Achievement Motiva-tion". *Contemporary Educational Psychology*, 25(1), 2000, pp. 68–81.

Susana Gonçalves

New Prospects in Higher Education: Hybrid Learning Environments and Creative Teaching

Abstract: General changes and specific changes through the Pandemic situation cause t cause the need to create learning environments with creative means. The paper considers the nature of creativity that can be used to create appropriate learning scenarios. The focus in this contribution is on hybrid learning environments to overcome social distancing.

Keywords: Alternative teaching methods, challenges in higher education, creativity, hybrid learning and teaching

The Covid 19 pandemic led to an unprecedented public health crisis and affected all areas of social life and institutions. Universities could not escape this crisis. It was the occasion for numerous emergency measures and a great dose of creativity, which despite these obstacles, allowed students to continue their learning paths and researchers to continue their studies. The world has not stopped and the changes have no return.

Crisis is always an occasion for transformation and poses many ethical, economic and social questions. For instance:

- Business opportunities emerge and the enrichment and professional success of some people becomes unprecedented, while many others are impoverished, fail and the quality of their life declines dramatically. How to reconcile these facts?
- The economic recession jeopardizes the right to education for all, with many leaving behind their educational paths and ambitions due to inability to meet the compulsory costs, such as paying school fees and school supplies or their families suffer from unemployment and loss of other sources of income.
- Crises always bring about a synthesis of the old and the new. People in crisis of life may fall into permanent hopelessness or become stronger. It is the same with social institutions. Some disintegrate, while others are renewed and become more stable. What have we seen during this pandemic crisis? First, there was a search for a vaccine and a solution to problems in a collective sphere, like overcoming fear and gaining more solidarity, and more cooperation; we saw how a renewed science services society and collectively we began to reflect on sustainable behavior and the importance of saving in

consumption: public affairs are more important than private interests are! Over the next few months, we also witness fatigue, forgetfulness, criticism, opportunism and authoritarianism. Through these events, we have learned several lessons and confirmed others that have already arisen before the pandemic. These lessons are about: great adaptability and survivability of technologies;
- compulsory development of digital skills for all;
- public health, which should be considered the heritage of humanity;
- Internationalization, which can exist even without physical mobility;
- an inevitable force that is human creativity.

The pandemic accelerated the paradigm shift that was already underway in the Higher Education area, and urged the preparation of tutors for the new demands of society. Teaching staff needs, more than before, to be able to produce resources for blended learning and alternative teaching and assessment modalities (e. g. flipped classroom), to use more adapted, creative and relevant teaching methods (like Learning by Projects or Problem Based Learning).

Auscultation of public organizations and industry is required. In addition, SOTL (Scholarship of Teaching and Learning) plays a predominant role. SOTL includes three elements (Information, inquiry and dissemination) aimed at both students who want to learn and succeed and teachers who want to better fulfill their roles, adjusting strategies and teaching schemes to their classes (cf. Leeds-Hurwitz / Hoff, 2012). Another shift from the traditional paradigm is the ability and desire to integrate cognition and emotion in the process of teaching and learning and the pedagogical endeavor.

Challenges to Higher Education Today

Some of the challenges that higher education institutions face today are the following:

a) Understand all aspects of globalization, including the impact on public health, mass mobility of people for tourism, business and migration, the digital cross-border market as well as the unique worldviews and behavior patterns of new generations;

b) not only develop society through science and education, but also be sustainable, especially to promote sustainable education (taking into account the four interrelated pillars: economy, culture, ecology and society);

c) Adapt the value system of the academic community to a world at risk and in transformation.

d) Reasonably adapt their foundations and procedures to the continuous battle between the interests of society and the interests of the economy;

e) Support and acknowledge the difficult role of teachers nowadays, who, unlike most other professions, are both learners (for instance learning how teach in new digital environments already using them), researchers and innovators;

f) Anticipate the implications of History being made today (Today is History) when preparing curriculum and activities for students as well as developing its mission and action plans;

g) Re-create the curriculum to promote students' digital, social and civic competences;

h) No time, no space: distance learning (blended and e-learning) challenges the dimensions of time and space and somehow puts teaching and learning in the fifth dimension, also with a new language (like gamification, which reminds us of technological wonders like holograms and avatars, the blogosphere, google earth, video games or consumption behavior mediated by algorithms).

Distance and Blended Learning

Distance learning, blended learning and hybrid teaching and learning environments are among the educational shifts from university teaching traditions. The trend towards more digital education was already evident at all levels of formal and non-formal education before the pandemic, but it has been intensified and now seems irreversible. Technological accessibility has become a reality for almost everyone, with more and better technological tools (cf. Sharples et al. 2015) shortening distances and increasingly serving the interests of students and teachers. Distance learning eliminates time and space constraints, reaches more people and facilitates autonomous learning management. But what are the problems associated with social and physical distance? What challenges do we face regarding the teaching and learning process? What competences and skills (in addition to digital literacy) will we have to develop to be successful in the new higher education models? During the Covid pandemic, these issues generated numerous studies and publications around the world, and the academic community developed an unprecedented collective effort to effectively move from traditional face-to-face teaching to hybrid and distance-learning models (cf. Gonçalves / Majhanovich 2021a, 2021b).

Distance learning subverts the notions of time and space as we knew it and, in the case of teaching and learning environments, poses special challenges, such as:

- *Virtual space*: implies physical and social distance, with possible effects on the motivation and involvement of students, especially those who are more sociable/extroverted or who prefer to learn in social and cooperative environments. On the other hand, these environments may be favorable to students that are more introverted and those who prefer to learn autonomously and in socially neutral environments. Online communication is another challenge, as it leads to many misunderstandings and requires the learning of its own codes and netiquette.
- *Virtual time*: the asynchronous modality of teaching and learning and remote work are clearly favorable to student-workers and those with different learning paces and different priorities in the study. However, it can also promote procrastination and discouragement due to the absence of social stimuli and immediate feedback.

Other issues are about curriculum and adaptability of pedagogical methods and resources, when teachers are required to transform, adapt and modify a lot of the materials and procedures they have successfully used in traditional face-to-face teaching modalities. In addition, role expectations must change, with a more autonomous learning experience on the part of students and a more tutorial style on the part of teachers. Moreover, social interactions and values have been challenged, including issues such as assessment and plagiarism, less exposure to direct patterns of behavior and redefinition of learning and reflection communities, which used to be one of the strengths of student life in more orthodox education. Previously universities were social spaces where students tested and developed their personal and professional identities. They also worked as laboratories for the application of social and civic skills, the advancement of cultural interests, the development of civic and political experience and the promotion of the understanding and application of ethical and deontology principles in behavior. How to replace these traditional roles of higher education institutions in hybrid or distance education? Creative pedagogy and curriculum are needed in this new model. As Moreira and Ferreira refer:

> More than integrating physical and virtual learning environments, hybrid learning must affirm itself as a full learning concept characterised by the use of combined solutions, involving the interaction between different models, pedagogical approaches and technological resources. The interaction of pedagogical approaches is a direct and indirect consequence of the combination of various resources within differentiated spaces. [...] The adoption of different technological resources is one of the ways of rendering the dialogue between these different approaches effective, as each resource implies not only specific forms of knowledge management, but also specific forms of interaction. (2021, p. 10).

Also, as I mentioned elsewhere

> We do not need to reinvent the will when it comes to discussing education and how universities approach teaching and pedagogy. However, it is strongly recommended to take into account both the educational data and students' opinions on how to organize the learning environment (including classroom space), the proposed learning activities and content to foster student engagement and deep learning. (Gonçalves 2021, p. 38).

Creative and innovative teaching need not be revolutionary. It must only reject a model that does not take into account pedagogical theories, current life contingencies, the possibilities offered by technologies, the need for synergies in the community and, of course, the voice of students, verified through SOTL.

Today's global challenges demand creative solutions, and higher education is the right place to nurture creative minds for a better future. Many universities around the world already promote these types of teaching and opportunities for students, with assignments such as entrepreneurship contests, internships and collaborations with corporations, student integration in research projects, or problem-based learning.

Creative Teaching and Learning

Being creative may be seen as a habit, meaning, something that can be learned and integrated as normal approach to the problems posed by work and daily life. According to Csikszentmihalyi (1997) creative people combine playfulness with discipline, alternate fantasy with a good sense of reality, are both humble and proud, and passionate about their work and goals. According to Gregoire (2017) and Kaufman and Gregoire (2015) the practices and habits of mind that promote creative thinking can be contradictory, including both mindfulness and daydreaming, seriousness and play, openness and sensitivity, and loneliness and collaboration, such practices open minds to the world of possibilities and the complexity of the natural and spiritual phenomena.

The study of cases of creative people widely recognized for their outstanding work (like painter Pablo Picasso, novelist Marcel Proust, scientist Thomas Edison, actress Josephine Baker, musician John Lennon, chess champion Josh Waitzkin or video-game designer Shigeru Miyamoto) helped understand creativity as a mental framework that translates in special habits, qualities, and behaviors. These include imaginative play, passion, daydreaming, loneliness, intuition, openness to experience, mindfulness, and sensitivity, turning adversity into an advantage and a way of thinking differently. In higher education, this is what should stimulate teaching if the goal is to prepare students to become creative professionals. How do creative people create? There are many paths, but the following are common (Jeffrey 2006):

- By trials and errors
- Being experimentalist
- With effort and persistence
- Accepting mistakes
- Integrating the new into the old
- Collecting ideas
- Using a repertoire of techniques
- Observing peers
- Learning from effective work
- Copying and adapting;
- Managing his own power;
- Self-exposure to criticism.

Creativity is not about being an artist. It is about being adaptable, resilient, wise and able to solve problems in a good manner. Creative people see the point, they connect things and understand causality, they also express themselves in multiple ways and are constantly curious about the world. We are all biologically programed to be creative but experience and social restrictions block this potential, and many end up giving in to conformism and routine.

Conventional socialization and obstacles to imagination and independent thinking can weaken creativity and ideational fluency (Simonton 1994). Traditionally, education systems have played an important role in defining the social, cultural and economic conventions and in orienting students' minds towards the *status quo*. This is especially evident in liberal mass education. However, currently, with unprecedented global ecological, economic, social and political problems, ground-breaking ideas, with a sense of social purpose need to be encouraged and it is urgent to find innovative and unconventional solutions that go beyond the conformist perceptiveness.

These ideas lead us to the matter of creative teaching and creative teachers. Creative experiences (these include relevance, ownership and control) lead to innovation and a possible transformation of learners (Woods 1995). The study by Horng et al. (2005) confirmed that creativity can be taught and that effective teaching strategies for students before college are:

- student-centered activities,
- a connection between teaching contents and real life,
- management of skills in class,

- open-ended questions,
- an encouragement of creative thinking and
- use of technology and multimedia.

All of these strategies are well documented as they are also applied at the university level. The findings by Paek / Sumners (2017) also point to the important role of fixed and evolving creative thinking in teachers while developing creativity in the classroom. An interesting case study by Lilly and Bramwell (2004) reveals the forces behind the creative process in teaching: high energy, motivation, and commitment to a career are critical. Moreover, a teaching style that provides a safe learning climate, stimulates flexibility, and includes regular feedback, fosters an atmosphere of curiosity and stimulates students' creative independence and a risk-taking attitude to innovate without fear of failure. Apart from teachers' attitudes and personality, teaching strategies are of extreme importance.

Creative teaching and learning happen mostly with critical events, such as (Jeffrey 2006):

- school environment improvements and analysis;
- coordinated international projects;
- computer toy constructions for major competitions;
- business case studies;
- re-enactments of social issues and
- local histories and the examination of lives from different cultures.

These events usually involve strategic co-operations and external engagement (advisors, specialists, workshop providers, artists, visits...) and can either be incorporated into existing programs or replace them. The stages of teaching with critical events are conceptualization, preparation and planning, divergence and convergence, consolidation, and, finally, celebration. The process involves:

- intense intellectual inquiry (problem finding and solving and productive speculation)
- engaged productivity – learners focus on process and production of products

  - craft their innovatory ideas and artifacts over a period of time
  - select and review ideas from peers
  - work focusing on purpose and ownership
  - take control of the techniques and processes,
  - using others' ideas, a form of collective scaffolding
  - engage in learning by doing and discovery learning
  - use examples, metaphors and analogies to describe their creations

  – engaged productivity resulting in high levels of concentration and interest.
- process and product review – students

  – revisited their products and investigations with a fresh eye and evaluate whether they were achieving their objectives
  – discuss mistakes as a productive part of the process
  – look for different alternatives arising from their evaluations
  – review breakdowns in learning situations
  – evaluate teaching and learning strategies

During this process, teachers present open-ended problems and solution actions in which learners explore resources, ideas, tools and patterns. They also model creativity by stimulating and glorifying students' ideas, investing time in discussion and criticism, appreciating the importance of experimentation, working with external agents, modeling learning itself by taking part in the research/ explorations processes as learners, demonstrating the pleasure of innovatory ideas, actions and demonstration of personal involvement. Finally, they organize the learning environment so that the students get the most out of critical events, which may involve creative use of space (or even moving to unusual locations to facilitate more creative practice) and adjusting time boundaries for time spent on activities that go beyond the lessons.

Hybrid and Creative Learning Environments

From what we have just mentioned, the shift to a highly computer-mediated, hybrid teaching and learning seems to be inevitable, in which teachers work more as tutors, knowledge curators and creators of pedagogical resources than traditional lecturers do. It also seems that more and more innovative and creative forms of teaching are required, which allow students to develop the capacity for autonomous learning, problem solving (both individually and in teams) and using abundant divergent thinking and pertinent innovation.

Flipped classrooms fit well teaching in hybrid environments, where students collaborating with each other and with the teacher to debate and solve real problems. Gamification is a fun teaching method adjusted to new generations of students, having shown excellent results. Brainstorming, concept mapping, storytelling, collaborative worksheets, online debates and presentations, students' cooperation (for instance for reciprocal assignments assessment), taking students on virtual tours, inviting experts to give online lectures, using apps and software for virtual pools and other (usually fun) group activities… these are all well-known strategies that work well and that stimulate students' involvement and active learning.

In addition, teaching with critical events can easily be adapted to a blended (even to a distance) learning environment, thus promoting student intellectual inquiry, engaged productivity and process and product review. The teacher's effort is much less to revolutionize teaching. Rather, it is an effort to adapt and renew their methodologies and expectations about what good teaching is and about their own roles as an educator.

Conclusion

The roles of educators are changing and we should now see teachers more like influencers/ stimulators for creative learning, taking on tasks that are more related to guiding/mentoring than to exposing knowledge. To do this, the teacher needs to master technologies and human relations and they need to establish connection with their academic and professional community and be continuous learners in a world that is constantly transforming. Not an easy task. Anyway, Education has always taken place in times of crisis and complexity.

Literature

Csikszentmihalyi, Mihaly: *Creativity: Flow and the Psychology of Discovery and Invention.* Harper Collins Publishers: New York, 1997.

Gonçalves, Susana: "Contemporary Approaches to Teaching in Higher Education". In: Wang, Dan / Chen, Xiaoxin (eds.): *Framing Challenges in Higher Education: Bridging the Gap Between Russia, China and Europe.* International Research Conference Proceedings. University of Sanya: Hainan, 2021, pp. 37–38.

Gonçalves, Susana / Majhanovich, Suzanne (eds.): *Ensino Superior em Transição: Estudantes Online. Higher Education in Transition: Students Online.* CINEP/IPC: Coimbra, 2021a.

Gonçalves, Susana / Majhanovich, Suzanne (eds.): *Pandemic and Remote Teaching in Higher Education.* CINEP/IPC: Coimbra, 2021b.

Gregoire, Carolyn: "18 Things Highly Creative People Do Differently", 2014/ 2017 retrieved 11.9.2021 from https://www.huffpost.com/entry/creativity-habits_n_4859769.

Hong, Jan-Chao et al.: "Creative Teachers and Creative Teaching Strategies". *International Journal of Consumer Studies*, 29(4), 2005, pp. 352–358, retrieved 11.9.2021 from https://doi.org/10.1111/j.1470-6431.2005.00445.x.

Jeffrey, Bob: "Creative Teaching and Learning: Towards a Common Discourse and Practice". *Cambridge Journal of Education*, 36(3), 2006, pp. 399–414.

Kaufman, Scott B. / Gregoire, Carolyn: *Wired to Create: Unravelling the Mysteries of the Creative Mind*. TarcherPerigee: New York, 2015.

Leeds-Hurwitz, Wendy / Hoff, P. S. *Arquitetura Pedagógica para a mudança no Ensino Superior*. [Pedagogical Architecture Changes for Higher Education]. Instituto Politécnico de Coimbra: Coimbra, 2012.

Lilly, Frank R. / Bramwell, Gillian: "The Dynamics of Creative Teaching". *The Journal of Creative Behavior*, 38(2), 2004.

Moreira, José A. / Ferreira, Antonio G.: "Blended and Hybrid Environments in Higher Education in Times of the Pandemic". In: Gonçalves, Susana / Majhanovich, Suzanne (eds.): *Pandemic and Remote Teaching in Higher Education*. CINEP/IPC: Coimbra, pp. 9–20.

Paek, Sue-Hyeon / Sumners, Sarah E.: "The Indirect Effect of Teachers' Creative Mindsets on Teaching Creativity". *The Journal of Creative Behavior*, 53(3), 2017, pp. 298–311, retrieved from https://doi.org/10.1002/jocb.180.

Sharples, Mike et al.: "Innovating Pedagogy: Exploring New Forms of Teaching, Learning and Assessment, to Guide Educators and Policy Makers". *Open University Innovation Report* 4, 2015 retrieved 11.9.2021 from https://iet.open.ac.uk/file/innovating_pedagogy_2015.pdf.

Simonton, Dean K.: *Greatness: Who Makes History and Why*. Guilford Press: New York, 1994.

Woods, Peter: Creative Teachers in Primary Schools. Open University Press: Buckingham, Philadelphia, 1995.

Irina Pervukhina, Marina Vidrevich, Natalia Vlasova

Impact of the COVID-19 Pandemic on Modern Management Technologies in Higher Education as Knowledge-Intensive Activity

Abstract: The COVID-19 pandemic has presented a challenge to the entire higher education: to 'migrate' from traditional in-class face-to-face education to online education in a matter of days. The paper explores the wave of responses to COVID-19 from universities in the international and country-specific perspective. We focus on how management, faculty and students in Russian higher education institutions were affected by the COVID-19 global pandemic. It is concluded that there is an urgent need for new online teaching and learning strategies, management approaches, didactic materials and techniques in order to overcome the difficulties caused by transferring traditional methods of teaching, learning and assessment from the face-to-face classroom to the virtual environment.

Keywords: Effects and challenges of Covid-19, university management, digital learning strategies, digital assessment, international and comparative perspective

Introduction

In a matter of weeks, the coronavirus disease known as COVID-19 has changed how students are educated around the world. The impact on academic higher education system with its conservative, centuries-old, lecture-based approaches to teaching has been unprecedented. COVID-19 has become a catalyst for educational institutions worldwide to search for innovative solutions in terms of teaching and learning and management technologies in a relatively short period of time.

According to UNESCO, on 1 April 2020, schools and higher education institutions (HEIs) were closed in 185 countries, affecting 1 542 412 000 learners, which constitute 89.4 % of total enrolled learners (Marinoni / van't Land / Jensen 2020). This has proven challenging for both university managers, students and educators, who have to deal with the emotional, physical and economic difficulties posed by this disease. This global crisis has triggered a reconceptualization of education provision at all levels. The intensive use of different technological platforms and resources to ensure continuity of learning outside HEIs is the boldest experiment in educational technology – albeit unexpected and unplanned (UNESCO-IESALC 2020).

Many scholars questioned if higher education was prepared for the forthcoming digital era of learning (Houlden / Veletsianos 2020; DeVaney et al. 2020). The data (Mitchell 2020) show that 60 % of HEIs reported online learning provisions in their strategic planning prior to COVID-19, but only one-third appeared to provide full online courses in some form.

Developing robust online platforms has become necessary to offer continuity in learning. Yet in many countries the shift to 'going digital' has not been easy due to disparity in socio-economic backgrounds of students and the quality of educational institutions. Faculties are being called upon to redesign curricula and redefine learning outcomes in order to meet the current and future needs and to develop effective tools that will ensure students stay involved and active in the learning process. Moving away from traditional pedagogies in most HEIs and the demand for quality educators will shape the way higher education moves forward from this crisis.

This paper begins a conversation by exploring the wave of responses to COVID-19 from universities globally. We continue to address this in our discussion of universities in Russia, highlighting the country-specific approaches to higher education and focus on how Russian universities were coping with the changes brought in by the COVID-19 global pandemic.

Materials and Methods

This paper adopts a desktop analysis approach with the careful consideration as to quality of the information source. In order to create an effective status update for universities globally, it is critical that we seek to use reliable sources given the general fluctuation of information regarding COVID-19. The emphasis was put on the use of direct university and government sources supplemented by news articles, higher education news outlets, and other forms of communication. We went down from the top to the bottom, starting from the Russian national level, and focused on the cases of several universities, including the Ural State University of Economics (USUE), located in Ekaterinburg.

The impact of the COVID pandemic was studied through various parameters and factors. The emphasis placed on administrative regulations and changing institutional conditions, analysis of changes in the tertiary sector. Since Russia, due to its vastness, presents significant interregional differentiation in terms of the availability of and access to quality education and educational resources, the focal point was formed by spatial and inter-university responses to the emergency remote teaching. The authors used the findings of different surveys conducted in Russian universities and public organizations in order to identify the attitude of students and teachers to the challenges posed by COVID-19. In general, there were three key sources of statistical data:

1. The large-scale surveys conducted by the National Research University-Higher School of Economics and aimed at examining Russian students' reaction to the emerging demand for the sudden shift to online learning environment. The first round of the research was carried out at the beginning of the transition period, from March 24 to April 1, 2020, with a sample of 10 938 respondents. The second set of data was collected from May 24 to June 1 at the end of the semester when students had been distance learning for several weeks, and included 24 428 respondents.

2. The 2020 survey of 6 000 students from 153 Russian universities, conducted by the RAEX Rating Review (2020). The survey questions were designed to assess student's perception on a wide range of topics related to the COVID-19 outbreak, including anxiety towards having moved to strictly online learning off campus, level of emergency preparedness, students' level of experience in the learning environment, and the impact of COVID-19 on the learning process.

3. USUE in-house students' survey, carried out by the Department of Applied Sociology in December 2020. The population was made up by 199 senior students (Year 4). One of the objectives was to find out how satisfied undergraduates were with the studies at USUE; what problems they were facing during university studies; and their preferences in terms of education delivery modes.

Special attention was paid to the choice of technologies, which are affected by the local situation and the emergence of needs for new online meta-skills (McCarty 2020), which may result in a significant change not only in the daily class management, but also in the adaptation of courses taught currently, as well as educational programs in general.

Results and Discussion

Responses to COVID-19: International Perspective

The IAU Global Survey on the impact of COVID-19 on Higher Education (Marinoni et al. 2020) involving 424 universities around the world revealed that institutions were affected by the pandemic in terms of research, conferences, international mobility and education delivery. Most universities stating that they had to adopt online learning and had to face many challenges, the most important being access to technology and teachers' ability to deliver online courses. During this time, the method of education delivery has often been modified to provide students with alternative learning opportunities and, in many cases, learning delivery has been shifted to online platforms.

The immediate actions that HEIs worldwide were taking to address the emerging circumstances were roughly the same irrespective of the level of economic development, size of the country and political regime. Most countries implemented the following measures counteracting and slowing down the COVID spread (Crawford et al. 2020; Rumbley 2020). Universities were instructed to shut down after the coronavirus was declared a public health emergency in many countries (Ozili / Arun 2020). Students were sent home and teachers had to cancel classroom teaching. The technology infrastructure was rapidly progressing towards online teaching and learning. However, there was a cost in terms of teachers' personal and professional lives. The shift from face-to-face to distance teaching did not come without challenges, the main ones being access to technical infrastructure, competences and pedagogies for distance learning and the requirements of specific fields of study (Marinoni et al. 2020). National governments issued regulations enforcing measures for self-isolation. They worked out recommendations and guidelines for remote instruction delivery, in particular with regard to standardized tests and examinations. Examination arrangements were changed. Information channels for students and academic staff were designed and social and emotional support was provided. Fee payments were postponed in order to assist students.

Responses to COVID-19: Russia's Perspective

At the same time, Russian HEIs deployed measures that demonstrate a different response to a complex challenge. University closure skyrocketed the demand for distance learning. The country's Ministry of Higher Education and Science (hereafter: the Ministry) recommended all universities switch to distance learning as a preventive measure against the spread of coronavirus (Shtorm pervyh nedel 2020).

The pandemic has revealed great non-uniformity and the risk of widening the gap between Russian universities. By the mid-March 2020 only 11 % of Russian universities had the necessary technological and technical infrastructure to support virtual courses. Every tenth university had no resources or digital capacity to move to full online delivery.

The gap between Russian universities is also strongly affected by their locality. Students in urban areas have a significantly different distance learning

Table 1: Households possessing PC and Internet access by type of locality (2015–2019)

Type of locality	Households with PCs (% of total)			Households with broadband network (% of total)		
	2015	2018	2019	2015	2018	2019
Urban	76.8	76.2	73.6	71.6	77.3	77.7
Rural	59.2	60.5	56.4	51.9	60.7	60.9

Source: https://rosstat.gov.ru/folder/210/document/13251.

experience than students in peri-urban and rural areas. The more the HEI has been integrated in the world educational context, the higher is the degree of loyalty to the online modality. Accessibility to the internet and personal computers for students in urban and rural regions differ significantly. There is still large differentiation in the number of Russian households possessing PCs and having access to the internet by their locality (Table 1).

Nevertheless, it is apparent from Table 1 that the gap between urban and rural population in terms of internet access is gradually narrowing. A similar process is observed with regard to PC ownership, but the gap is filling much slower. To a certain degree it is due to spacial disparity in personal incomes. While in 2018 an average income per urban household member was 31.4 thousand roubles, in rural locality this income accounted for 19.2 thousand roubles only, with a proportion of food expenditures standing at 33 % in the urban household budget and at 41.6 % in the rural household budget.

By the end of March, 60 % of Russian universities provided distance learning without major interruptions. Another quarter of HEIs offered studying from home, but experienced occasional problems. Many universities worked out guidelines to assist academic staff in delivering teaching and learning with the use of online technologies.

In order to respond to the COVID challenge and effectively reformat the educational process by introducing e-learning and distance learning, the Ministry launched the federal project – Modern Digital Educational Environment in the Russian Federation – aimed at providing access to free online courses for all categories of citizens and for educational organizations of all levels. This digital educational environment unites 69 online platforms, developed and used by public and educational organizations, and contains more than 1600 online courses offered at 111 universities of the Russian Federation. This Portal may reinforce the solution to the following tasks:

- introduction and application of the unified identification and authentication system;
- search for online courses in the online course registry;
- quality assurance of online courses;
- rating of online course;
- building of students' digital portfolios and recognition of the achievements of online training by educational organizations and employers.

From the beginning, Russia's HEIs took measures to safeguard health on campus and in buildings. One of the measures was to enact requirements for social isolation for academic staff aged 65+. Studies ceased for a week, from 28 March to 5 April 2020. A two-week vacation for students was declared from 28 March to 5 April. The period from March 30 to April 3 was announced 'the stay-at-home' at one's full pay both for faculty and non-teaching staff (Shtorm pervyh nedel 2020). The faculty had to use this break to design teaching materials and placing them on the university portal to make them available for all students, both Russian and international.

In addition to work on ensuring an adequate transition to the remote learning format, universities and the Ministry also had to address arising social problems. More than half of all students experienced income loss, which prompted universities to adopt programs for supporting student employment on campus in order to alleviate the strain and provide students with additional opportunities to earn money and continue their education. Several initiatives were taken to limit inequalities regarding access to technology: some universities fully subsidized the cost of internet connection in dormitories to ensure continuous access to distance learning.

Enrollment for the New Academic Year

The outbreak also disrupted the admissions process for 2020/2021 entry. Some universities began planning and using virtual webinars and tours to support perspective students in the admission process. Universities focused on introducing more flexible admission processes, delayed start dates and relaxed some entry requirements. A new mode of application – online application – was introduced. The mandatory national tests for high school leavers having originally been scheduled for the end of June were rescheduled for a month later, to July. High school students who were not planning to enter the university were allowed not to take the national test. According to the statistics, 12 % of school leavers seized this opportunity.

Impact on Students

A number of researchers have discussed the psychological impact of the COVID-19 epidemic on college and university students in different countries (e. g. Cao et al. 2020; Al-Tammemi et al. 2020; Prakhov 2021). Moving learning from classrooms to homes at scale and in a hurry has presented enormous challenges for Russian students as well. In the hierarchy of concerns they have given priority to three areas (Uroki "stress-testa" 2020), which is in line with international studies: (1) the replacement of face-to-face classes with online learning, which does not encourage self-regulated learning; (2) the immediate effect on students' day-to-day schedule, and financial issues caused by decrease in or loss of income; (3) suspension of out-of-class activities, which led to social isolation and lack of communication with peers and teachers.

The quality of the distance teaching provided in response to the emergency situation varied a lot, depending on the infrastructure in place, the capacities of the teaching staff to adapt to the online teaching and on the field of study. According to the available data, the majority of Russian university students thought that the shift to the new system was done on time. Overall, Master's students were more satisfied with the new way of attending classes than Bachelor's students. However, student responses differed depending on the field of study. Students majoring in computer and social sciences, as well as humanities, economy and management rated their institution preparedness for a transition to and optimization of online learning more positively than arts, music and design students, future engineers, and doctors where practical lessons cannot be replaced by distance teaching and learning. Students were quick to evaluate online instruction as worse than face-to-face teaching they received.

The first-year students seemed to find it most difficult to adapt to online learning, as they had not yet acquired sufficient experience in academic study. They felt overwhelmed with too much information and faced problems of self-discipline, time management and prioritizing tasks since they had to create their own learning environment and control their learning. Over half of the responses indicated that students needed more time to prepare for classes. The majority (80 %) replied that they had to spend more time in front of the computer than before the pandemic. Among the concerns that students most often reported, in addition to technical interruptions and poor internet connection, was lack of personal interaction with group mates and professors. Students felt uncomfortable and shy to answer teachers' questions or to ask for clarification during online classes. It was harder to focus and more difficult to understand new material.

Table 2: Undergraduates' satisfaction with studying at USUE (% of respondents)

Level of satisfaction	2019	2020
Fully satisfied	17.9	9.5
Fairly satisfied	56.0	57.8
Rather not satisfied than satisfied	12.0	18.2
Not satisfied	7.6	8.5
Don't know	6.5	6.0

Similar responses were obtained by the survey conducted by RAEX Rating Review (2020). University students identified several persistent factors that limited their off-class learning engagement. Inadequate facilities (from poor communication, unavailability and accessibility issues to low application functionality) appeared to be the highest impediment to online education during the pandemic. Only a low number of students (13.6 %) stated that they were fully satisfied with technical solutions. 35.7 % of students felt that teachers were not prepared for an emergency. They reported an increase in the amount of work they had to do out of class and less contact with teachers. The transition to a new format was assessed negatively for organizational reasons by approximately one-third of respondents.

Among the most commonly used tools of online communication between students and teaching staff, were e-mail and virtual learning portal. Academic staff often assigned online assignments and interactive tasks (tests, surveys, etc.). The tools that most educators used for training purposes were chats, forums and online questionnaires. Less than 70 % of respondents agreed that university professors used online lectures and seminars for information transfer. At the same time, this percentage might vary from one region to another: 82.4 % in Moscow and half as low outside megapolises – only 40.3 %.

The answers of USUE undergraduate students showed that the level of their satisfaction with the university studies decreased in 2020 compared to 2019, which is largely due to the move to online-only instruction versus what they were previously more accustomed to – in-class learning environment (Table 2).

However, in spite of the above-mentioned difficulties, two-thirds of students are satisfied with how online learning is organized at their university. Over 33 % of university students prefer online over face-to-face learning since the virtual modality brings in some advantages: they have more time for sleep and leisure; and they feel less tired.

At the beginning of the pandemic over 10 % of Russian students had problems accessing effective technology including working laptops and reliable high-speed internet. The Ministry published a guide with general recommendations on providing support to these groups of students; however, the decision on forms of support was assigned to institutions.

In addition to the technical support, which gave students the opportunity to continue their studies, most universities strongly focused on mental wellbeing and community engagement and supported solidarity among students, citizens and institutions. Many universities provided support using the staff of specialized departments (e. g. Psychology Department) in the format of mixed teacher-student volunteer teams. These teams provided educational and psychological assistance to the academic community; helped students to organize their time and concentrate on studies. Universities were forced to look for different forms of handling extracurricular activities and community engagement in order to allow students to maintain their usual hobbies in isolation. The interest groups met in the online format, using a variety of platforms and modifying communication algorithms.

Impact on Faculty

Teachers also experienced a significant impact at work and in their professional life. The most evident impact on teachers is the expectation, if not the requirement, that they continue to teach using the virtual mode. While the survey of the teaching staff of the leading Russian universities showed that they had not looked upon distance learning as a complete substitute of a traditional face-to-face mode, since the use of IT incurred some risks, including low student motivation and a threat of de-professionalism of the staff.

Unfortunately, not all teachers had the necessary technical skills and they did not manage to adapt their teaching style in such a short time, or properly interacted with students in the online environment in order to assure high standards of the teaching process. Confirming the necessary infrastructure and logistics are in place students gave low scores to teaching staff in aspects related to pedagogical knowledge and content regarding the use of Information and Communication Technologies (ICT) in their classroom. 86.4 % of students stated that teachers frequently used a limited number of tools provided by the E-learning platform: they used only the basic tools, which were almost mandatory for conducting the courses.

Researchers analyze the relationships between various demographic, social, economic, and other factors and the development of digital competencies.

Though Basantes-Andrade et al. (2020, p. 210) acknowledge that the results of their research do not reflect with certainty the relevance of generation for the development of digital competence, the authors believe that the statement that as "the age of educators increases their level of digital competence decreases; hence, the young professors have a greater level of technological knowledge" may be valid.

The report on the stress test of Russian HEIs (Uroki "stress-testa" 2020) identifies four groups of faculty members with regard to their attitude towards online teaching and learning:

1. The faculty members teaching subjects, which include the development of students' professional competences through practice (clinics, technical sciences, arts). This group is not numerous (5 % of the total teaching staff) and has responded to the change in teaching and learning modality very negatively and argue that many traditional university activities cannot be moved to the online mode without a significant drop in their effectiveness.
2. Teachers having significant previous experience in using digital technologies (including online courses and resources) (25 % on average). These teachers are flexible and believe that the online course can have the same quality as the traditional university studies.
3. Teachers having some previous 'digital' experience (such as information search and e-mailing) (40 %). This group reports that they are tired of growing workload, complexity and pressure of learning new technologies. Teachers in this group do not advocate a significant increase in online education, but do realize that digital platforms and digital resources can supplement the teaching practice. They developed the so called *Emergency Remote Teaching*, or *Coronateaching* (UNESCO-IESALC 2020): they transform the existing classes to a virtual mode, but do not modify the curriculum or the methodology.
4. Teachers without any previous experience in distance education. This group may make up from 5 % to 30 % depending on the university. For these teaching staff the abrupt entry into a complex teaching mode with multiple technological and pedagogical options has resulted in frustration and overwhelm since they are resistive to change and unable to adapt to a new educational modality due to lack of corresponding digital skills and training. For them the only alternative is to reprogram the face-to-face offer.

Digital Pedagogy and Quality of Learning

Some Russian universities already had made extensive use of online teaching tools and this facilitated the transition to full online teaching. Universities with a strong emphasis on classroom and laboratory-based education and where online learning had been implemented mostly in a supplementary function to classroom activities, reported that the closure of the university has exposed a number of critical weaknesses to this approach.

Although the use of technology in teaching has been implemented in Russia for almost two decades, solely online teaching is new to lecturers and students (Vydrevich / Pervukhina 2020). In general, most universities regard the online teaching approach as a temporary solution and expect to resume face-to-face teaching after the crisis. Migrating from traditional or blended learning to a fully virtual and online delivery strategy is associated with many challenges (COVID-19 crisis and curriculum 2020; Crawford et al. 2020), such as the lack of 'home office' infrastructure; the organization of student infrastructure; availability of teachers with the appropriate capacities and skills needed to professionally design online courses; and monitoring of quality assurance, to name just a few.

The pandemic has raised the question of developing a new pedagogy. Going digital does not only mean to have teachers lecture in front of a camera; to take the didactic materials from the conventional course and post them onto a university portal, and/or to upload lessons from the internet. It has become clear that HEIs are in need of completely new didactics, completely new ways of upholding motivation, individualization, interactivity, and student involvement (Crawford et al. 2020).

Surveys of Russian students and teachers showed (Prakhov 2021; Uroki "stress-testa" 2020) that in order to adapt their teaching style to the online environment, educators used the video conference function where students could actively participate. More advanced formats incorporating the use of online lectures and discussion questions have been identified as online teaching strategies, which engage students, reduce anxiety while also increasing knowledge acquisition. However, the percentage of using these formats might vary from one region to another: the highest in Moscow – 82.4 % and half as low outside megapolises – only 40.3 %.

Among the mostly used types of online communication between students and teaching staff, respondents indicated e-mail and virtual learning portal. Academic staff often gave online assignments and interactive tasks (tests, surveys, etc.). Most faculty members experienced problems at the first stage of the transition to online learning and teaching due to the lack of experience with online learning platforms. For example, to offer students the possibility to work in teams during seminars an educator needs to be able to create 'rooms', to allocate students into groups, to monitor by using virtual tools, to visualize the results of discussions, etc. These technical skills also refer to the teacher's ability to present topics through screen sharing, to use synchronous chat during presentations, to post various links on the platform with reference to various sources of information, to make short videos for laboratories/seminars and to upload them on the platform.

Universities had to quickly provide assistance and useful instructions to the university community, as well as fast track training in online teaching and learning methodologies. Technical assistance teams offered user support hotlines for faculty members to ask any questions about working remotely; devoted e-mail addresses for students and/or staff who have questions or are facing difficulties regarding online courses or are experiencing technical issues. However, the further acquisition of more advanced digital skills remains almost entirely in the area of teacher responsibility and depends on their desire and willingness to immerse themselves in the world of technologies.

According to the statistical data, 15 % of students mentioned that academic staff did not have the necessary skills and they did not seem eager to improve their teaching skills in the online environment. Furthermore, 22.5 % of students mentioned that the main issue they encountered was the lack of adaptation of the teaching style to the online environment, this having a negative impact on their ability to assimilate and understand the subjects taught during the courses.

Nevertheless, over 40 % of Russian university teachers believe that they are equipped with skills sufficient for working in a remote format. 81.3 % of educators reported that teaching in a new technical environment did not cause any difficulties. At the same time, 33.5 % believe that they need to improve their digital skills in order to enhance their teaching in the online modality. Other categories of required knowledge and skills are pedagogy of remote classes (59.4 %), awareness and application of ICT (47.8 %), handling electronic databases, including library resources (42.6 %).

An obvious negative side effect of the transition to distance learning is an increase in the workload: 66 % of university teachers stated that they feel more tired as they have to spend more time on working with a computer and preparing for classes, 58.3 % faced the problem of major modifications to teaching materials. 67 % of faculty members agreed that there is a need to introduce biomedical and psychological recommendations for working in a new mode.

On the other hand, the transition to online learning has opened up more opportunities for the development of educational platforms and massive open online courses (MOOCs) in Russia. Leading Russian universities joined the MOOC experiment in 2013. In experts' opinion, the use of MOOCs may broaden student opportunities for building individual educational trajectories, and adjust university curricula to the demands of the labor market. However, until now, only a small number of teachers have included MOOCs in their courses. This is partly due to the lack of awareness of MOOCs advantages, the lack of relevant skills to administer MOOCs as well as a need to restructure educational and managerial processes at the university and the lack of regulatory rules (Bekova et al. 2021).

This situation has forced educator to re-assess a set of skills essential for students and promote the digital competence, or digital literacy, which implies the ability to use digital technologies consciously and critically (Sá / Serpa 2020) as well as soft skills, such as adaptability, ability to learn and communication skills. The importance of soft skills is also highlighted by employers' community. Their graduate skills list is topped with communication skills, an ability to critically assess information, team working, responsibility and leadership qualities (Agranivich 2020), which conforms to global trends (Omoth 2021).

The importance of the digital literacy due to the transition to Society 5.0 was discussed by both researchers and practitioners back prior to COVID-19 (Zermeño 2020), but the situation caused by the pandemic forces to address these requirements urgently. To meet rapidly changing demands, teaching professionals in Russia can use the European Framework for the Digital Competence of Educators (DigCompEdu) (EU Science Hub 2021), a scientifically sound framework describing what it means for educators to be digitally competent. It provides a general reference frame to support the development of educator-specific digital competences in Europe. DigCompEdu is directed towards educators at all levels of education, from early childhood to higher and adult education, including general and vocational education and training, special needs education, and non-formal learning contexts. DigCompEdu defines common terminology and can be adjusted to national and regional teaching needs.

The professional digital competence (PDC) of teachers constitutes the backbone of pedagogical training (Guillén-Gámez / Mayorga-Fernández 2020). However, faculty members integrate ICT into their teaching practice in different ways that are affected by the level of individual digital competence. By the end of the online–only period of studies over 60 % of Russian academic staff reported that they still did not feel confident in using LMS and scored their level of digital competence 3.2 points out of 5.

Thus, PDC plays a fundamental role in the teacher's profile as experience in using ICT will directly affect the level of digital competence of their students. To be successful, the university course needs to foster effective student engagement and be digitally dynamic. This is not possible without appropriate teacher preparation. Such university professors who taught effectively in the face-to-face classroom environment may not find it effective or easy to deliver content digitally. They are likely required to undergo professional development training to rapidly move to online delivery.

The 2020/2021 Academic Year

The decision to reopen Russian universities was taken at a national level and done in consultation with the Ministry of Health and other relevant stakeholders. The new 2020/2021 academic year for all Russian universities started with no delay although significant uncertainty continued as the current COVID-19 climate affected the type of teaching and learning modality. Following the recommendations of the Ministry, universities had to choose the approach, which falls into one of the two categories:

1. Moving to Online-Only Instruction: As of October 2020, of 1278 Russian universities, 152 universities were operating online-only during the winter semester (Remezova 2020).
2. Creating a Hybrid Model: The rest of the universities were using a blend of in-person and online learning.

As the epidemiological climate was improving, at the end of January 2021, the Ministry announced a return to in-person training. The spring semester exams for the 2020–2021 academic year were held in a traditional face-to-face mode.

Though returning to the classroom provides opportunities for socialization that students missed so much, their feelings about the return to in-person teaching were complicated. Most often, students noted that during the quarantine restrictions, they simply lost the habit of traditional classroom studies. Now they have to leave a quiet and comfortable place of study at their homes and to adapt to 'a new normality': a traditional classroom learning. The average rate of students who opted to not attend in person is 21 %.

Conclusions

The pandemic has provided a better understanding of our current education systems' vulnerabilities and shortcomings. COVID-19 is causing us to challenge deep-rooted notions of when, where, and how we deliver education, of the role of HEIs, the importance of lifelong learning, and the distinction we draw between traditional and non-traditional learners (Kandri 2020). It remains to be seen how the quality of learning will be affected by the shift from face-to-face to online teaching. The 2020/2021 academic year was a blend of e-learning and mainstream face-to-face, and it will require more effort by both HEIs and students, and a close dialogue between them, in order to provide a meaningful learning experience in the future.

There is an urgent need for new online teaching and learning strategies, management approaches, didactic materials and techniques in order to overcome the difficulties caused by transferring traditional methods of teaching, learning and assessment from the face-to-face classroom to the virtual environment.

So far, the current situation has deepened the digital gap between regions, giving better chances to large universities for the introduction of new technologies. On the other hand, the fast and rigid transition to remote teaching and learning has challenged the professional status of the teacher as an educator. They have to bear the burden of a dual responsibility: on the one hand, they are obliged to improve their level of pedagogical digital competence, and, on the other hand, they must contribute to enhanced development of the pedagogical digital competence of their students (Guillén-Gámez / Mayorga-Fernánde 2020). During the online-only period, the proportion of staff members who see new opportunities for education in digital technologies increased from 30 % to 70 %. 41.2 % of university academic staff believe that in the future teachers will have even more freedom in selecting teaching methods and techniques (Uroki "stress-testa" 2020). Unfortunately, for many academic members, the task is almost impossible to complete and is limited by transferring lectures or seminars to an online format only.

The pandemic has led to a growing awareness of the need to develop new digital competencies not only among faculty members but also among students. This urgency has prompted the HEI management to modify the existing courses by adding digital components and to introduce new subjects and new programs related to the digital competence in the university curricula (e. g. digital economy, digital governance). The transition to online teaching and learning opens up more opportunities for promoting personalized learning and offering individual educational trajectories.

During the pandemic caused by COVID-19, the university has largely lost its role as a place of social communication and socialization. The educational function of higher education to develop and apply role models is diminishing, especially in regional universities. Therefore, 'compensating' techniques and new forms of socialization, relevant for online learning are needed.

Teachers are getting more willing to include online modules and open online courses in their teaching, but it may be possible if some issues are solved. For instance, it might be essential to find out which organizational models should be used in order to build MOOCs into Russian university curricula. It is also worth identifying what skills students should have to successfully complete MOOCs; whether MOOCs can successfully substitute –fully or partly –traditional courses, and how the integration of MOOCs may affect student learning outcomes.

All these aspects will definitely require restructuring of both the educational and management processes in Russian universities. During the pandemic, universities began to actively update their management systems by offering IT platforms that can be used for support and management of the educational process.

At the initial stage to respond to the challenges posed by the coronavirus crisis, the Ministry declared a nationwide suspension of face-to-face teaching and advised to follow the overall government's recommendations for the organization of the educational process. However, the independent decision-making process based on the current regional situation has been left to university management. To a certain extent, this approach is justified by such factors as the country size and regional differentiation in terms of local morbidity rates. Nevertheless, in response to HEIs needs, more coherent, comprehensive and sometimes innovative policy initiatives in building the national digital educational environment for teaching and learning, should be taken.

Literature

Agranovich, Maria: "Rabotodateli rasskazali, kakih vypusknikov vuzov zhdut na rabotu." [Employers told what kind of university graduates they are looking]. RGRU 15.6.2020, retrieved 15.5.2021, from https://rg.ru/2020/07/14/rabot odateli-rasskazali-kakih-vypusknikov-vuzov-zhdut-na-rabotu.html.

Al-Tammemi, Ala'a B. / Akour, Amal / Alfalah, Laith: "Is It Just About Physical Health? An Online Cross-Sectional Study Exploring the Psychological Distress Among University Students in Jordan in the Midst of COVID-19 Pandemic." *Frontiers in Psychology*, 11 2020, 562213, retrieved 4.4.2021, from DOI 10.3389/fpsyg.2020.562213.

Basantes-Andrade, Andrea / Cabezas-González, Marcos / Casillas-Martín, Sonia: "Digital Competences Relationship Between Gender and Generation of University Professors." *International Journal on Advanced Science, Engineering and Information Technology*, 10(1), 2020, pp. 205–211, retrieved 18.4.2021, from DOI 10.18517/ijaseit.10.1.10806.

Bekova, Saule et al.: *Online, Don't Panic! Models and Effectiveness of Integration of Massive Open Online Courses into Russian Universities.* Higher School of Economics. National Research University. Institute of Education: Moscow, 2021, retrieved 20.4.2021, from https://ioe.hse.ru/data/2020/05/28/155 0145876/Онлайн%20без%20паники.%20Модели%20и%20эффективн ост..рсов%20в%20российских%20университетах.pdf.

Cao, Wenjun et al.: "The Psychological Impact of the COVID-10 Epidemic on College Students in China". *Psychiatry Research,* 287, 2020, 112934, retrieved 4.4.2021, from DOI 10.1016/j.psychres.2020.112934.

COVID-19 crisis and curriculum: sustaining quality outcomes in the context of remote learning. (COVID-19 Education Response. Education Sector issue notes 4.2). UNESCO, 2020. retrieved 1.1.2021, from https://unesdoc.unesco. org/ark:/48223/pf0000373273.

Crawford, Joseph et al.: "COVID-19: 20 Countries' Higher Education Intra-Period Digital Pedagogy Responses". *Journal of Applied Teaching and Learning,* 3(1), 2020, pp. 1–20, retrieved 4.12.2020, from DOI 10.37074/jalt.2020.3.1.7.

DeVaney, James et al.: "Higher Ed Needs a Long-Term Plan for Virtual Learning". *Harvard Business Review,* 5.5.2020, retrieved 12.3.2021, from https://hbr.org/ 2020/05/higher-ed-needs-a-long-term-plan-for-virtual-learning.

EU Science Hub: DigCompEdu The European Framework for the Digital Competence of Educators, retrieved 28.4.2021, from https://ec.europa.eu/ jrc/en/digcompedu#:~:text=The%20European%20Framework%20for%20 the,specific%20digital%20competences%20in%20Europe.

Guillén-Gámez, Francisco D. / Mayorga-Fernández, María J.: "Prediction of Factors That Affect the Knowledge and Use Higher Education Professors from Spain Make of ICT Resources to Teach, Evaluate and Research: A Study with Research Methods in Educational Technology". *Education Sciences,* 10, 2020, pp. 276, retrieved 28.4.2021, from DOI 10.3390/educsci10100276.

Houlden, Shandell / Veletsianos, George: "Coronavirus Pushes Universities to Switch to Online Classes – But Are They Ready?" The Conversation 12.3.2020, retrieved 12.3.2021, from https://theconversation.com/coronaviruspushes-universities-to-switch-to-online-classes-but-arethey-ready-132728.

Kandri, Salah-Eddine: "How COVID-19 Is Driving a Long-Overdue Revolution in Education". World Economic Forum 12.5.2020, retrieved 4.11.2020, from https://www.weforum.org/agenda/2020/05/how-covid-19-is-sparking-a-rev olution-in-higher-education/.

Marinoni, Giorgio / van't Land, Hilligje / Jensen, Trine: *The Impact of COVID-19 on Higher Education Around the World. (IAU Global Survey Report).* IAU: France, 2020, retrieved 12.12.2020, from https://www.iau-aiu.net/IMG/ pdf/iau_covid19_and_he_survey_report_final_may_2020.pdf.

McCarty, Steve: "Post-Pandemic Pedagogy". *The Journal of Online Education (JOE)*. Special Issue on Teaching Online during the 2020 Coronavirus Pandemic May 2020. New York University, retrieved 14.4.2021, from https://www.researchgate.net/publication/349592254_ Post-Pandemic_Pedagogy.

Mitchell, Nic: "Universities Not Ready for Online Learning. U-Multirank". *University World News*, 9.6.2020, retrieved 12.1.2021, from https://www.university worldnews.com/post.php?story=20200609183303614.

Omoth, Tyler: "9 Soft Skills Employers Are Looking for in 2021". TopResume, updated January 2021, retrieved 2.3.2021, from https://www.topresume.com/-career-advice/6-soft-skills-employers-are-looking-for.

Ozili, Peterson K. / Arun, Thankom: Spillover of COVID-19: Impact on the Global Economy. SSRN 2020, retrieved 4.12.2020, from http://dx.doi.org/10.2139/ssrn.-3562570.

Prakhov, Ilya: *Studenty vuzov v uslovijah pandemii: distancionnoe obuchenie, trudovye traektorii i vosprijatie ogranichenij.* [*University Students in a Pandemic: Distance Learning, Employment Trajectories and Perception of Limitations*]. Monitoring jekonomiki obrazovanija 1. Higher School of Economics. National Research University: Moscwa, 2021.

RAEX Rating Review: Deficit obshhenija i rost uchebnoj nagruzki–sledstvija perehoda studentov na «udaljonku» [The lack of communication and the growth of the academic load are the consequences of the transition to online mode], retrieved 2.3.2021, from https://raex-a.ru/releases/2020/05June.

Remezova, Tatyana: "Perehod na udalenku: ministr Fal'kov objasnil, kak budut uchit'sja student" ["Switching to online: Minister Falkov Explains How Students Will Study"]. Vesti.Ru 28.10.2020, retrieved 4.11.2020, from https://www.vesti.ru/article/2478405.

Rumbley, Laura E.: Coping with COVID-19: International Higher Education in Europe. European Association for International Education (EAIE), 2020, retrieved 4.12.2020, from https://www.eaie.org/our-resources/library/publication/Research-and-trends/Coping-with-COVID-19--International-higher-education-in-Europe.html.

Sá, Maria J. / Serpa, Sandro: "COVID-19 and the Promotion of Digital Competences in Education". *Universal Journal of Educational Research*, 8(10), 2020, pp. 4520–4528, retrieved 2.2.2021, from DOI 10.13189/ujer.2020.081020.

Shtorm pervyh nedel': kak vysshee obrazovanie shagnulo v real'nost' pandemii [Storm of the First Weeks: How the Higher Education Stepped into the Reality of the Pandemic]. (Sovremennaja analitika obrazovanija 6(36)). Higher School of Economics. National Research University: Moskwa, 2020, retrieved

4.10.2020, from https://publications.hse.ru/mirror/pubs/share/direct/368821 792.pdf.

UNESCO-IESALC: *COVID-19 and Higher Education: Today and Tomorrow. Impact Analysis, Policy Responses and Recommendations*. IESALC: Caracas, 2020, retrieved 12.12.2020, from http://www.iesalc.unesco.org/en/wp-cont ent/uploads/2020/04/COVID-19-EN-090420-2.pdf.

Uroki "stress-testa": *Vuzy v uslovijahpandemiiiposle nee*. [Universities in the Context of the Pandemic and after It]. Ministry of Science and Higher Education: Moskwa, 2020, retrieved 4.10.2020, from https://drive.google. com/file/d/1GMcB-IoP8ITzE_WDVh4nFksX6lceotZY3/view.

Vydrevich, Marina / Pervukhina, Irina: "The Role of the COVID-19 Pandemic in the Development of Remote Education in Universities in Russia". In: *Proceedings of the Research Technologies of Pandemic Coronavirus Impact (RTCOV). Advances in Social Science, Education and Humanities Research 486*. Atlantis Press: Dordrecht et al. 2020, pp. 344–349, retrieved 4.1.2021, from https://doi.org/10.2991/assehr.k.201105.062.

Zermeño, Gomez M. G.: "Massive Open Online Courses as a Digital Learning Strategy of Education for Sustainable Development". *Journal of Sustainable Development of Energy, Water and Environment Systems*, 8(3), 2020, pp. 577–589, retrieved 5.5.2021, from http://dx.doi.org/10.13044/j.sdewes.d7.0311.

Tatiana Tregubova, Irina Ainoutdinova, Vadim Kozlov

Transformation from Conventional Methods to Web-based Technologies: Enhancing FLT/ FLL Practices in Russian Universities

Abstract: This chapter analyzes the ongoing transformation of the methodology of teaching and learning foreign languages (FLT / FLL) and the changing needs, roles, skills and competencies of teachers in Russian universities. The evolution of the FLT / FLL paradigm spans from conventional methods to web-based technologies and takes place in the context of globalization, informatization and digitalization. Major disasters, including the COVID-19 pandemic, are also having impact on education systems around the world. This contribution was carried out in the framework of contextual, social, pedagogical, integrative and competency-based approaches.

Keywords: Foreign language learning and teaching, digital learning, MOOCs, language learning approaches and methods

Introduction

This Section provides an overview of the main multicultural trends and recognized methods of FLT / FLL at the turn of the 20th – 21st centuries, applicable in Russia (Direct, Audio-lingual, Immersion, Total Physical Response, Communicative, Task-based Learning, etc.).

The scientific and technological revolution of 1940–1970, which entailed an explosion of information and the need for its transmission (Perez 2003, p. 224), led to the involvement of a large number of Russian scientists, teachers and educators into scientific and practical collaboration, cultural and business contacts with international partners around the world. Communication in those days was limited to mechanical and analog electronic technologies such as old landline telephones, audio tapes, photocopiers, etc. Digital revolution of 1975 to-the-present has accelerated the transition of human civilization from its industrial phase to the technologically advanced stage of development (Bell 1979) and has filled the living space with digital devices and really fast communication technologies. Computers, laptops, microprocessors, memory chips, digital cell phones and the Internet have revolutionized every aspect of our lives, including the way we teach, learn and communicate (Castells 2009, p. 656).

In the context of expanding globalization and digitalization, the need has arisen to create new, faster and more reliable communication channels for dissemination and exchange of scientific knowledge and best practices among stakeholders living at a distance. Data transmission is now carried out through various telecommunication networks, including the Internet. Educators and teachers, as well as members of other social groups, began to establish, maintain and develop professional and interpersonal contacts through social sites, online associations, and professional groups, communicating in different languages from different countries.

Adequate networking in such multicultural environment is unthinkable without proper means of communication, the main of which is language. Likewise, it is impossible for scientists and researchers to maintain useful contacts without sufficient knowledge of foreign languages. It is expected that specialists who are fluent in foreign languages will use them for various purposes: in research work, when working with authentic sources that allow them to read, extract and analyze information, in joint projects with foreign partners, when communicating on social networks or speaking publicly in front of a foreign audience without an interpreter, etc. Given that knowledge of at least one foreign language is becoming a social, cultural and digital demand, there is an urgent need to popularize its value, improve the quality of teaching and motivate adult learners to study it on a regular basis and in the frame of a "new culture of learning and teaching" paradigm (Warschauer / Kern 2012, p. 256).

It becomes obvious that a foreign language is becoming a necessary component not only of the educational system, the scientific sphere, but also the key to successful professional growth and development of any competitive specialist. The possibilities of a foreign language are expanding, turning it into: a means of foreign languages teaching and learning (FLT/ FLL) and continuous individual development; a means of access to information in foreign languages, which is associated with the supranational nature of scientific knowledge, which has become the property of all mankind; and a means of implementing intercultural communication in the context of people's professional and daily activities (Moeller / Catalano 2015).

Implementation of the Bologna Declaration, Russia's disposition to enter into the world and European educational environment led to intensification of intercultural communication and significantly increased the importance of FLL for specialists in various fields. Today, the key task of FLT at the university is the formation of the ability to use foreign languages as a tool for communication in the dialogue of different cultures and civilizations of the world. A foreign language is also seen as an instrument for European and global cooperation, and as a means of bilingual and multicultural self-development. This is especially important in modern realities, when fusion of people, languages and cultures has reached its climax and the digital technologies have contributed to this. At the same time, there is an acute problem of fostering tolerance, interest and respect for other cultures and overcoming feelings of irritation from redundancy, insufficiency, or simply the dissimilarity of other nations and cultures (Phillips 2007).

Some Recognized Methods of FLT / FLL in the 20th–21st Centuries in Russia

Until recently, FLT/ FLL in Russia was mainly about reading texts. At the university level, for example, this process was carried out based on reading outdated newspaper articles, when students had to read "in thousands of words" incomprehensible texts, which did not correspond to either the theme of their future profession or the requirements of the day. Communicative initiatives were limited to memorizing primitive "topics", such as: "In the hotel", "In the restaurant", "At the post office", etc. With this method, only one language function, the information or messaging function, was implemented, but in a very narrow form. In addition, only one passive, recognition-oriented skill associated with the foreign language proficiency – reading – was in sight, and the other three skills – writing, speaking and listening comprehension – were totally ignored (Ter-Minasova 2013).

FLT/ FLL, however, cannot be narrowed down only to transfer of certain signs, rules, their combination or a fixed set of language stereotypes necessary for communication, because, along with mastering the language, the learner must penetrate into a different system of values and life guidelines and integrate it into his/ her own picture of the world. Consequently, it is necessary to search for alternative educational methods and technologies that could optimize FLT/ FLL and make it possible to form a bilingual or "secondary linguistic personality" with linguistic, communicative and intercultural competencies (Ainoutdinova 2017, p. 456).

It is important to note that in the entire history of humanity many different educational methods have been developed. At first, all methods of FLT were borrowed from programs designed to teach the so-called "dead languages" – Latin and Greek, within which almost the entire educational process was limited to reading and translation. This method, the foundations of which were laid by the enlighteners at the end of the 18th century, took shape by the middle of the 20th century under the name "Grammar-translational method". In the classroom, students mainly did grammar exercises and translated texts into a foreign language and vice versa. The teacher explained grammar most often in their native language, scolded learners for mistakes and tried to correct them all to the last. If the student could not correct his mistake himself, the teacher did it for him (Ter-Minasova 2013).

According to this method, language proficiency is based on grammar and vocabulary. Hence, with time, students formed the idea that a foreign language is a set of boring and difficult grammatical rules or some long lists of words that need to be memorized. As for the text, these usually were the so-called artificial texts, in which almost no meaning was given to the content, according to the principle – "it is not so important what you say, it is important how you say it". As a result, students received knowledge about the language and its structure, and not the language itself, not being able to conduct a full-fledged dialogue. The main disadvantage of this method was that it created ideal prerequisites for the emergence of the so-called language barrier, since a person in the process of learning stopped expressing himself/ herself and began not to speak, but simply to combine words by means of some rules and memorized clichés (Ainoutdinova 2017, p. 456).

In the mid-1950s, it became obvious that the traditional method did not meet the requirements of linguistics that had formed by that time. The result was the birth of a huge number of alternative methods and techniques (ibid.). Speaking about non-traditional or alternative methods of FLT/ FLL of that period, two main features should be distinguished that characterize them. First, some of these methods were based on the principles of suggestopedia; they used the effect of over-memorization, when a person perceived and assimilated information without critical understanding (for example, the works of Bulgarian scientist G. Lozanov) (Kharismawati 2014). These methods are also based on the work of the subconscious. For example, the widespread "25 frame" method is nothing more than a subconscious perception of information in the form of pairs of words in Russian and English. However, practice has proven that such a variant of simply memorizing the meaning of words cannot help to speak and duly communicate (Bancroft 1998).

Another example of a highly controversial method is learning languages while sleeping. The possibility of learning foreign languages in a dream, according to the supporters, is not a fiction at all but it requires an alliance between a teacher and hypnologist. The learning process is based on the brain's ability to remember and reproduce. A person recalls, for example, all pieces of English speech that have ever been heard – phrases from songs, films, scraps of school knowledge, and so on. After all, our brain remembers absolutely everything that we saw, heard and felt, only most of this information is hidden so deeply that in the normal state we cannot extract it. However, under hypnosis, all these "masses of information" return to consciousness and become active. Thus, a large number of new words could be memorized without any difficulty. This method can only be compared with teaching in early childhood, when memory, like a sponge, instantly absorbs everything heard and seen. Therefore, the knowledge gained in childhood or under hypnosis can also be forgotten only under hypnosis (Batterink et al. 2014). Secondly, these unconventional methods are most often focused on a quick and intensive task of language acquisition, where theoretical aspects are either minimized or absent altogether, and the emphasis is on live communication, for example, spoken language, without special rules (Ainoutdinova 2017, p. 456).

In Russia, there are currently about 20 different well-developed and tested methods of FLT/ FLL. Each has its pros and cons that limit its use. Let's have a broader look at some of these methods. In the late 1970s – 1980s, there was a boom in suggestopedia. The method itself used by Bulgarian psychiatrist G. Lozanov means "treatment by suggestion or by hypnosis". With regard to FLT/ FLL, suggestopedia attaches great importance to the psychological mood and emotional state of students while learning. The role of teachers is extremely important and complex there: they must create an atmosphere in which there is no place for shyness, timidity, fear of mistakes, and in which self-confidence increases. This technique actively uses music, movements, stage actions, etc. (Bancroft 1998). Unfortunately, this method often took a caricatured form in Russia, mainly due to the insufficient qualifications of teachers. At present, discussions about the suggestopedic approach have become rare and have lost their former tension, although some further research on the methodology of pedagogical suggestionology and its application in education continues in research laboratories in Bulgaria and some other countries. These ongoing studies are likely to indicate that some of the conceptual assumptions about suggestopedics for FLT/ FLL do have value (ibid.; Batterink et al. 2014).

The systems of FLT / FLL by G. Kitaygorodskaya and I. Shekhter were developed partly under the influence of G. Lozanov's ideas. The main point of language learning, according to G. Kitaigorodskaya, is "learning through communication" (1986, p. 176). Students work in groups of 10–12 people under the guidance of a teacher. In the classroom, role-playing games are conducted with lots of movement, and specially selected music. The main goal is to learn to communicate in foreign languages, and get rid of the language barrier. However, the method of Kitaygorodskaya, called the method of "activating the reserve capabilities of the individual and the team", provides only group training. In addition, it is not suitable for students who begin learning foreign languages "from scratch", since in order to be actively involved into the process as an "equal player", it is necessary to have at least a passive basic level of foreign language proficiency (ibid.). Shekhter's method is based on emotional and semantic language acquisition. Igor Shekhter is an ardent opponent of learning languages by "constructing sentences using patterns", which, by the way, is one of the fundamental elements of the grammatical-translation method. Shekhter's ideas about FLL (he calls it "mastering") are at odds with the traditional ones. His theory seriously contradicts the provisions of the classical methodology. Shekhter's method is based on the hypothesis that a foreign language should be perceived as a native one. To achieve this goal, students are first taught to express their thoughts in the form of statements related to various hypothetical situations, and only later grammatical materials are added to serve as bridges between three levels of training. It is assumed that after the first stage students will not get lost in the country of the studied language, after the second – they will not get lost in grammar in their own monologues, and after the third stage – they will become equal participants in any discussion. However, Igor Shekhter's "emotional-semantic" method is not suitable for students under the age of 16, since students are expected to "master the basics of grammar on their own", and in the classroom, they are expected to express their thoughts within the framework of hypothetical situations, which is not so easy. However, Shekhter declares that free language communication between the teacher and the student is possible from the first lesson (Shekhter 2005).

The "cognitive-motivational method" by linguist and psychologist Denis Runov is based on teaching grammar using graphic symbols and memorizing new words using the method of direct associations (Zelenin / Kovalyova 2011). This method can hardly be used with students under the age of 14, as it requires a sufficiently developed student's thinking; thus, this method is doomed to an age-limited audience. The author declares the creation of original approach to FLT based on unique ways of presenting information via technology for compressing and presenting it, and special ways of learning words by using memory support methods. According to the author, any person can master foreign languages from scratch using this method at a high level in just 8 months. There is an opinion that at the moment teaching foreign languages using this method is distorted in Russia in comparison with the initial postulates that were put forward by Denis Runov himself (ibid.).

Mikhail Shestov's methodology "Blitz Courses of English – Supreme Learning" can only be used for individual training (2007, p. 66). The course provides a high-speed integrated study (mastering "from scratch") of a fluent oral and written language or improvement of any level of English proficiency with parallel mastering of the system "How to teach yourself to learn" (an effective step-by-step instruction for mastering any skill or subject developed by M. Shestov). Being engaged in "Supreme Learning", doing for 1–3 months simple exercises designed in accordance with the elementary scheme: "key phrases correctly pronounced – are correctly spelled or recorded", any student, according to the author, will simultaneously learn how to understand well any oral or written texts, speak correctly and write well in English, while the student is completely relieved of the need to think, memorize or make at least any elementary efforts. The method evokes ambiguous assessments and justified skepticism.

Vladislav Milashevich's method made it possible to master the grammatical structure of the language in a very short time (up to 30 hours) (Bronzova 2013). This knowledge is supposed to be sufficient to learn how to quickly and competently translate texts of any complexity, in particular, scientific and technical literature. This method was developed only for Russian-speaking students who have already studied the chosen foreign language at least at school. The disadvantage of the method is that it includes only the grammatical aspect of a foreign language. Thus, in order to learn how to speak a foreign language, learners would have to take another course. Techniques created according to Milashevich's method are from time to time practised in Russia, but only to provide mainly basic knowledge in the structure of the language, grammar and vocabulary (Bronzova 2013).

Next, let's examine the so-called "method of immersion" (suggest-pedia). According to this method, a student can master a foreign language by becoming (at least for the period of study) a completely different person. This method involves the student's refusal to communicate in his/ her native language, in addition, the student chooses a different name for himself, associating himself with a completely different person – to impersonate a fictional native speaker (Wilkinson 1998). As a result, the illusion is created that learners are in the world of the language being studied; they completely relax, take on other roles and their speech becomes as similar to the authentic as possible. A session of "immersion" in a foreign language environment is one of the variants of the suggestive technique. This technique is believed to have a special effect on a person and liberates him/ her. However, the same technique is used in the systems of Kitaygorodskaya and Shekhter. The economic realities of today make this teaching method inaccessible to most learners due to the high cost of courses. It is also necessary to clarify that not a single methodological approach has been subjected to such distortion and even perversion as the method of "immersion". Probably, this is because "immersion" requires the highest professional level from the teacher, which few can match.

Another method, called the "Silent way" (the method of silence) appeared in the mid-60s. Its principle of FLT was as follows: "knowledge of the language is inherent in the one who wants to learn it", and, most importantly, teachers must neither interfere with the intentions of students nor impose any obligatory point of view on them (Stevick 2000). Following this method, teachers initially do not say anything, and only pronunciation is trained at the first level. Teachers use complex color tables, in which each color or symbol denotes a certain sound, and in this way new words are presented. For example, to "say" the word table, you must first show the box for the sound "t", then the square for the sound "a", and so on. Thus, by manipulating all these squares, sticks and similar symbols, the student works out the material. What is the advantage of this method? Since the level of the teacher's knowledge has practically no effect on the level of the student's outcomes, it may turn out in the end that the student through learning with due diligence will know the language better than the teacher will. In addition, throughout the entire educational process, students have all the opportunities to freely express their thoughts. This method can be attractive for high-tech adepts.

The next way to learn foreign languages appeared in the late 1970s. It is called "Audio-lingual method" (audiolinguistic method). Its essence is that at the first stage, students repeat over and over again what they have heard after the teacher or phonogram. And only starting from the second level, students are allowed to speak one or two phrases from themselves, most of the other practice consisted of endless repetitions (Mart 2013). With the advent of the audio-lingual method, language lab courses and language lab classes have become very popular where students did endless and boring laboratory work with headphones: for example, it was necessary to make mechanical replacements in the sentence structure, etc. Classes, as a rule, were also both boring and unpromising with little or no feedback. The proponents of the method believed that students need to memorize the grammatical and phraseological structures by repeating them many times in ready-made educational dialogues, and then, according to experts, students will use them automatically at the right time and right place. However, the experience of many trainees having used this method shows that in a real situation, as a rule, a person cannot use a phrase or speech pattern that he/ she once learned that way.

Another interesting method is called "Total-physical response" (TPR or method of physical response). The basic rule of this method is: "you cannot understand what you have not passed through yourself." According to this theory, students at the early stages of learning do not say anything (Oflaz 2019). First, they receive a sufficient amount of knowledge, which becomes their passive store. For about 20 lessons, students constantly listen to a foreign speech, read something, but do not speak a word in the target language. Then, in the process of learning, there comes a period when students should already react to what they heard or read – but they can only react with actions. Usually, training starts with requests for physical movement. For example, when students learn the word "get up", everyone gets up; "sit down" – they sit down, etc. Only then, when students have accumulated a sufficient amount of information (first they listen, then move), they become ready to start talking. This method is attractive, first of all, because students feel comfortable in the learning process, as they communicate not only with the teacher, but also with each other. The necessary effect is achieved by the fact that a person passes all the information received through himself/ herself (ibid.).

Today the world-recognized "communicative method" (Canale / Swain 1980, p. 1) is widely used in Russia. For English learners, a different name is often used – "Oxford" or "Cambridge" method, as it was jointly developed by linguistic teachers and psychologists from these leading British universities. However, its methodology is now quite popular in teaching any other language, not just English. Such popular training courses as "Headway" and "New Cambridge English Course" (English), "Teumen neu" (German), and "Le Nouvelle sans Frontiers" (French) have been written on the basis of the communicative method, which is aimed at the simultaneous development of basic language skills (speaking, writing, grammar, reading and listening) in the process of lively, easy communication. Teaching the student to communicate in a foreign language is the main task of the teacher. Vocabulary, grammatical constructions, expressions in foreign languages are presented to students in the context of real, emotionally colored situations, which contributes to the rapid and long-term memorization of the studied material (Savignon 2000).

The communicative method serves to break down the psychological barrier between teachers and students. And when the students cease to feel the "distance" between them and the teacher (ibid.), then they become involved and feel free in communication: this is how people begin to speak a foreign language with ease and desire. Numerous play-based learning elements promote classroom interaction, maintain a positive emotional atmosphere and increase student motivation. Collaborative work "in pairs", "in triplets", participation in debates and discussions on topics of interest to students – all these practices allows the teacher to approach the learning process taking into account the individual characteristics and learning styles of their students, make classes creative and exciting, and at the same time it gives the teacher the opportunity to, invisibly for the students, exercise full control over the learning process and learning progress of the learners.

The systems of independent mastering of foreign languages are becoming popular in Russia today. For example, a "sequential system" method that includes the best developments in scientific and popular linguistics, psychology, and applied sciences, including the author's method of visual modeling of English grammar, as well as materials supporting motivation and organization of the process. Or the method of "Active development of foreign languages" – the first step-by-step, structured electronic course by Sergei Vasilenkov on the Russian Internet on how to independently and effectively master any foreign language in 4–6 months (Kolisnichenko / Yatsun 2018). The next example is "How to easily and quickly learn any foreign language" – a kind of magic seminar by Igor Serov, who supposedly offers really working principles and techniques, which teachers never talk about, but that allows freely mastering any language in a quite short period of time (Turaeva 2019). Another educational resource for self-study of foreign languages is Ivan Poloneichik's "Forced mastering of foreign languages" – a selection of useful techniques, methods and approaches to learning languages of varying degrees of complexity (Ivanovskaya / Nefyodov 2016).

Knowledge of a foreign language involves the use of different aspects of language and communication: speaking, listening (with understanding), writing, and reading with comprehension. Each of these aspects is based on its own methods of achievement. Therefore, from the point of view of different tasks and objectives, any method may have its own strengths and weaknesses. However, the greatest effect in learning a foreign language is achieved with the integrated or eclectical use of all of the above methods, which allows students to study all aspects of the language together and with the best results. Next, in this chapter we will consider how the old methods are being replaced by innovative digital technologies for FLT/ FLL and what factors do influence this paradigm shift.

Impact of Globalization & Digitalization on FLT/ FLL Paradigm Shift

> *This section is devoted to an in-depth analysis of the means, methods and technologies of FLT/FLL at university in the context of modern realities: globalization, digitalization, etc. (ICT-based, Computer Assisted Language Learning (CALL), Web-based (WBL), MOOCs, etc.). Best European practices and results of international*

integration with our partners have been also taken into account.

In Russia, both the state policy on education and the related national legislation on education depend on many external and internal socio-economic, political and cultural factors and with time tend to give rise to tremendous changes in the sphere of education and its practices. These alterations correlate with various global processes and trends, including globalization, technologization, and digitalization, that influence at large the state and society, labor markets and educational institutions. These shifts further contextually impose high burden on the education system and, similarly, on FLT/ FLL practices (Stepanenko et al. 2020). Moreover, each era generates its own vision of educational standards, as well as its own teaching and learning methods and technologies. For example, the first generation of educational technologies in FLT/ FLL in Russia was regarded as traditional or conventional; second and third generation involved mainly structured and block-based learning systems, while the fourth generation of educational technologies can be classified as innovative, integral or integrative technologies (Ainoutdinova / Ainoutdinova 2017). So, why do we need innovative approaches, models, technologies and do we really need them today, if there is a certain developed concept of integrative learning; and the arsenal of almost every teacher is properly equipped with a set of traditionally used teaching methods, which, moreover, have proven themselves quite well? In answering this question, we declare that the world we live in has changed completely over the past half-century. The global economic relations are constantly growing in volume, expanding in content and actualizing the need for universal personnel (specialists) with professional training at national universities. This leads to the fact that the content of national systems of higher education naturally tends to the so-called universal world standards developed by science and technology. New modern technologies with their powerful infrastructure and resources make information available to almost all corners of the globe, universalize the content of higher education, and provide knowledge transfer and learning from anywhere, at any time and for everyone (Tregubova et al. 2017).

Globalization, despite differences of opinion, is an objective current reality that requires a new paradigm orientation of national higher education systems, taking into account the need for international cooperation and collaboration based on the common values of human ethics, respect and dignity. The spread of democracy in almost all countries of the world is strengthening the legal status of the state, which, in turn, increases the role of education in teaching young people and adults in the spirit of democratic citizenship. The best features originally inherent in science and higher education, including the ideas of academic freedom and equality, are then gradually transferred to the entire society, universalizing its political structure in different countries of the world (Ainoutdinova 2017; Ainoutdinova / Ainoutdinova 2017; Tregubova et al. 2017). The formation of new socio-cultural values shared by most countries, such as a civilized free market and the humanization of public relations, not only changes the structure of higher education in Russia, expanding the training of economists, managers, lawyers, sociologists, political scientists, etc., but also changes the entire paradigm of higher education as a system of globally accepted ideas, views and concepts. The new educational paradigm, in this context, crowns the transition from scientism (Hyslop-Margison / Naseem 2007, p. 134) (a belief system that asserts the fundamental role of science as a source of knowledge and decision-making about the world) to homocentrism (Horsthemke 2019) (a belief system that means the advancement of human rights and interests). At the same time, this new educational paradigm does not put obstacles to the moral freedom of specialists, does not force them to give an unambiguous answer to the question "what is good and what is bad", but requires appropriate and competent behavior in everyday and professional life in accordance with the circumstances and requirements of the day (Ainoutdinova 2017; Ainoutdinova / Ainoutdinova 2017; Tregubova et al. 2017).It is well known that foreign languages are one of the most important driving forces of human progress. Foreign languages are necessary to acquire new knowledge and skills that allow for intercultural, interdisciplinary, academic and professional communication. Therefore, educational programs of universities consider teaching a foreign language as one of the main components of training highly qualified specialists for all areas of science and technology. This is done in order to ensure the innovative development of the country and its economy. This implies that throughout the entire period of study at university, students must intensively and effectively study foreign languages. In this regard, the question of optimization and intensification of the educational process arises.

There are various methodological prerequisites for learning foreign languages in the innovative learning environment, which offers students and teachers new ideas, flexibility, agency, ubiquity, and connectedness (Osborne 2016). In particular, the improvement of FLT / FLL practices at the university level depends, according to A.I. Fefilov, on the implementation of certain principles of optimization of the educational process (Fefilov 2014, p. 188), which include: rejection of the authoritarian teaching style and transition to a learner-centered teaching paradigm; focus on the personal qualities of the student, his/ her learning expectations, needs and styles; improvement of teaching technologies and shift from the monologue to polylogue and dialogue; using communication not only as a means of data transfer but as an incentive for some action; taking knowledge as a set of skills that are actualized in the course of the subject's activity; exclusion from the educational process any situation marked by mercantilism or consumerism; exclusion of any situation causing replacement of learning by training of the language memory; awareness that "language proficiency" should not be replaced by "knowledge about the language"; recognition of the need to regularly practice reproductive language aspects, such as speaking, listening, reading, and writing; recognition of the need to understand the conceptual content expressed with the help of language; awareness that only consistency, integrity of knowledge obtained in an interdisciplinary context can guarantee the successful mastering and achievement of the set goals and learning objectives (Ainoutdinova 2017).

Today, according to experts, the best examples of sustainable innovative and disruptive technology-based FLT/ FLL methods include: Web-based learning (WBL) (Ainoutdinova / Ainoutdinova 2017), computer-assisted language learning (CALL), e-Learning, blended learning, mobile (M-Learning), open and distance learning, etc. (Tregubova et al. 2017). All these methods include ICT-based educational activities and practices that should not be perceived as a direct substitute for conventional FLT/ FLL strategies though they have dramatically reshaped traditional classrooms, fostered learner's autonomy and motivation, created a wide range of options for authentic interaction and communication in a technology-mediated learning environment, etc. (Ghasemi / Hashemi 2011). Let's have a broader look at some methods, keeping in mind that any experienced teacher will always take an eclectic approach to language teaching, allowing for a combination of different approaches and methods, depending on the goals of the lesson and the abilities of the students, in order to match the dynamics of the times (Tabassum et al. 2018).

Information Communications Technologies (ICT) in Education

ICT – is an acronym that stands for Information Communications Technology. The phrase ICT had been used by academic researchers since the 1980s, but it became popular after it was used in a report to the UK government by Dennis Stevenson in 1997. Addressing the UK government Stevenson emphasized that both teachers and students must be "confident and highly competent" (Stevenson 1997, p. 44) in using ICTs "in all aspects of their daily life" as well as in all other routine and specific areas that can contribute to their teaching practice and learning experience. ICT (information and communications technology or technologies) – is an umbrella term that includes any communication device, digital infrastructures or applications, like radio, digital television, networks, satellite systems, personal computers, laptops, printers, scanners, software programs, data projectors, cellular phones, interactive teaching box, robots and so on, as well as various services and applications associated with them, such as video-conferencing or distance learning tools. In other words, ICT concerns the uses of digital technology to help individuals, businesses and organizations to use information.

Generally speaking, ICT – covers any product that will store, retrieve (access information from memory or other storage devices), manipulate (control), transmit or receive information electronically in a digital form. So, ICT – is concerned with storage, retrieval, manipulation, transmission or receipt of digital data. It is also concerned with the way these different tools can work or interact with each other (Chapelle 2001, p. 236). In its broader sense, ICTs are defined as a "diverse set of technological tools and resources used to communicate, and to create, disseminate, store, and manage information" (Stevenson 1997, p. 44). Thus, information and communication technologies (ICTs) include both hardware, software, networks, and media used to collect, store, process, transmit, and present information in the form of voice, data, text, images, animations, etc. ICT also refers to technologies that provide access to information through telecommunications. In this sense, it is similar to Information Technology (IT), but focuses primarily on communication channels: the Internet, wireless networks, smartphones, and other communication mediums. It should be noted that ICT and computers are not the same thing, the latter being just the hardware as a part of some ICT-based system. ICTs are often categorized into two broad types: traditional computer-based technologies, which require the use of specific hardware, software, and micro processing features available on a computer or mobile device; and the more recent, and fast-growing range of technologies, which allow communicating and sharing information digitally.

In the past few decades, ICTs have provided the world population with a vast array of new communication capabilities. For example, people can communicate in real-time or synchronously with others from different countries using technologies, such as instant messaging, voice over IP (VoIP), or video-conferencing (Zoom, Teams, Voov, etc.). People can also communicate globally via electronically mediated asynchronous means of communication, so the participants in this case do not communicate concurrently. Forums, e-mail, bulletin board systems, chats, etc. allow the participants to send or post messages at different times. Social networking websites, like Facebook, Twitter, Skype, etc. allow users from all over the world to be in touch and communicate on a regular basis. Modern ICTs are said to have created a "global village", in which people can communicate with the others across the distances as if they were living next door. In this regard, ICTs are often spoken of in the context of how modern information and communication technologies affect the entire society.

ICTs – are also often spoken of in a particular context, such as ICTs for development, ICTs in education, ICTs for environmental sustainability, ICTs in health care, ICTs for libraries, ICTs in business or organizations, etc. In recent years, academics, educators and teachers have taken a particular interest in how best to use computers and the Internet to improve the efficiency and effectiveness of education at all levels in both formal and informal settings. Different technologies, tools and resources are usually tested and used here in combination, rather than as the only knowledge and instruction delivery system. Technologies are specifically used to enable teachers and students to communicate, create, disseminate, store, and manage information. In some contexts, ICT has also become integral to the FLT/ FLL interaction, through such approaches as e-Learning, blended learning, web-based learning, computer-based learning, distance learning, etc.

It is also worth mentioning that ICT can be seen as the third revolution in learning and teaching, the first of which is associated with the invention of the written language, and the second with the development of movable fonts and books. ICTs make both the content of learning and teaching interactive and available anytime, anywhere and for everyone. According to the 2013 European Commission "Survey of schools: ICT in education. Benchmarking access, use and attitudes to technology in Europe's schools", the importance of ICTs lies less in the technology itself rather than in its ability to create greater access to information and communication for people living in different parts of the world with or without digital literacy and skills to utilize media and the Internet.

Computer Assisted Language Learning (CALL) in FLT/ FLL

Computer-assisted language learning (CALL) – is not a new development in language teaching and learning, as it has been used since the 1960s and 70s. Recently, though, computers have become so widespread in schools and homes and their uses have expanded so dramatically that the majority of language teachers must now begin to think about the implications of computers for language teaching and learning. The term CALI (computer-assisted language instruction) was in use before CALL, reflecting its origin as a subset of the general term CAI (computer-assisted instruction). CALL was the expression agreed upon at the 1983 TESOL (Teachers of English to Speakers of Other Languages) convention in a meeting of all interested participants (Chapelle 2001, p. 236). However, CALL still lacks concise research methods and a clear definition. The purpose of this section is to try to give a more specific definition of CALL, to study the main stages of the development of CALL, to find out how computers were used and are used for FLT / FLL; and discuss the most recent issues arising from the use of CALL in education.

So, what is CALL? Broadly speaking, Computer-assisted language learning (CALL) – is an approach to FLT/ FLL in which a computer is used as an aid for instruction, presentation, reinforcement and assessment of material to be learned, usually including a substantial interactive element. According to Carol A. Chapelle from Iowa State University (Chapelle 2001, p. 236), CALL – is a term widely used to refer to the area of technology and second language teaching and learning. Michael Levy defined CALL as the search for and study of computer-based applications in FLT/ FLL (Levy 1997, p. 320). According to Ken Beatty, any definition of CALL should accommodate its changing nature and reflect the broad process of what may go on in a CALL environment, where learners use computers and improve their language skills (Beatty 2003, p. 304). Since then CALL has come to encompass many other issues about materials, design, technologies, pedagogical theories and modes of instruction associated with the use of computers. Materials for CALL include those, which are purpose-made for FLL, and those, which adapt the already existing computer-based materials.

Why do teachers use CALL? Research and practice suggest that, appropriately implemented, computer-assisted and network-based technology can significantly contribute to the specific areas in FLT/ FLL (ibid.). *Experiential learning* – is conducted as students can tackle a huge amount of human experience from the Internet; in such a way, they learn by doing things themselves, become the creators and not just receivers of knowledge, they develop thinking skills and choose what to explore. *Motivation* – is attained either because computers are most popular among students as they are associated with fun and games or because they are considered to be fashionable and handy to use. *Enhanced students' achievements* – are gained since network-based instruction helps strengthen their linguistic skills, self-confidence and self-reflection; advance their learning attitudes and autonomy. *Authentic materials for study* – allow students to use various resources or reading materials either at university or from their home 24 / 7 at a relatively low cost or free of charge. *Wider interaction* is achieved through regular access to the Web that disrupts the linear flow of learning; for example, by sending emails or joining newsgroups where students can chat with group mates, friends, or people they have never met; likewise, some online activities provide positive or negative feedback, offering students ample opportunities to share their views and expectations, or automatically adjusting their online activities, etc. *Individualization and personalization* allow some shy or inhibited students to take advantage of collaborative learning focused on ensuring that everyone can reach their full potential, as long as their peers do not interfere with their work at their own pace. *Independence from a single source of information* – is achieved through access to thousands of information sources on the Internet along with paper books, which allows avoiding "canned" knowledge and satisfies the need for interdisciplinary learning in a multicultural world. *Global understanding* – is achieved in a multicultural context with extensive use of the Internet, making students feel like citizens of a "global village" that allows them to communicate globally (Warschauer 1996).

The history and practice of CALL suggests that computers can serve a variety of uses for FLT/ FLL. It can be a "tutor" to offer language drills or skill practice; a "stimulus" – for discussion and interaction; or a "tool" – used for writing, research and even playing games. With the advent of the Internet, it can also serve as a "medium of global communication" and a "source of unlimited authentic materials". But as Nina Garrett points it out, "the use of the computer does not constitute a method"; rather, it is a "medium in which a variety of methods, approaches, and pedagogical philosophies may be implemented" (Garrett 1991). Thus, the effectiveness of CALL depends not only on the medium itself, but also on the way it is used; and those who expect great results simply from installing computer systems are likely to be disappointed. But those who use computer technology in the service of good pedagogy will undoubtedly find ways to enrich their curriculum and learning opportunities for their students. Principles for the design and use of CALL programs in FLT/ FLL include: a student/ learner-centered approach – to promote a learner autonomy; meaningful purpose; comprehensive and authentic input; sufficient level of stimulation – both cognitively and emotionally; multiple modalities – to support different learning styles and strategies; high level of interaction (human-machine; human-human); and a wide range of applicable methods and techniques.

Mark Warschauer from the University of California (USA) conducted a profound research in the sphere of CALL from the pedagogical perspective, and came to conclusion, that its development can be divided into three distinct phases: behaviorist, communicative and integrative. It is important that these stages do not occur in a rigid sequence; as each new stage emerges, the previous stages continue to exist and operate. *Behaviorist or Structural CALL* – was first implemented in the 1960s and 70s, when the Grammar-Translation and Audio-lingual method were mostly used. It was introduced with a view of a foreign language as a formal structural system (Structural approach), and computer was mostly used as a tutor for drill and repetitive practice, the principal objective being the accuracy. *Communicative/ Cognitive CALL* was based on the communicative approach to FLT/ FLL, which became popular in the 1970s-90s. It viewed language as a mentally constructed system through interaction, in which computer is used as a tutor – to practice the language but in a non-drill format, by giving students choices, control and interaction; as a stimulus – to provide computer programs that stimulate writing or discussions; and as a tool – to teach to apply language knowledge in practice, as with a word processor, grammar checkers, etc.

Integrative (Sociocognitive or Socioconstructive) CALL (1990s to present time) – is the current approach based on two important technological developments of the last decade: multimedia computers supported by CD-ROMs and the Internet. *Multimedia CALL* creates a more authentic learning environment based on a variety of multimedia, including hypermedia, allowing language skills to be developed easily and autonomously. *Web-based CALL* – includes Computer-Mediated Communication (CMC) and the Internet-based CALL. *CMC* – provides authentic one-to-one, one-to-many, or many-to-one synchronous and asynchronous communication channels in modes. *The Internet* – provides students with opportunities to search through millions of files around the world to locate and access authentic materials exactly tailored to their own personal interests, e. g., to publish their materials or media, to share them with peers or the general public. Both approaches in Web-based CALL use computers to perform real-life tasks (as a tutor, stimulus or tool), the main objective of which is some kind of meaningful action and decision-making. Language is viewed as a social interaction through discourse. The teaching paradigm is based on a content-based ESP (English for specific purposes) or EAP (English for academic purposes) methods.

How Can Computers Be Used in FLT/ FLL?

Some of the options include: teaching on a single computer in the classroom for content delivery (PowerPoint); classroom activities and discussions (Interactive whiteboard); training in a computer networked environment (task-based group work, synchronous or asynchronous CMC, tandem training, etc.); self-access/ independent learning for drills, exercises, word processing, resource search, etc.; distance/ remote learning for online course content delivery, CMC activities, e-mail, discussion forums, chat rooms, "crowdsourcing", etc.; integration of Internet activities into the curriculum to create a specific language environment with many technical and technological tools, authentic options and resources, etc. The choice of the type of CALL, relevant programs or applications and their use depends on the goals facing the stakeholders when using computers in FLT/

FLL. Computer as a Tutor – requires programs and apps for training separate aspects of language (listening, reading, writing, and speaking). Computer as a Stimulus – employs software generating analysis, critical thinking, discussion or simulations (SimCity, Second Life). Computer as a Tool – uses programs for hands-on experiential activities – as word processing (Microsoft Word, Open Office Writer), grammar checkers (Grammarly, Ginger), collaborative writing apps (Google Docs, Dropbox Paper), authoring tools with templates (Hot Potatoes, iSpring), etc.

Web-based Learning (WBL) in Teaching and Learning of Foreign Languages

Web-based Learning (WBL) – is considered the most popular and vibrant approach to higher education today due to the active use of advanced computer technology, related tools, resources and the Internet. WBL is a new powerful, flexible and efficient way for technology-enhanced FLT/ FLL. Professor Badrul Huda Khan, a well-known US educator and consultant in the field of e-learning, first coined the phrase "Web-based instruction" in his 1997 book of the same name (Khan 1997, p. 480). Later Khan defined WBL as "a hypermedia-based educational program which utilizes the attributes and resources of the World Wide Web to create a meaningful learning environment where learning is fostered and supported" (Khan 2001, p. 599).

Web-based learning environment could be defined in this context as a sum of the internal and external circumstances and influences surrounding and affecting a person's mode of learning. Recognized scholars and experts B. Gillani and A. Relan defined WBL as an "application of a repertoire of cognitively oriented instructional strategies within a constructivist and collaborative language learning environment, utilizing the attributes and resources of the World Wide Web" (Relan / Gillani 1997). Herbert H. Clark, professor of psychology from Stanford University, defined WBL as "an individualized instruction delivered over public or private computer networks and displayed by a Web browser" (Clark 1996, p. 432). All of these definitions have one thing in common: the inclusion of the Internet or the World Wide Web.

From pedagogical perspective, WBL provides benefits to FLT/ FLL as it supports the shift from the traditional teacher-centered classroom to a learner-centered environment. In addition, learning over the Internet is a powerful interactive resource that expands learners' knowledge and guarantees the quantity and quality of language input and output. Web-based learning is often integrated with conventional, face-to-face teaching. This is normally done via the Intranet, which is usually "password protected" and accessible only to registered users. In this way, it is possible to protect the copyright of open online resources and materials and maintain confidential exchange of information between the interested parties. Web-based learning allows quick access to digital libraries (for example, to order books or journals), online databases, and electronic journals. These services on the Internet are particularly useful for research and other scientific activities (Hartley 1988).

D.L. Johnson of North Carolina State University (Johnson et al. 2002, p. 240) revealed some of the unique characteristics of the Web, namely, that information here is interactive in nature; and that the Web often makes use of multimedia, including graphics, sound, or animation. The Web provides more effective and efficient searching tools than traditional searches in libraries, and the pages retrieved from the Web are more attractive and appealing than traditional printed media. Moreover, multimedia capabilities probably make the Web more user-friendly to many people.

In terms of pedagogical features of the Internet, WBL facilitates communication, enhances interaction, provides student-centered, self-paced and collaborative learning, disseminates and shares information, and reaches out to global communities. Research has also shown that the long-term effects of learning via computers encourage students' interaction and involvement during the whole learning process. Barbara Grabowski of Pennsylvania State University presented an analysis and assessment of WBL and concluded that including web-mediated lessons and activities is a new way for teachers to use computer technology, increase student motivation and improve their learning outcomes (Grabowski et al. 1998, p. 62). Therefore, it looks like the Internet offers another new way of learning that students would rather use. Therefore, more and more teachers experiment with educational websites to make their teaching practice quite interactive and engaging for students.

With the advent of Web 2.0, the Internet is viewed as a medium in which interactive experience in the form of blogs, wikis, discussion forums, podcasts, social networking, data sharing, etc., plays a more important role than simply accessing information. The 1997 Dearing Report, formally known as the reports of the National Committee of Inquiry into the UK Higher Education (a series of major reports addressed to the government of the United Kingdom) pointed out that through the Internet-based and computer-based networks it is possible to offer different forms of opportunities and provide access to many highly effective learning materials that were previously unavailable to many students (Stevenson 1997).

What Are Computer Networks?

A computer network – also a data network – is a group of computer systems and other computing hardware devices that are linked together through communication channels to exchange data, and facilitate interaction and resource-sharing among a wide range of users. The best-known network is a global system of interconnected computers, called the Internet.

What Is Computer Networking?

In its broadest sense, it is linking two or more computing devices for the purpose of sharing data. Computer networking in language classrooms – can be categorized into two important technological and interactive developments: computer-mediated communication (CMC), and the globally linked hypertexts, both providing different ways for communication and exchange of data. CMC – can be practised in both synchronous and asynchronous modes supported by the related activities; globally linked hypertexts are often written in HTML (Hypertext Markup Language), where web pages are connected by hyperlinks, typically activated by a mouse click.

The FLT/ FLL process can be enhanced with one or all of 5 well-known educational web tools such as: *Hot List or Topic Hotlist* – a collection of websites on a specific unit or topic being taught (Dejica et al. 2016, p. 270); *Multimedia Scrapbook* – a collection of multimedia links to photographs, maps, stories, facts, quotations, sound clips, videos, virtual reality tours, etc. (Erenchinova / Proudchenko 2017); *Treasure Hunt* – an inquiry-based game in which learners act upon successive clues and are directed to a "prize" (A Big Question); *Subject Sampler* – a teacher's collection of links to multimedia resources or websites pertaining to a certain topic for students to choose from (Mustakim et al. 2014); and *WebQuest* – an inquiry-based teamwork activity or mini-project in which a large percentage of the input and material is supplied by the Internet.

A Paradigm Shift towards Massive Open Online Courses (MOOCs)

In recent years Massive Open Online Courses (MOOCs), which UNESCO named among the 30 most promising trends or drivers in the development of education until 2028, are of particular interest in Russia. It is believed that namely xMOOCs and cMOOCs open up new opportunities in the field of distance education today (Dzhurinskiy 2017, p. 240). In its form, xMOOC is, in fact, an open electronic educational resource (educational e-course or teaching methodological complex), which includes video lectures with subtitles, lecture notes, homework tasks, tests and final exams.

Unlike traditional electronic educational resources, which are actively created and used for students of certain areas of training at the university, in particular, by the authors of this chapter, MOOCs are global in nature and operate outside of one university. Most MOOC authors are also teachers and professors of the world's leading universities, but courses are posted on the sites of popular educational online resources, courses are often created by huge clusters of universities, either on a territorial or thematic basis. In addition, MOOCs are addressed to a wide range of potential students, trainees and teachers, who are their target audience. The process involves mainly large American and British universities, which are actively involved in the creation and distribution of educational resources, training courses and programs, including open and free content; they are also actively exploring the commercial market for e-learning courses and services Kuzmina 2015).

The cMOOC model as a supplement to the structure of distance learning organization according to a more traditional xMOOC model, extensively implements various tools and means of social online communication via the Internet, creates open forums, chats and blogs for users (students, teachers and tutors), both for maintaining online communication within the community, and to assist and solve possible problems of a technical or pedagogical nature or both (Hollands / Tirthali 2014, p. 211).

The first mention of MOOCs appeared in 2008, when, independently of each other, two experts in the field of education from the United States and Canada, Bryan Alexander and Dave Cormier coined the word "MOOC" (Ainoutdinova / Blagoveshchenskaya 2017) to describe the essence of the then open online course "Connectivism and connective knowledge (CCK08)" developed by George Siemens and Stephen Downes on the basis of the University of Manitoba, Canada, to attract as many insolvent students as possible from different parts of the world (Cormier / Siemens 2010). As a result, the CCK08 attracted more than 2300 students who received training content via RSS feeds (Really Simple Syndication); all the extensive information was collected, processed and presented in this format by aggregator software and online services, which allowed users to receive news instantly and in a convenient form from virtually any site, without having to access the site itself. The course also offered other convenient Web-based learning tools, including LMS Moodle (Learning Management System), blogs, communication in the 3D virtual world with elements of the social network "Second Life", as well as unlimited online meetings and chats in real time.

The idea underlying the title and content of the course "CCK08" – is important for understanding the phenomenon of cMOOC, since the course was devoted to the study of the theory of connectivity or connectivism itself (Cormier / Stewart 2010), took its roots in it and was built on its fundamental principles, which in general terms convey the following message:

> Teaching and learning in the modern era will be successful if people learn to build the necessary relationships, provide communication and connections mediated by the goals and objectives of cooperation and interaction via electronic networking (Downes 2006).

The idea of creating networks of like-minded people or networking communities, connecting people for developing and gaining knowledge, and therefore creating a "knowledge society" – is one of the key and fundamental characteristics of MOOCs (Kop / Hill 2008). According to Downes, connectivism shows that "knowledge is distributed across a network of connections", and therefore "learning consists of the ability to construct and traverse such networks".

Over the past years, the number and popularity of MOOCs among the university students in Russia has increased manifold. Statistics show that the number of students registered at various MOOCs ranges from several hundred to hundreds of thousands. Among the most popular MOOCs are still Coursera with more than 77 million registered users; Udemy; Udacity; Khan Academy, etc. In Europe, the leading position in the field of MOOCs is still held by the British University of Open Education (the Open University, UK). One of the analogues of the MOOCs platforms in Runet (Russian Net) is the project by the Internet University of Information Technologies, which provides a free-of-charge distance learning at the National Open University "INTUIT". Another Russian system of online education, built on the MOOCs technology, is Universarium. It was launched on the Internet in 2013 to provide free educational courses conducted by teachers and professors from the leading Russian universities (Lomonosov Moscow State University, Moscow Institute of Physics and Technology, etc.). Universarium offers full-fledged free courses designed according to the highest e-learning standards. The other successful Russian MOOCs platforms are: Courson – the Russian equivalent of Udemy; project Lectorium; the leader in FLT/ FLL – Lingualeo with 13 million users; the leader in teaching of programming – GeekBrains, etc.

High reputation of MOOCs is because here FLT/ FLL takes place in communities of like-minded people connected not only by network interaction, but also by common goals, views, motivation and interests. The network communities are made up of people, each of whom are separate networks and can choose the most appropriate individual approach to learning and cognition. In this way, the personal knowledge of each student also constitutes a network that supports the overall development of the community, which in turn develops both the network, stimulates the learning needs, and improves the learning outcomes of individual learners. It is equally important that teaching through MOOCs is carried out in the interconnection of many disciplines and professions, which is aimed at reproducing the application of a certain scientific discipline or subject in the real world.

FLT/ FLL during the COVID-19 Pandemic in Russia and Europe

This Section contains a description and assessment of the effectiveness of various FLT / FLL resources, methods and technologies during the period caused by the COVID-19 pandemic in Russia and Europe, with priority being given to remote and online initiatives and strategies. A comparison has been made between traditional and innovative means, methods and technologies in both Russian and European universities, taking into account the advantages and disadvantages of both approaches to FLT / FLL in higher education.

Several factors have prompted the need to rethink the role, place and purpose of university education, the most recent and dramatic being the COVID-19 pandemic and its unprecedented impact on the lifestyles of billions of people around the world. The recent spread of the COVID-19 turned to be a strong stress test for education systems throughout the globe with an increasing number of countries closing their institutions of learning as a response to the pandemic. In order to keep the doors of learning open there were large-scale efforts on the part of the governments, authorities, international and local organizations, educational institutions, etc. to utilize technology in support of remote modes of teaching and learning. Thus, various forms of distance and online initiatives were mobilized to replace the traditional forms of training future specialists (Ainoutdinova et al. 2021).

In the urgent circumstances of the unexpected lockdown, most universities were forced to change not only the teaching and learning format but also their curricula and look for adaptive methods and forms using various web-based resources and digital platforms such as Microsoft Teams, Zoom, VooV, etc. This happened both in synchronous mode (through online training with a mandatory Internet connection on the Teams and Zoom platforms), and through asynchronous network interaction via LMS Moodle, blogs, chats, forums, electronic resources hosted on internal and external educational sites (Cronje 2016). This made it possible to implement distance and online learning into the educational process and make it an integral part. As a result, the emphasis on FLT/ FLL has shifted from the individual to collective, massive, open, equitable and technology-enhanced teaching and learning, which placed a heavy burden on teachers and education systems at large (Li / Lalani 2020).

Although even before COVID-19 there was already a high increase in the interest of some Russian educators and teachers in various electronic forms of teaching and learning, we can assume that it was COVID-19 that, oddly enough, has given impetus to popularization and practical use of distance and online education in Russia. Also, despite all the efforts, it became obvious that many universities were only partially ready to switch to online broadcasting of their programs. This was due to pedagogical, psychological, communicative and purely technical problems that arose many times in the process of transforming to the new teaching format. For example, there were interruptions in the broadcast of lectures and practical classes due to the poor Internet connection; the online platforms did not meet expectations of the users (it turned out that Skype cannot serve large groups, Zoom may turn off after 40 minutes, and Microsoft Teams is excessively energy-intensive and consumes too much of the computer's internal memory); the equipment involved was also either outdated or technically not up to the required parameters of a high-quality online connection. This is just a small part of the questions that daily accompanied the educational process during that period.

At the same time, there was some panic noted among the older generation of professors, whose basic ICT-literacy skills, competencies and knowledge of the Internet or web-based applications revealed their poor readiness for full-fledged work in the new digital conditions. Due to unexpected but inevitable transition to distance and online education, some members of academic community were taken aback and worried whether such mode of learning would remain in post-pandemic conditions and how such shift could affect the education market and services, educational opportunities and general concept of knowledge acquisition.

Particular emphasis was placed on the question of how to teach in the age of Google, when search engines provide answers even before students have finished typing their question, and what, in fact, is left to be learned (Li / Lalani 2020). Various pedagogical issues related to the selection of methods, technologies and designs that could simultaneously meet the requirements of the day and serve the traditional goals and objectives of fundamental university education were also in focus. It turned out that many teachers experienced difficulties while moving from offline (face-to-face) to online work, as this forced them to radically change their approaches and attitudes to issues of knowledge transfer and its acquisition.

Many found it difficult to develop relevant and effective content that would not only encompass the curriculum, but could also engage students and motivate them to study with diligence for a multitude of axiologies (values) and ontologies (ways of being) (Affouneh et al. 2020). Ensuring that digital equity was also crucial, teachers were to modify their teaching paradigm to meet all students` needs and provide equitable digital learning opportunities by encouraging learners to create their own personal learning environments (PLE) and personal learning paths in a technology-based and information-rich context albeit without direct instruction or teacher supervision. Likewise, many disputes arose regarding psychological and communicative readiness of teachers and students for the upcoming changes, etc.

Most university educators and practitioners recognize the potential of distance and online education, especially during the COVID-19 pandemic. Distance learning helps overcome obstacles related to distance, time, human and material resources that can limit access to learning opportunities in emergencies. However, if the goal of a distance program is still learning (rather than entertainment), then that program should provide an instruction design that fosters creative interaction between students and their teachers. In short, when universities choose distance learning programs for any of many reasons, they must be very careful in selection of didactic materials, teaching aids, resources, methods and technologies designed to achieve the goals of quality university education.

Teaching aids and resources are quite important in this respect. For example, Dave Cormier (who is the author of a successful MOOC titled "#rhizo14" based on the principles of rhizomatic learning) divided them into four types, from the most stupid (anonymous sources like Wikipedia) to the most useful (the unique content created by students or teachers) (Cormier 2008). Cormier regards anonymous sources useless, since in the absence of a particular author's responsibility for the quality of the data, it is difficult to discuss the content. Most of all he praises individual research project or textbooks created by individual or collective students or teachers that allows discussion of topics of interest in a multicultural environment (Cormier 2021).

To help online teachers and instructors establish best distance practices and achieve performance expectations of Generation Z students, the core principles of effective online teaching were developed at Penn State's World Campus in 2012 and published later in the Special Report presented by Faculty Focus (Ragan

2010, p. 26) . This document was primarily focused on the overlap between concepts of "distance education" and "online education", as there are many similarities between courses that describe themselves as online learning and others that call themselves distance learning. These concepts have much in common; their meanings often interchange, although the way content is delivered is still slightly different. A distance learning course will usually have more independent study than a course describing itself as online learning. This is because online courses usually include lectures or tutorials delivered via online video conferencing with a mandatory Internet connection. For distance learning, lectures or tutorials can be pre-recorded, with reading materials provided additionally; however, distance learning courses always include an online learning component and access to online learning materials. Likewise, both modes have online forums where students discuss course-related topics and engage in interaction with lecturers for immediate feedback (Sampson 2003).

In an online classroom, the set of objectives and tasks is completely different. Failure to learn how to properly manage the online learning environment can lead to frustration and negative experience for teacher and student. According to Penn State's World Campus, effective online and distance FLT/ FLL can be realized if a few reminders are taken into account. First, teachers should not simply guide students through the course, although it may already be developed and ready for online delivery. On the contrary, they have to practice active course management strategies and always set and communicate the pace and outline of the course to students. Teachers are also expected to inform students about any accidental or unexpected changes in the course syllabus and respond to student requests (feedback) in a timely manner. Teachers need to be clear in their messages and instructions to avoid misunderstanding. Similarly, they are expected to maintain positive progress in students' studies and provide adequate quality of online learning resources, instructional design strategies, while the technological infrastructure of online classrooms shall meet the needs and expectations of Generation Z students.

The New Roles, Needs and Competencies of FLT/ FLL Teachers

This Section presents the results of an empirical study, which reveals new and updated roles, needs and competencies of teachers. This part also contains relevant data on the levels of ICT literacy and ICT competence acquired by 56 teacher-respondents and considered necessary for realization of the goals and objectives of

FLT / FLL at university. The author's system for assessing ICT-literacy and ICT-competence of teachers, sufficient for effective and expanded pedagogical practice in modern social, economic, political and cultural contexts, is provided.

Recognizing that technologies have firmly entered our lives, and the use of ICTs is an obligatory component of most educational programs in all areas of training in higher education, including foreign languages, we will hereafter consider some of the new and updated roles, needs and competencies of university teachers in the ICT-mediated educational settings in Russia. Research and analysis of thematic literature and education-related documents by UNESCO (1999 Report, ICT CFT 2011 and ICT CFT 2018) and the European Commission (2021) allowed us to assume that there are certain reasons why teachers' roles must change in the ICT-mediated classroom and beyond. First, the ongoing expansion of ICT will cause certain existing technical resources to become obsolete; overhead projectors or chalkboards, for example, may no longer be necessary if all learners have access to the same networked resources on which the teacher is presenting information, especially if students are not physically in the same location.

Second, ICT – can make some assessment methods redundant; online tests, for example, can provide the teacher with considerably more information than traditional multiple-choice tests. Third, ICT – will cause that it is no longer sufficient for teachers to impart content knowledge, since they must encourage higher levels of cognitive skills, promote information literacy, and nurture collaborative working practices. Fourth, ICT – will enable a technically competent teacher: to operate computers and use basic software for word processing, spreadsheets, email, etc.; to evaluate and use computers and related ICT tools for instruction; to create hypertext documents and multimedia content to support instruction; to apply current instructional principles, research, and appropriate assessment practices to the use of ICTs. Fifth, ICT – will enable a technically competent teacher: to evaluate educational software; to create effective computer-based presentations; to search the Internet for resources; to integrate ICT tools into student activities across the curriculum; to demonstrate knowledge of ethics and equity issues related to technology; to keep up-to-date as far as educational technology is concerned.

The media literate teacher will, then, have to acquire, develop and master a wide range of new skills and competencies in order to meet the transforming goals and objectives of education as it opens new opportunities to the stakeholders and creates a wide range of teaching and learning strategies that enable to dynamically explore contrasts, to make comparisons and to establish connections. These new perspectives are greatly facilitated by the integration of ICTs into FLT/ FLL process. Our research allowed us to identify the current roles that teachers of foreign languages already have and continue to acquire, ranging from "instructors", "facilitators", "coaches", "constructors" to "creators" of rich ICT-mediated learning environments. However, a genuine and sophisticated incorporation of new skills and roles of teachers in the wake of ICT is necessary even before teachers start their practice, so teacher training becomes crucial in this regard. Teachers are also expected to improve their knowledge and acquire new skills and competencies as they take on new roles during their professional development and growth. Teachers can look for new opportunities in the following areas of occupation: pedagogy, education and curriculum development; strategies for full ICT integration into curriculum; staff development; support systems, etc. (Rokenes / Krumsvik 2014).

Based on the empirical approach, we interviewed teachers of foreign languages working at the Russian universities, namely, Kazan (Volga region) Federal University (KFU) and Kazan National Research Technical University (KAI). We aimed to determine teachers` attitudes and needs in the changing ICT-mediated conditions. The total number of teachers surveyed was more than 50, aged from 25 to 60 years. The survey was conducted by distributing individual questionnaires issued to each participant. The event was held after the teachers` working hours, all of them having been previously instructed on the rules and goals of the survey. Participation in the study was voluntary and confidential. This survey does not pretend to show any in-deep scientific data; rather, it was an attempt to collect primary information to confirm our hypotheses about the importance of ICTs in education and about their obvious impact on the teaching profession.

The data-driven analysis of the results of the survey proved that participants (56 teachers of foreign languages from two high-ranking Russian universities) could be divided almost equally into three groups as follows: those who fully support ICT integration into educational settings and possess positive attitudes toward ICT (42 %); those who oppose ICT and show negative attitudes toward ICT (34 %); and those who generally possess positive attitudes towards ICT, but feel scared when it comes to ICT integration into educational process at university due to various reasons (24 %). The questionnaire contained 30 questions in four sections. Both open-ended and close-ended questions (as fixed alternative, multiple choice and matrix questions, the latter offering identical response options arranged one after the other, as: Strongly satisfied; Satisfied; Neutral; Unsatisfied; Strongly unsatisfied) were used during the survey (Player-Koro 2012).

The first section covered standard questions concerning age, gender, educational level and access to ICT at home and at work (university). The second
section consisted of fixed alternative questions regarding teachers' private use
of ICT outside their profession; their perceived self-efficacy in using ICT and
why and how often ICT is used for private purposes. In the third section, fixed-
alternative questions about teachers' use of ICT in classroom practice were formulated as were questions about their self-efficacy in using ICT in classroom
practice and why and how often they make use of ICT-based technologies there.
Finally, questions about teachers' attitudes to ICT use in education were asked.
These questions contained fixed queries and the respondents were asked to agree
or disagree with a series of statements. The respondents also had opportunity to
add responses in their own words in a number of open-ended questions after
each of the sequences in the questionnaire to ensure that no relevant response
was missed.

The results of our empirical research confirmed that the majority of teachers
realize the need for ICT integration into higher education as a driver for its successful reforming (82 %); admit that ICT has totally changed the way teachers
work in the classroom (77 %); agree that ICT facilitates students' learning pace
and styles (75 %); favor ICT in education since it contributes to cooperation
between colleagues (68 %). Some teachers believe that a true professionalism
of their students is only achievable in multidisciplinary settings where ICT
promotes subject integration and makes students' work in the active, experiential and problem-based formats (64 %); increases students' awareness of the
range of possibilities of ICT for their future profession (59 %), increases students'
readiness for their future career (57 %); serves as an important factor in preparing students for active social and public life (53 %). Only a small number of
the respondents do not see the need to integrate ICT into higher education (8 %),
since it takes time away from other important learning activities (10 %). At the
same time, they admit that ICTs might make teaching and learning funnier and
more attractive to their students (12 %), and, as a result, increase students' motivation and learning outcomes (15 %).

The survey also showed that at least four factors: confidence, ICT literacy,
gender and age – should be taken into account when measuring teachers' attitudes
toward digital technologies (Eickelmann / Vennemann 2017). Though age and
gender do not have direct influence on confidence, knowledge or attitudes
toward ICT, they sometimes obstruct and limit integration of technology in
academic environment of university. Our study also helped to clarify what an
competent teacher is expected to perform or demonstrate in the ICT-mediated

learning environment of an university. 67 % of the teachers' respondents agreed that ICTs do support pedagogical development and growth.

Conclusion

> *This section contains practical steps to popularize and implement the best tools, methods and technologies for effective FLT/ FLL in both European and Russian universities. Recommendations and strategies for further improvement of practices, skills and competencies of Russian teachers were presented, taking into account what has been achieved in the field of higher education in Europe. We hope, this study will be interesting and useful for both European project partners and Russian colleagues, so that they will apply our findings in their FLT / FLL practice, thereby supporting and developing international integration, collaboration and cooperation.*

Causes and effects of the new or updated roles, skills and competencies are different for an adequate functioning of foreign language teachers in the ICT-mediated learning environment of a university; this causes additional questions and debates. Each teacher goes through a range of training activities in order to reach a certain level of ICT-literacy or ICT-competency. Mastering of the skills takes time, efforts and finances. The author's scale of gradation of the levels of teachers' proficiency in ICT covers six levels of performance, presented from the lowest permissible to the highest/ mastery, namely: basic (nominal), normative (standard), instrumental, conceptual, cultural and analytical. Each level of ICT proficiency achieved in a given period of time is directly related to the new ICT-based knowledge and skills that a teacher is expected to acquire at that particular stage. The ICT skill levels normally correlate with the achievements teachers had received in the previous stages, before they attained mastery or simply began to actively use ICT in their professional practice. The mode of assessment of levels of ICT proficiency can be carried out by external experts in the process of testing teachers' skills and performance in practice, or by teachers themselves in the framework of self-reflection.

The lowest level does not inspire optimism, since it indicates that the teacher was not able to achieve even the basic or nominal level of ICT proficiency. Failure to acquire even basic ICT skills means that although the teacher tried, he/ she failed. The negative result can be caused by a variety of external and internal factors, one being the absence of any experience of earlier use of technical or digital devices or just total technical illiteracy. This, of course, is an extremely rare case for educated people. More often, the causes of failure are beyond the teacher's control and may include, for example, the overly complex design of the semantic technology, technically difficult instructions or instability of technology, as liability of the Internet. Other limitations may include incompatibility of the technology with the aims and tasks of teachers within the university curriculum. There are also cases of culturological discrepancy between the teacher and the learning environment mediated by ICT. Difficulties and limitations in this case always dominate the goals (Maloy 2016).

The next level confirms acquisition of standard or normative ICT skills needed to efficiently use the elementary functions of ICTs in order to assess and retrieve, store and produce, present or exchange information (Facer / Owen 2012, p. 6). Also, these ICT-based skills will allow communicating and participating in collaborative and social networks via the Internet. Standard skills are still insufficient to fully employ ICTs that could contribute to the best practices of FLT/ FLL. The next, third level of ICT proficiency demonstrates instrumental skills. It is assumed that the teacher will be fluent in computing devices and other digital technologies, to be able to download software, use electronic textbooks and other manuals on disks and flash memory. It is expected that teachers at this stage will also acquire elementary skills that allow them to create their own electronic didactic materials with subsequent posting on the Internet and demonstrating to the target audience, etc. The fourth level of ICT proficiency comprises conceptual skills that enable the use of ICT tools and resources innovatively and in a new Web-based context. Such skills will enable to create and develop the ICT-enriched learning scenarios, cases and projects to promote creative and collaborative learning, with technologies being integrated into disciplinary, interdisciplinary or interpersonal relationships. Thus, conceptual skills infuse instrumental skills with new creative meanings and empirical knowledge.

Attainment of the fifth level of ICT proficiency involves cultural skills, which implies synergy or interaction of instrumental and conceptual skills in conjunction with the concept of a "new culture of learning and teaching" (Warschauer / Kern 2012 p. 256). Possession of such cultural skills related to ICT allows for easy transition from the traditional modes of learning to innovative web-based FLT/ FLL formats. These skills also provide a smooth paradigm shift from teacher-centered forms to student-centered forms of FLT/ FLL that offer students more learning opportunities and autonomy in knowledge acquisition. At the apex of teachers ICT proficiency are achievements in analytical skills. This is the highest level of ICT proficiency, though some educators believe that analytical skills should be in the arsenal of every university teacher by default. Teachers with analytical skills are expected to make quick decisions about the suitability and usability of various ICT-based tools and resources in education, and even have a basic knowledge of computer programming to enable them to write simple codes or use open source code to create author's electronic programs or digital courses. They also need to be aware of cyber threats and cybersecurity issues, as well as intellectual property and copyright related to cyberspace.

The described roles of teachers, their ICT-related skills and competencies, gradation of levels of ICT proficiency should be regarded as the authors` design models. Provided that the learning environment of modern university is organized in accordance with the requests of information society based on knowledge, technology and networking, the submitted study can be useful for both teachers and administrators for better understanding their new mission and place in the educational process.

Acknowledgment

This is to thank our European ENTEP partners for collaboration and support.

Literature

Affouneh, Saida / Salha, Soheil / Khlaif, Zuheir: "Designing Quality E-Learning Environments for Emergency Remote Teaching in Coronavirus Crisis." *Interdisciplinary Journal of Virtual Learning in Medical Sciences*, 11(2), 2020, pp. 135–137.

Ainoutdinova, Irina N.: "Innovacionnye technologii v obuchenii inostrannym jazykam v vuze: integracija professional'noj i inojazychnoj podgotovki konkurentosposobnogo specia-lista: zarubezhnyj i rossijskij opyt. (= "Innovative Technologies in Teaching Foreign Languages at University: Integration of Professional and Foreign Language Training of a Competitive Specialist: Foreign and Russian Experience"). In: Ainoutdinova I. N. (ed.): *Nastol'naja kniga pedagoga-novatora (= Handbook of the Teacher-Innovator)*. Kazan University Publishing House: Kazan, 2017 (2nd Edition).

Ainoutdinova, Irina N. / Ainoutdinova, K.A.: "Web-Based Tools for Efficient Foreign Language Training at University". *Modern Journal of Language Teaching Methods*, 7(7), 2017, pp. 130–145.

Ainoutdinova, I.N., & Blagoveshchenskaya, A.A.: "The Potential of Massive Open Online Courses (MOOCs) for Revival of Distance Education in Russia". In: *ICERI2017 Proceedings: The 10th Annual International Conference of Education, Research and Innovation*. Sevilla, 2017, pp. 8335–8344.

Ainoutdinova, Irina N. et al.: "Rhizomatic Model of Online University Education in the Context of the COVID-19 Pandemic in Russia". In: *INTED2021 Proceedings: 15th Annual International Technology, Education and Development Conference.* IATED; Valencia, 2021, pp. 6962–6968.

Bancroft, W. Jane: *Suggestopedia and Language Acquisition.* Routledge: Amsterdam, 1998.

Batterink, L.J. et al.: "Sleep Facilitates Learning a New Linguistic Rule". *Neuropsychologia*, 65, 2014, pp. 169–179.

Beatty, K.: *Teaching and Researching Computer-Assisted Language Learning.* Routledge: New York, 2003 (2nd Edition).

Bell, Daniel: "The Social Framework of the Information Society". In: Dertoozos, Michael L. / Moses, Joel (eds.): *The Computer Age: A 20 Year View.*: MIT Press: Cambridge, MA, 1979, pp. 500–549.

Bronzova L.I. (2013): "Using V. Milashevich's Method in Teaching Translation from English". *Bulletin of the Tula State University. Humanities*, 2, 2013, pp. 313–320.

Canale, Merrill / Swain, Michael: "Theoretical Bases of Communicative Approaches to Second Language Teaching and Testing". *Applied Linguistics*, I, 1980, pp. 1–47.

Castells, Manuel: *The Rise of the Network Society, The Information Age: Economy, Society and Culture, Vol. I.* Blackwell: Malden (MA) / Oxford, 2009 (2nd Edition).

Chapelle, Carol A.: *Computer Applications in Second Language Acquisition (Cambridge Applied Linguistics).* Cambridge University Press: Cambridge, 2001.

Clark, Herbert H.: *Using Language.* Cambridge University Press: Cambridge, 1996.

Cormier, Dave: "Rhizomatic Education: Community as Curriculum". *Innovate – Journal of Online Education*, 4(5), 2008, pp. 1–6.

Cormier, Dave: *Making the Community the Curriculum: A Rhizomatic Learning Companion.* Pressbooks EDU: Montreal, 2021, retrieved 07.06.2021, from http://davecormier.com/edblog.

Cormier, Dave / Siemens, George: "Through the Open Door: Open Courses as Research, Learning, and Engagement". *Educause*, 45(4), 2010, pp. 30–39.

Cormier, Dave / Stewart, Bonnie: "Life in the Open: 21st Century Learning & Teaching". In: Murray Shannon (ed.): Proceedings of the Atlantic Universities' Teaching Showcase, Vol. 14, 2010, Association of Atlantic Universities: Halifax, pp. 24–31.

Cronje, Johannes C.: "Twenty-first-Century Learning, Rhizome Theory, and Integrating Opposing Paradigms in the Design of Personal Learning Systems/

Johannes C. Cronje". In: Spector, Michael J. / Lockee, Barbara B. / Childress Marcus D. (eds.): *Learning, Design, and Technology. An International Compendium of Theory, Research, Practice, and Policy.* Springer: Cham, 2016, pp. 1–22.

Dejica, D. et al.: *Language in the Digital Era. Challenges and Perspectives.* De Gruyter: Warsaw / Berlin, 2016.

Downes, Stephen: "Learning Networks and Connective Knowledge". In: Harrison Hao Yang & Steve Chi-Yin Yuen (eds.): *Collective Intelligence and E-Learning 2.0: Implications of Web-based Communities and Networking.* IGI Global: Pennsylvania, 2006, pp. 1–26.

Dzhurinskiy, A.N.: *Higher Education in the Modern World: Trends and Problems.* Prometey Publishing House: Moscow, 2017.Eickelmann, Birgit / Vennemann, Mario: "Teachers Attitudes and Beliefs Regarding ICT in Teaching and Learning in European". *European Educational Research Journal,* 16(6), 2017, pp. 733–761.

Erenchinova, E. / Proudchenko, E.: "Advantages of WEB Resources use in Learning Process. Proceedings of the 7th International Scientific and Practical Conference 'Current Issues of Linguistics and Didactics: The Interdisciplinary Approach in Humanities'" (CILDIAH 2017), retrieved 07.05.2021, from https://dx.doi.org/10.2991/cildiah-17.2017.18.

Facer, Keri / Owen, Martin: *The Potential Role of ICT in Modern Foreign Languages Learning 5-19. A Discussion Paper.* The National Foundation for Educational Research in England & Wales, 2012.

Fefilov, Aleksander I.: *Fenomen jazyka v filosofii i lingvistike: ucheb. posobie* (= The Phenomenon of Language in Philosophy and Linguistics: Tutorial). FLINT: Moscow, 2014.

Garrett N.: "Technology in the Service of Language Learning: Trends and Issues". *The Modern Language Journal,* 75, 1991, pp. 74–101.

Ghasemi, Babak / Hashemi, Masoud: "ICT: Newwave in English Language Learning/Teaching." *Procedia – Social and Behavioral Sciences,* 15, 2011, pp. 3098–3102.

Grabowski, Barbara / McCarthy, Marianne / Koszalka, Tiffany: *Web-Based Instruction and Learning: Analysis and Needs Assessment. Project: Designing Online Instruction.* NASA. Dryden Flight Research Center, National Aeronautics and Space Administration: Washington, D.C., 1998.

Hartley, J. R.: "Learning from Computer Based Learning in Science". *Studies in Science Education,* 15(1), 1988, pp. 55–76.

Hollands, Fiona M. / Tirthali, Devayani: *MOOCs: Expectations and Reality. Full Report.* Center for Benefit-Cost Studies of Education: Columbia University, 2014.

Horsthemke, Kai: "Anthropocentrism, Education and the (post-)Anthropocene. On_Education." *Journal for Research and Debate*, 2(4), 2019, pp. 1–3.

Hyslop-Margison, Emery J. / Naseem, Ayaz: *Scientism and Education: Empirical Research as Neo-Liberal Ideology.* Springer Netherlands: Dordrecht, 2007 (1st Edition).

Johnson, D. LaMont et al.: *Evaluation and Assessment in Educational Information Technology.* The Haworth Press: New York et al. 2002.

Khan, Badrul H.: "Web-Based Instruction". In: Khan, Badrul H. (ed.): *Web-based Instruction.* Educational Technology Publications: Englewood Cliffs (NJ), 1997.

Khan, Badrul H.: "Web-Based Training". In: Khan, Badrul H. (ed.): *Web-based Training.* Educational Technology Publications: Englewood Cliffs (NJ), 2001.

Kharismawati, Ragil: "Suggestopedia Method in the Teaching and Learning Process". *Research on English Language Teaching in Indonesia*, 2(1), 2014, pp. 1–11.

Kitaygorodskaya, Galina A.: *Methodical Bases of Intensive Teaching of Foreign Languages.* Moscow State University Publishing House: Moscow, 1986.

Kolisnichenko, N. N. / Yatsun, Y. M. (2018): "Four Basic Methods of Teaching English in a Chronological Order of Their Development: Application in the System of Public Administration Training." *Public Governance*, 2(12), 2018, pp. 149–166.

Kop, Rita / Hill, Adrian: "Connectivism: Learning Theory of the Future or Vestige of the Past?" *International Review of Research in Open and Distributed Learning (IRRODL)*, 9(3), 2008, pp. 1–13.

Kuzmina, O.V.: "Massive Open Online Courses (MOOCs): Problems and Prospects". *IMS-2015 Proceedings 'Internet and Contemporary Society'.* University of ITMO: St. Petersburg, 2015, pp. 88–95.

Levy, Michael: *Computer-Assisted Language Learning: Context and Conceptualization.* Oxford University Press: Oxford, 1997.

Maloy, Robert W.: "Commentary: Building Web Research Strategies for Teachers and Students". *Contemporary Issues in Technology and Teacher Education*, 16(2), 2016, pp. 172–183.

Mart, Cagri T.: "The Audio-Lingual Method: An Easy Way of Achieving Speech". *International Journal of Academic Research in Business and Social Sciences*, 3(12), 2013, pp. 63–65.

Moeller, Aaleidine J. / Catalano, Theresa (2015): "Foreign Language Teaching and Learning". In: Wright James, D. (ed.): *International Encyclopedia for Social and Behavioral Sciences*. Pergamon Press: Oxford, 2015 (2nd Edition), pp. 327–332.

Mustakim, S.S. et al.: "Teacher's Approaches in Teaching Literature: Observations of ESL Classroom." *Malaysian Online Journal of Educational Science (MOJES)*, 2(4), 2014, pp. 35–44.

Oflaz, Adnan: "The Foreign Language Anxiety in Learning German and the Effects of Total Physical Response Method on Students' Speaking Skill." *Journal of Language and Linguistic Studies*, 15(1), 2019, pp. 70–82.

Perez, Carlota: *Technological Revolutions and Financial Capital: The Dynamics of Bubbles and Golden Ages*. Edward Elgar: Cheltenham (UK) / Northampton (MA), 2003.

Phillips, June K.: "Foreign Language Education: Whose Definition?" *The Modern Language Journal*, 91(2), 2007, pp. 266–268.

Player-Koro, Catarina: "Factors Influencing Teachers' Use of ICT in Education." *Education Inquiry*, 3(1), 2012, pp. 93–108.

Ragan, Lawrence C.: "10 Principles of Effective Online Teaching: Best Practices in Distance Education". In: Hill, Christopher (ed.): *Distance Education Report*. Wsconsin: Magna Publication, 2010.

Relan, Anju / Gillani, Bijan B.: "Web-Based Instruction and the Traditional Classroom: Similarities and Differences. In: Khan, Badrul H. (ed.): *Web-based Instruction*. Educational Technology Publications: Englewood Cliffs (NJ), 1997, pp. 25–37.

Rokenes, Fredrik M. / Krumsvik, Rune: "Development of Student Teachers' Digital Competence in Teacher Education – A Literature Review". *Nordic Journal of Digital Literacy*, 9(4), 2014, pp. 250–280.

Sampson, Nicholas: "Meeting the Needs of Distance Learners". *Language Learning & Technology*, 7(3), 2003, pp. 103–118.

Savignon, Sandra: "Communicative Language Teaching". In: Byram, Michael (ed.): *Routledge Encyclopedia of Language Teaching and Learning*. Routledge: London, 2000, pp. 125–129.

Shekhter, Igor Y.: "Zhivoj jazyk" (= Living Language). In: Shekhter, Igor Y. (ed.): M.: REKTOR Kirov: Open Joint Stock Company House of the Press: Vyatka, 2005, 240 p.

Shestov, M. Yu: *Yes! You Can Learn Any Language and Teach Yourself to Learn Effectively*. Wayward Ventures Publishing: New York, 2007

Stepanenko, Ravia / Ainoutdinova, Irina N. / Krotkova, Natalya V.: "Distance and Online Learning Solutions in the Context of Modern Legal Educational Policy". *Cuestiones Políticas*, 38(2), 2020, pp. 239–250.

Stevenson, D. *Information and Communications Technology in UK Schools: An Independent Inquiry*. The Independent ICT in Schools Commission: London, 1997.

Stevick, Earl W.: "Review of Teaching Foreign Languages in the Schools: The Silent Way". *TESOL Quarterly*, 8(3), 2000, pp. 305–313.

Tabassum, Rabia / Najeeb, Ullah / Ullah, Irfan: "Effect of the Eclectic Approach of Teaching on English Communication Skills at Elementary Level." *Modern Journal of Language Teaching Methods*, 8, 2018, pp. 138–146.

Ter-Minasova, Svetlana: "Learning and Teaching Languages in Russia: Old Traditions and New Problems". *Linguistics and Intercultural Communication: Moscow University Bulletin*, 19(2), 2013, pp. 9–19.

Tregubova, Tatiana / Ainoutdinova, Irina / Khuziakhmetov, Anvar: "Advantages and Disadvantages of Distance Education for University Students in Russia". *Modern Journal of Language Teaching Methods*, 7(9/2), 2017, pp. 72–86.

Turaeva, M.A.: "Method of Teaching a Foreign Language as an Independent Theoretical and Applied Science". *Young Scientist*, 28(266), 2019, pp. 261–263.

UNESCO: ICT Competency Framework for Teachers – ICT CFT. UNESCO publishing: Paris, 2011 (2nd Edition).

UNESCO: ICT Competency Framework for Teachers – ICT CFT. UNESCO publishing: Paris, 2018 (3rd Edition).

Warschauer, Mark: "Computer Assisted Language Learning: An Introduction". In: Fotos S. (ed.): *Multimedia Language Teaching*. Logos International: Tokyo, 1996, pp. 3–20.

Warschauer, Mark / Kern, Richard: "Introduction: Theory and Practice of Network-Based Language Teaching". In: Mark Warschauer / Richard Kern (eds.): *Network-based Language Teaching: Concepts and Practices*. Cambridge Applied Linguistics Series. Cambridge University Press: Cambridge, 2012.

Wilkinson, Sharon: "On the Nature of Immersion During Study Abroad: Some Participant Perspectives". *Frontiers: The Interdisciplinary Journal of Study Abroad*, 4(1), 1998, pp. 121–138.

Zelenin, G. / Kovalyova, Y.: "A Survey of Innovative Foreign Language Teaching Methods in the XX-XXIth Century". *Problems of Engineering and Pedagogical Education*, 32/33, 2011, pp. 172–177.

Further Reading

European Union – European Commission: Education and Training: Digital Education Action Plan (2021–2027), retrieved 07.05.2021, from https://ec.eur opa.eu/education/education-in-the-eu/digital-education-action-plan_en

Hawkins, Melissa: "Self-Directed Learning as Related to Learning Strategies, Self-Regulation, and Autonomy in an English Language Program: A Local Application with Global Implications". *Studies in Second Language Learning and Teaching*, 8, 2018, 452–456.

Li, Cathy / Lalani, Farah: "The COVID-19 Pandemic Has Changed Education Forever. This Is How", retrieved 01.05.2021, from https://www.weforum. org/agenda/2020/04/coronavirus-education-global-covid19-online-digital-learning/.

Osborne, Mark: "Innovative Learning Environments. CORE Education's White Papers", retrieved 30.09.2021, from https://core-ed.org/assets/PDFs/Innovat ive-Learning-Environments.pdf.

UNESCO: World Communication and Information Report 1999. UNESCO publishing: Paris, 2000.

Sergei Vasin, Konstantin Korolev, Tatiana Razuvaeva

Enhancing Teaching Practice in HEIs through the Development of University Learning and Teaching Strategy

Abstract: The article describes PSU practices in the context of enhancing learning and teaching. PSU experience shows that one-off events and partial involvement of university units cannot catalyze redesigning of higher education. The proposed Learning and Teaching strategy is a ground for systemic transformations, as it embraces various levels (designing curricula, improving digital learning environment, providing quality assurance, etc.) and aims at increasing relevance and visibility of HE at PSU.

Keywords: Teaching and learning policy, curriculum design, digital learning, learning and teaching strategy

Currently, the higher education system faces the task of proactively respond to any changes occurring in the world in order to ensure sustainable development. The competitive features of higher education in general and of its institutions in particular are the quality, speed and flexibility in adapting to global trends and challenges. The great political and social expectations regarding the role and contribution of higher education to solving modern problems in society are triggered by profound transformations taking place in the modern world:

- growing population in the developing countries and aging population in the developed countries,
- globalization,
- digital revolution,
- fast-paced development, transfer and application of new knowledge and information.

Today, the activity of higher education institutions should be built with the view to the radical changes in the external environment, which determine the new realities for the functioning of higher education:

- steady growth of student numbers and increased diversification of student population (gender, age, social origin and status, type and level of qualifications before admission, disabilities, migrant / refugee status, religion, multicultural diversity),

- considerable difference of learning styles among students (combined with motivational problems and insufficient sensitivity to traditional teacher-centered learning and teaching),
- rising demand for civic education and active citizenship, as well as for building 21st-century skills, including the ability to learn from field-specific skills and knowledge.

The global challenges require students to fulfill the following tasks, which are adequate to the changing conditions:

- advancing the ability to learn and continue learning and to adapt to trans-formations throughout their career,
- developing critical thinking and capacity to effectively process huge amounts of digital information,
- acquiring concept-based skills in their professional career,
- enhancing international experience and constantly adjusting to the global environment around them.

In turn, higher education institutions should in these conditions:

- build the effective learning and teaching system,
- create innovative ecosystems to train students for their future professional career, broaden 21st-century skills and promote active citizenship,
- tailor and customize the academic process, ensure the curricula flexibility and develop the potential to interpret knowledge in new and creative ways, including a wide range of educational tools and learning styles,
- provide assistance and career guidance to students from admission to graduation,
- encourage, stimulate and recognize professional development and growth of staff in the field of learning and teaching, support staff in improving their ped-agogical skills.

These trends are of the global nature. They shape the evolution of the educational systems around the world. The European Higher Education Area is no excep-tion. Despite the differences among the national educational systems, methods of their regulation, requirements for higher education institutions in different countries, as well as variability within the systems and educational institutions, it is currently obvious that the reforms at the national, regional and institutional levels mainly focus on learning and teaching enhancement.

Meanwhile, within the general trend in the development of higher education, it is necessary to take into account the country-specific features in the functioning of the educational systems, varying progress in their reformation, and introduction of specific tools of the Bologna Process. For example, the analysis of the Russian higher education system may illustrate a number of challenges that it is currently facing.

There is a gap between the legal frameworks and existing practices of learning and teaching. Regular updating of the educational standards designed to ensure a favorable environment for the academic process in higher education institutions actually turns into paper work overload for teaching staff and an increased amount of documents for administrative staff. The accreditation of degree programs, which should guarantee their quality at the external level, does not include assessing the implementation procedures, but checking the regulation and availability of documents of a certain form and content.

In the context of the increased workload of the teaching staff (the annual teaching load is at the level of 850–900 academic hours), the internal procedures for ensuring the quality of education are more declarative and not able to maintain the quality of learning and teaching in higher education institutions.

In addition, there is a mismatch between degree programs and / or their graduates and needs of the labor market. The higher education system disregards industry and business – 91 % of employers note a lack of practical knowledge among graduates (Boutenko et al. 2017, p. 40).

The absence of units in the higher education institutions, which provide organizational and methodological support for the teaching staff, including young teachers, and lack of professional development programs for the teaching staff to improve their pedagogical skills indicate the need for staffing the learning and teaching process at a brand new level.

Another problem was the transition to distance learning in the context of the COVID-19 pandemic. The transformation of higher education was unprecedented. For example, it affected over 4 million students and 235 thousand teachers in Russia in the 2019–2020 academic year. The transition of higher education institutions to distance learning during the pandemic has become the most discussed topic, especially given the difficult epidemiological situation in the country and in the world in late 2020.

CourseBurg conducted a study "Online Education 2020: Which Russian HEIs are Ready for Distance Learning" and analyzed 710 online courses published by 19 Russian higher education institutions. The data were taken at the time of the study from the official report of the Ministry of Science and Higher Education of the Russian Federation, based on the courses available at the Modern Digital

Educational Environment website[4]. The results showed that only 19 HEIs across the country took an active part in the transition to distance learning, and the majority of them are located in Moscow and St. Petersburg. Many higher education institutions were not ready for a large-scale transition to the distance education mode, since they delivered online lectures for students just on their closed platforms.

The intensified work of the teaching staff and lack of time for the remaining workload standards led to their discontent and low satisfaction with their work. According to the NAFI Analytical Center, more than 70 % of school and university teachers reported an increased workload, 26 % of them informed on poorly organized transition to distance learning and reduced quality of the academic process[5]. Due to the shift to distance learning, the majority (85.7 %) of teachers had less free time, and the idea of increased workload arose. As a result, 67.2 % of teachers do not consider the distance education mode to be convenient and comfortable for them, 59.9 % of the teachers do not see the distance education mode to be convenient and comfortable for students. In general, the overwhelming majority of teachers (87.8 %) believe that it is better to conduct their classes in the face-to-face mode.

According to the results of conducted studies, there are three types of major problems faced by the teachers:

- practical (need for computers and other equipment, stable Internet connection),
- methodological (need to redesign and upload training materials for distance learning),
- psychological (lack of live communication with students and colleagues) (Shtykhno et al. 2020, p. 77).

These facts allow concluding that the transition to distance learning also requires a new reality and modality of the educational systems and their institutions, which should be taken into account when reassessing the mission of higher education institutions and carrying out long-term transformations in learning and teaching.

Obviously, higher education institutions need comprehensive strategies, mechanisms and tools to introduce initiatives contributing to the academic and

---

4   https://online.edu.ru/public/promo.
5   https://nafi.ru/analytics/sistema-obrazovaniya-okazalas-ne-gotova-k-perekhodu-na-distantsionnoe-obuchenie-v-usloviyakh-pandemi/.

scientific excellence, continuous innovation, transformed governance and sustainable development. They should focus more on learning and teaching both within the strategic plans and through the new learning and teaching strategies. The adaptation to global changes should be interpreted in terms of the areas of strength and areas for improvement with great emphasis on digitizing, linking higher education to the labor market, promoting professional development of staff, aligning learning and teaching styles, improving assessment and feedback. The strategy is aimed to assist the administration of higher education institutions, heads of student affairs departments and staff of professional development departments in enhancing the quality, relevance and visibility of higher education.

An overview of learning and teaching in the European Higher Education Area shows that at present more than 90 % of European higher education institutions agree that they "now pay more attention to learning and teaching than in the past". All educational institutions in Austria, Greece, Spain, Italy, Switzerland, and the UK define learning and teaching as their top priority. In some countries, learning and teaching have been improved for a long time, which confirms the relevance of this focus. 86 % of educational institutions have a learning and teaching strategy or policy, mainly at the level of HEIs (46 %) or at the level of HEI and its faculty level (38 %). In general, only 3 % of higher education institutions do not have a learning and teaching strategy, and they do not plan to develop one (EACEA 2018, p. 48).

The size of education institutions matters, since 95 % of medium-size educational institutions have a learning and teaching strategy (at the institution or faculty level, or both). This is 10 % higher than in large or small institutions.

There are also differences between countries: in France, Greece, Ireland, Portugal, Romania, Turkey and Switzerland all institutions (100 %) have a strategy at the institutional or faculty level, or both.

The most frequently used concepts in describing the learning and teaching strategies of European higher education institutions are "teaching excellence", "excellent education", "top level", "outstanding", "world class", "first class" or "high quality teaching", which characterize the ambition and position of the institutions in a competitive environment. Most higher education institutions focus on such aspects as:

- introducing research-based approaches to teaching and learning, emphasizing the importance of strengthening the links between research and teaching,
- managing quality and developing an internal quality assurance system as a strategic goal of learning and teaching,

- offering career prospects for graduates, enhancing opportunities for their civic and professional development in terms of values, skills and competencies arising from learning (about half of HEIs highlight the employment opportunities for graduates, careers or relationships with future employers are part of their strategies).

The most frequently cited areas in their strategies are:

- pedagogical innovation, academic process improvement, pedagogical development, recognition and support of teaching,
- use of international practices in the development and enhancement of learning and teaching through the international cooperation programs, academic mobility, internationalization at home, including the engagement of foreign staff and students, expansion of degree programs implemented in the English language,
- consideration of international trends in learning and teaching such as active learning and student-centered learning, as well as full implementation of the Bologna Process reforms within the European Higher Education Area.

In general, this confirms the importance of cooperation in learning and teaching, as well as added value, which European and international partners can bring to institutional and national learning and teaching strategies.

In terms of management, learning and teaching enhancement is a collaborative and collegial process involving cooperation within and across the higher education institution, when its administration plays an important role by actively promoting higher education and contributing to its development. The vice-rectors for academic affairs should focus on the strategic function of guiding and coordinating the learning and teaching policies within the institution.

Thus, the institutional learning and teaching strategies are an effective tool for managing and innovating the academic process through the continuous professional development of teaching staff, enhancement of pedagogical competencies and support for teaching.

The review of the learning and teaching strategies in European higher education institutions enables identifying the key elements that should form the basis for the design of this strategy at an institution where it is absent or represented by limited components (Vasin et al. 2021):

- policy on teaching staff development,
- opportunities for international cooperation,
- measures to enhance learning and teaching,

- procedures for developing, approving and evaluating degree programs and their components,
- student support services,
- formation of the learning environment,
- modern educational technologies,
- opportunities for lifelong learning,
- quantitative indicators for measuring strategy goals,
- operational plans for implementing strategy.

Further, each component of the strategy is examined in detail.

The policy on teaching staff development includes a description of key goals, forms and mechanisms of enhancing capabilities of the teaching staff. The policy aims at stimulating staff development, including professional growth within the higher education institution and beyond it, providing support for regular professional development courses and internships not only in the field of teaching, but also in the field of research. The policy shapes the specific tools and mechanisms to foster and reinforce the advancement of teaching and researching skills of staff:

- designing and operating the system of continuous professional development and growth of teaching staff in the higher education institution, including mechanisms of internal and external motivation,
- building the system for mentoring young teachers in order to provide methodological and psychological support to them,
- recognizing the completion of professional development courses as a part of the regular workload of teaching staff, acknowledged during the re-election of teaching staff (every 5 years),
- organizing and conducting professional development courses for teaching staff on the basis of the higher education institution at the expense of its budget,
- supporting teaching staff engaged in research on learning and teaching and in implementation of educational projects in order to improve the quality of the academic process.

The creation of opportunities for international cooperation presupposes listing the specific mechanisms and measures to encourage and promote the international collaboration and to enhance the involvement of teaching staff and students in academic mobility programs, educational and research projects with foreign partners, namely:

- including indicators of international activity in the annual evaluation of teaching staff that result in bonus payments (publications in foreign indexed journals, participation in international conferences and other international events, completion of internships in foreign higher education institutions, submission of applications to international grant funds, implementation of educational and research projects together with foreign partners),

- adding the section on international activity in the performance reports of teaching staff, as well as performance reports and work plans of the heads of departments during election or re-election,
- providing service of language training for students, teaching and administrative staff of the higher education institution (both from the HEI budget and at the expense of trainees),
- setting up the integrated system to support academic mobility programs for students and teaching staff, to maintain the implementation of international projects, to submit applications for international funding,
- designing the internal opportunities to support academic mobility of students and teaching staff,
- creating conditions for cooperation with foreign higher education institutions and exchange of the best teaching practices in order to improve the academic process in the global education area,
- developing, launching and running double degree programs with foreign partners.

Measures to enhance learning and teaching involve the specific mechanisms and actions aimed at improving teaching and upgrading degree programs:

- actively promoting individual and flexible learning by activating and supporting the participation of students in academic mobility programs with Russian and foreign higher education institutions, as well as by designing variable modules within the degree programs,
- encouraging research-based learning in order to actively integrate modern scientific developments and achievements into the curricula,
- adding practice-oriented modules to the degree programs,
- internationalizing the curricula through increasing the number of modules delivered in the English language,
- introducing students questionnaires to assess the quality of learning and teaching,
- stimulating innovation by providing support and training in pedagogy, holding competitions for the best research on learning and teaching in order to integrate its results into the academic process,
- increasing the number of joint degree programs implemented with other higher education institutions / enterprises / research institutions, etc.,

- arranging teaching skills contests among teaching staff of higher education institutions,
- providing organizational and methodological support to the coordinators of degree programs, heads of departments and teaching staff in planning, developing and implementing modern degree programs,
- recognizing teaching by means of modern methods and best practices (rating assessment, awarding bonus payments, placing on the honor board, etc.).

The procedures for developing, approving and evaluating degree programs and their components are designed to improve the quality of the academic process in the higher education institutions through the following mechanisms:

- formulating the algorithms to update the degree programs and their components based on the needs of students and demands of employers,
- establishing the advisory council in order to involve students, employers, general public and other education institutions in developing the degree programs (as provided for by the Federal State Educational Standards of the new generation),
- preparing degree programs for the international accreditation,
- introducing up-to-date assessment and feedback tools aimed at learning and teaching enhancement in order to ensure attainability of learning outcomes within the degree programs and to contribute to a better understanding of learning pathways among students.

The student support services provide for the development of mechanisms and measures to assist students both in studies and employment:

- improving the system of tutoring and mentoring (formulating the tutor policy, providing support services to tutors and mentors, training academic personal tutors),
- developing assessment and feedback tools to monitor the system of tutoring and mentoring in order to establish constructive dialogue between students and teaching staff, including providing better academic support services for students,
- advancing and operating the system of tutoring for junior students by senior students (tutor school),
- designing and introducing distance technologies to track learning pathways of students,
- developing and implementing a set of career development courses for students to acquire necessary skills in assessing, planning, building and boosting their careers,

- setting up the system for supporting students' employment (creating carrier development units in the higher education institution, interacting with employers, e. g. by holding job fairs, accompanying graduates for 3 years after completing their studies),
- expanding the functions of the psychological service, which provides support to students on various issues and problems,
- creating the conflict commission designed to handle and resolve possible conflicts,
- taking actions to support volunteering among teaching staff and students,
- enlarging areas of extracurricular activities for students with the view to their individual interests and needs, improving the infrastructure for extracurricular activities.

The formation of the learning environment envisages measures to improve the academic infrastructure in the higher education institution, namely:

- developing mechanisms to ensure the availability of education for students with different abilities, health status, social background and welfare,
- designing the digital learning environment in order to open individual learning pathways for students, taking into account their needs, interests, characteristics, as well as to provide them with necessary infrastructure for following these pathways,
- providing opportunities for experiential learning on campus, in enterprises and businesses, in national and international organizations,
- giving access to national and international digital libraries, expanding library stocks in the higher education institution,
- advancing material, technical and virtual infrastructure of the higher education institution.

The quantitative indicators for measuring the strategy goals are the key markers of changes in the goals of the strategy, which depend on the objectives in each section of the institutional strategy for learning and teaching. The operational plan for implementing the strategy contains the lay-out for the use of the strategy. Most often these documents are made for 5 years and for 1 year, with an indication of specific activities, responsible persons, sources of funding, outputs and outcomes following the implementation of each activity.

It is obvious that the success of developing and adopting an institutional learning and teaching strategy depends on many internal factors, specific conditions and relationships within the higher education institution. To implement the strategy, it is necessary to make management decisions, restructure many existing processes in the higher education institution, initiate new processes, establish new links between structural units, since the achievement of a particular objective requires involving several structural units at once.

According to modern managers in the field of education, a very effective practice is project management, which implies creating project teams with the representatives of several structural units, whose joint work is necessary to meet the set objectives (Ginevri / Trilling 2017). In many Russian higher education institutions, a centralized management system prevails, when certain functions are assigned to different departments and services, which creates communication barriers and causes problems in allocating responsibilities in order to fulfill the objectives that require the engagement of several structural units at once. For this reason, effective management decisions of the higher education institution administration, formed project teams and increased transparency of communication between different management levels are needed. In addition, it is crucial to take into account the accumulated experience of a particular higher education institution in developing and implementing an institutional learning and teaching strategy.

At Penza State University, an understanding of the need to formulate and integrate an institutional learning and teaching strategy was formed thanks to the participation in the international projects within the Erasmus+ Program under Capacity Building and Strategic Partnerships (HARMONY, ENTEP). This indicates the importance of cooperation between Russian and leading European higher education institutions. The learning and teaching strategy is seen at PSU as a starting point for initiating the systemic transformations, as it embraces various levels (designing, implementing and evaluating curricula, introducing educational technologies, creating and improving digital learning environment, providing quality assurance, etc.).

The strategy should be built on the background that allows implementing innovative solutions in the field of management, reforming the system for quality assessment of the academic process and integrating the best learning, teaching and management practices. With regard to Penza State University, it is necessary to highlight the following features:

- wide range of degree programs within the 3-cycle system of higher education, as well as vocational secondary education programs, advanced training and retraining courses in the areas of engineering, humanities, pedagogy, medicine, natural science and others,
- several degree programs implemented in the English language,
- 2 double degree programs run together with foreign partners,

- stable partnerships with foreign higher education institutions, experience in carrying out academic mobility programs and implementing international grant projects,
- functioning of 4 international foreign language test centers (English – Pearson; German – Goethe-Zertifikat, TestDaf; French – DELF / DALF),
- operation of the Center for Teaching and Learning Erasmus+ established within the ENTEP project, which provides courses for enhancing learning and teaching among students, teaching and administrative staff with the view to the best European practices,
- experience in adopting and running the teaching recognition system using modern methods and best practices (rating assessment, awarding bonus payments, placing on the honor board, etc.),
- modernized system for supporting students employment,
- introduced system of tutoring and mentoring,
- adopted system for students to assess the quality of learning and teaching (questionnaires),
- provided service of language training for teaching staff (from the HEI budget),
- good practice of project management, particularly to improve the administration system, enhance the quality of the academic process.

Based on this experience and expertise, the learning and teaching strategy of Penza State University should ensure the achievement of the following objectives:

- enhancing image and gaining recognition in the Russian and international market of educational and scientific services as a quality provider,
- providing high quality learning and teaching,
- creating opportunities for students with different backgrounds and learning styles to receive quality education,
- equipping students with knowledge, skills and experiences, which will allow them to successfully study throughout their lives and to be competitive specialists in the global labor market.

Thus, in the context of modern society development, the higher education institutions face various challenges. Designing innovative ecosystems to support students in career development, enhancing their 21st-century skills, teaching citizenship and its value, tailoring and customizing academic process, maintaining flexibility of curricula, providing opportunities for interpreting knowledge in new and creative ways (through a wide range of educational tools and learning styles) require HEIs to develop brand new approaches to planning, managing, implementing and evaluating educational activities and to creating effective learning and teaching environments. The analysis of the best international educational practices shows that institutional learning and teaching strategies are an effective tool for managing and introducing innovations into the academic process. The design of such strategy in the HEI should be based on the specific elements, namely policy on teaching staff development, opportunities for international cooperation, measures to enhance learning and teaching, procedures for developing, approving and evaluating degree programs and their components, student support services, formation of the learning environment, quantitative indicators for measuring strategy goals, operational plans for implementing strategy, which were considered in this article. In addition, the development of the strategy requires taking into account the specific features, internal factors, conditions and relationships, as well as background of a particular higher education institution.

Literature

Boutenko, Vladislav et al.: *Russia 2025: Resetting the Talent Balance*. The Boston Consulting Group: 2017. https://web-assets.bcg.com/img-src/Skills_Outline_v1.8_preview_tcm9-175469.pdf (Last Access: 26.09.2022)

European Commission/EACEA/Eurydice: The European Higher Education Area in 2018: *Bologna Process Implementation Report*. Publications Office of the European Union: Luxemburg, 2018.

Ginevri, Walter / Trilling, Bernie: *Project Management for Education: The Bridge to 21st Century Learning*. Project Management Institute: Newton Square, Pensylvania, 2017.

Shtykhno, Dmitry / Konstantinova, Larisa / Gagiev, Nikolay: "Transition of Universities to Distance Mode. During the Pandemic: Problems and Possible Risks". *Open Education*, 24(5), 2020, pp. 72–81.

Vasin, Sergey / Razuvaeva, Tatiana / Korolev, Konstantin: "Enhancing teaching practices at Penza State University". International Scientific Conference "Delivering Impact in Higher Education Learning and Teaching: Enhancing Cross-Boarder Collaborations" (DIHELT 2021). SHS Web Conference, Vol. 99, 2021, retrieved from https://doi.org/10.1051/shsconf/20219901020.

Juan Fu

Improving Teaching Practice in Higher Education from the Perspective of Learning Science

Abstract: In the context of globalization, there has been a surge in interest in teaching excellence of higher education. The practice of teaching in higher education is the main way to develop the professional ability of university students. In addition, it is the mission of colleges and universities to strengthen the theoretical research and exploration of practical teaching. In order to optimize the whole process of talent training, this paper will establish a practical teaching system with complete content and reasonable structure in terms of teaching methods and tools.

Keywords: teaching practice, learning science, learning process, learning analysis, higher education, MOOCs, online class

Cultivating Applied Undergraduate Talents with International Perspective

In view of the current international situation, Chinese colleges and universities are actively exploring ways of teaching reform to adapt to the educational development of Chinese students by cultivating applied undergraduate talents with an international perspective. The characteristics of the current international education development include the following aspects: 1. Implement the priority development strategy of education and strive to build a country of talents; 2. Build and improve the lifelong education system, create a learning society and promote and implement lifelong education; 3. Promote the rapid development of education of the universal education and popularization of higher education; 4. Pursue educational equity and promote educational equity; 5. Enhance international competitiveness and promote the internationalization of education (Xiaoyan Cao 2015).

By creating a lifelong learning system based on modern international forms of education, Chinese education research brings together advanced education concepts both domestic and foreign to be explored and applied in teaching practice. This paper research and formulate an education system suitable for Chinese education. In order to adapt to the development of students and teachers in the context of China's economic development, especially in the international

Fig. 1: The Present situation and development trend of Chinese colleges and universities

Note: The number of graduate training institutions has not been announced yet

community, it impacts the employment situation and career development direction of students. The question, is whether students studying in Chinese colleges and universities can really adapt to contemporary society and bring their own value. Therefore, based on the current development of Chinese colleges and universities and the national development strategy of cultivating application-oriented undergraduate talents, this paper conducts research on how to improve teaching practice from the perspective of learning science.

Analysis of the Present Situation and Development Trend of Chinese Colleges and Universities

According to the news of the present situation and development trend of Chinese colleges and universities in 2021, since 2004, the number of colleges and universities and graduate training institutions in China has increased steadily year by year. In 2019, there were 828 graduate training units and 3,784 institutions of higher education of various forms nationwide. In 2020, there were 537,100 schools of various types, which at various levels and 1,270 regular undergraduate schools (including 21 vocational schools at the undergraduate level).

Among 1000 universities in the academic ranking of world universities in 2020, there were 168 from Chinese mainland. There was an increase of 14 over the previous year, accounting for 14.68 % of the world. There were 140 in first-class disciplines. There were four universities in the top 100, namely Tsinghua University, Peking University, Zhejiang University and Shanghai Jiao Tong University.

According to these data, the development of higher education in China has provided abundant human resources for Chinese economic and social development. However, compared with the developed countries and compared with the requirements of building a modern economic system and building an educational power, there are still a series of problems in Chinese higher education. For example, the standard of education system is not complete; the employ ability of students needs to be improved; the construction of colleges and universities needs more investment; the supporting policies conducive to technical talents need to be improved; the remuneration system for teachers need to be improved; the quality of running schools and the level of talent training are uneven. (Ministry of Education of the People's Republic of China 2014 / China State Council 2019)

The emergence of these problems directly affects the development of colleges and universities and the challenges they face. Based on the premise of the rapid development of economy, science and technology, it adapts to the current international situation in the field of education and deepens the strategic goal of revitalizing the country with the help of science and technology. In addition, teaching practice also needs to be more related to science and technology in order to cope with the coming changes of the new era. In the future, educational science will also become an important link in the development of science and technology. Further, the study of educational science is carried out with the aim of connecting international level of education to adapt to the development of education at the present time. In the recent years, the development of information technology has had a profound impact on education and various technology-supported education modes have started playing an increasingly important role in primary school, middle school, high school, university and colleges. People hope to realize educational reform and modernization with the help of new technology and accelerate the process of informational education. In order to promote China's education reform and development including higher education, promoting education modernization through informational education has become an important strategic choice.

As a result, the education information age has come. Especially in higher education, the development of MOOCs and the emergence of cloudy live teaching and online education have provided more opportunities for the reform and development of education in contemporary China. Research in the field of educational science plays a very important role in teaching practice and facilitates the improvement of Chinese educational system.

The Purpose of Learning Science in Higher Education

This paper presents a frontier learning process and learning analysis from the perspective of learning science. Combined with constructivism learning theory, it is a way to explore the teaching strategies and paths of modern higher education. In order to adapt to the new industrial structure and the vigorous development of China's emerging technology, it is necessary not only to improve the teaching level and quality of teachers, but also to improve the learning ability and enthusiasm of students. In addition, their understanding and operation of subject knowledge and analysis of learning ability need to be strengthened. Specifically, this study will integrate methods, based on the higher education teaching study analysis in the learning process. It integrated various analysis methods of the study of the theory in the actual teaching situation of the learning process. Moreover, teachers and students must provide supportive evidence and individualized feedback, to advance students towards knowledge related to understanding, analysis, feedback, research and practice. Through these methods, they cannot only improve students' ability for self-control, self-regulation, self-practice and self-reflection, but they can also improve the impact of teaching. The Study of Learning Science in Teaching Practice

Learning science originates from cognitive science, which was born in the 1970s, matured in the 1990s and prospered in the 21st century (Junjie Shang et al. 2015). Learning science is a science that studies how people learn scientifically and effectively. According to research, the background and problems of learning science and the development of learning science encompasses a variety of learning techniques and learning theory after more than 30 years (Khousa et al. 2015).

Through the definition, learning science is an emerging discipline that intersects education, computer science, psychology, anthropology, and other disciplines. Collaboration among different disciplines breeds new ideas, new methods and new ways (Nianjing Ding 2013). It integrates different fields of science to study and innovate new theoretical systems that adapt to the current situation. It is more convenient and timely to solve the problems facing the development of education in the context of the development of a modern economy, science and technology. The characteristics of learning science are ecological, situational and increasingly cultural, which not only help us to understand the physiological characteristics and internal mechanisms of adaptation through learning and development, but also help teachers and students to be effective in teaching and learning. Moreover, parents can deeply understand the university and principals can help the school develop effectively. At present, learning science has been used and achieved certain results in higher education teaching. However, there is still lack of experimentation and exploration, which is necessary to research and practice for the following period. Therefore, this research focuses on the teaching practice of higher education from two aspects of learning process and learning analysis, and makes a research and discussion on the enlightenment and role of higher education learning science.

The Role of the Learning Process of Learning Science in Teaching Practice

In order to efficiently improve teaching practice of higher education, the learning process plays a significant role in learning science. The learning process generally includes two aspects: cognitive process and intentional process. The cognitive process refers to the cyclic process of cognitive activity from "not knowing to knowing – knowing to doing – doing to knowing". The process of intention is the progress of human emotion, motive, will, and personality (Yongfeng Wang 2007).

In higher education, the study and exploration of knowledge, and then to the later practice of innovation and creation, the learning process is an indispensable and necessary section. Throughout the entire learning process, the section of the cognitive process, as well as the following elements directly or indirectly affect the cognitive level of students' knowledge. These are the teacher's teaching and curriculum development, classroom teaching skills, educational methods and so on. However, in terms of the process of intention, teachers only indirectly carry out guiding intervention. Based on the assimilation of a certain amount of basic knowledge by students, students are required to spontaneously contribute to the development of their emotions, motivation, will and personality with increasing learning time and learning ability. American psychologist Lindgren (1971) believes that the learning process consists of the things that students should do in the learning process, which includes not only visible behaviors, such as listening to lectures, reading, calculation and conversation, but also invisible behaviors such as thinking, understanding and recognition. Each process must be performed in teaching and learning and the educator must study and improve these methods. Therefore, the learning process is a crucial process in the field of learning science. At present, traditional classroom teaching has been unable to meet the needs of students in the learning process. With the development of MOOCs and the formation of live classes, a new learning method has been opened up. Combined with various activities, the learning process of students has been greatly enriched. Finally, the purpose of improving students' learning effect and academic performance has been achieved.

Especially during the epidemic situation, all kinds of online courses have become an essential teaching method and learning process. This raises many questions about the impact and function of online courses. Compared with the traditional offline teaching mode, whether the effect of online courses is effective and feasible and whether students can well acquire knowledge through the online course mode. In view of all kinds of problems, more and more people are studying the teaching mode of online courses. At the same time, the state has also formulated a series of policies to develop and improve the educational system of online classes.

This makes the development of MOOCs to have a qualitative leap. In addition, the combination of online and offline teaching mode is also a lead to the future direction of higher education development. Therefore, the development of learning process also directly affects the practical direction of teaching.

Robert Mills Gagné (Linglun 1983), an American psychologist, believes that the learning process is an information processing process, which is divided into eight stages: motivation, understanding, acquisition, retention, recall, generalization, homework and feedback. As a result, it requires more and more information technological including hardware and software skills to support these processes. At the same time, these processes need an educator to spend a certain amount of time to master.

Lyon Jieff (Shusheng Shen 2016), a psychologist from the former Soviet Union, believed that the learning process is a circular structure composed of three links: orientation, behavior and feedback. It also needs a closed loop operation to complete. For example, the principals provide all kinds of materials and resources for teachers and administrators. They can open the online and offline platform to carry out the whole learning system. Everyone's orientation, behavior and feedback are open and transparent and can be controlled within higher educational policy.

As we can see, the development of the learning process concerns the entire learning science and affects the result of the quality of higher education. Shen Shusheng (2016) believes that the learning process pursues the development of students and is a collection of many related learning behaviors of students over a certain period of time. Guoan Zhao (2015) believes that the learning process is a process in which students acquire knowledge, skills and attitudes.

Therefore, the author believes that the learning process is the core link for the teaching activities, which is the process and source of learning results and which is the basis and guarantee for the effective implementation of teaching practice and quality.

The Use of Learning Science in Learning Process

Mao Zedong is the main founder and leader of the Communist Party of China, his words are often widely circulated among scholars. One of his very popular phrases: "it is never too late to learn", which emphasizes that the learning process is a lifelong process both during learning and during work. It has become an integral part of the application and practice of learning science, but is also inseparable from the educational process of research and practice.

Keith Sawyer (Qingyou Hu 2008) believes that it is possible to improve the effectiveness of the learning process only through the use of learning science and effective design of learning environment and a deep understanding of the learning process can contribute to the effective promotion of student understanding. John D. Cloth (ibid.) has briefly pointed out to Ford in the course teaching, assessment and designing learning environment. The following focus on three aspects has become the basic principle of student classroom learning, curriculum, teaching plan and assessment. First, this is the understanding of the original knowledge. Second, the importance of self-monitoring and influencing factual knowledge. Third, it is the conceptual framework for understanding. (Qingyou Hu 2008) More and more emphasis is placed on the important position of understanding in the learning process. Understanding is the premise for students to acquire knowledge. At the same time, the transition from memorizing facts to understanding processes has become the focus of learning (ibid.).

Compared with cognitive science, learning science pays more attention to the learning process in real-life situations; it pays more attention to how students learn rather than how teachers teach; it pays more attention to the deep understanding of concepts, which includes the construction of knowledge combining with the original understanding and the creation of learning environment. Understanding learning is the most prominent manifestation of the learning process of learning science research. On the one hand, the essence of the learning process is not just memorization and accumulation of factual content (Zongkui Zhou 2007), but it emphasizes research and development of understanding. On the other hand, it is only when the focus is on the learning process, a deep understanding of students can be fully developed. To see the essence through the phenomenon and understand the process is the core ability of students in the learning process. This also reflects different audience groups, students' perception and understanding are also different in the same teaching environment. In particular, the effect of online classroom has undergone a major test in the process of understanding. It takes time to study and experiment whether the teaching and interaction mode through the screen can convey knowledge well and whether it can improve students' understanding and their learning level. In recent years, many colleges and universities began to actively explore the way of teaching reform. A large national investment in education hardware provides an effective guarantee for teaching reform. For example, the popular flipped classroom in recent years breaks the traditional teaching method and reconstructs the links between knowledge teaching and knowledge internalization. Related studies have proved that it can improve students' course participation and knowledge internalization. Another example is the combination of advantages of traditional classroom teaching and online learning through online and offline blended learning, which is the mainstream of information-based teaching at present.

Take MOOCs (Massive Open Online Courses), for example: the emergence of MOOCs has opened up new opportunities for the development of innovative teaching models. In addition, to foster the deep integration of MOOCs and traditional classroom teaching, SPOCs (Small Restricted Online Courses) are emerging at the historic moment. New teaching modes such as SPOC-based blended learning and SPOC-based flipped classroom have also been widely used in teaching practice in colleges and universities.

In addition, some researchers have also confirmed that innovative teaching based on Web platform and mobile teaching platform is an effective way to improve the quality of teaching. Through the new teaching model of flipped classroom, students' comprehension and knowledge application can be improved, to better solve various problems encountered in the learning process. Finally, the improvement of learning process based on the premise of learning science is achieved.

Furthermore, many factors have also become the focus of learning science research in the learning process, such as knowledge structure, autonomous learning, learning motivation and learning community, etc. (Qingyou Hu 2008). It also promotes the development of learning science while paying attention to the learning process of students.

The Use of Learning Science in Learning Analysis

Another important branch of learning science is learning analysis. The definition refers to a large amount of information, such as collecting and analyzing data about learners, the learning process and the learning environment. In addition, learning analysis can understand and optimize the learning process. This can help improve the learning environment and provide individualized feedback based on learners' characteristics (Shum 2012). Learning analysis is further studied from the perspective of learning science. Learning analysis techniques and learning analysis methods play an important role in the whole learning process. Learning analysis technology and methods can collect, excavate, organize, analyze, extract and visualize various types of complex data in the learning process. Moreover, it could provide individualized evidence-based feedback, so that learners can improve their self-learning management and understanding by leveraging the powerful brain memory effect, to achieve the optimal learning outcomes. Learning analysis can also deal with large text, time series, fragmentation, audio, video and other data in teaching. It can even deal with multi-dimensional data-sets. Thus, it can significantly reduce the number the man-hours exponentially generated by manual sorting of data and increase the ability to summarize data. Thus, the previous decision-making process based on artificial eyes and senses became an objective, efficient and data-driven process of processing information in real-time. Among them, the real-time big data generated in the learning process can be automatically recorded and automatically analyzed by algorithms. And then real-time reports can be generated and provided to teachers and students to improve the teaching process (Gobert et al. 2013).

At present, with the development of science and technology, the statistics of big data has become more and more advanced and comprehensive. In universities around the world, there are systems with different models to reserve and analyze the application of big data. This is very helpful in the learning process. These records including Real-time records of students' learning process, analysis of students' learning state and academic performance help teachers understand students' learning situation to t better assist them. Teachers' ability to classify and summarize help them improve the teaching process and subsequently improve the level of teaching practice. At the same time, students can also conduct self-assessment and testing using these data in order to improve their self-study ability. Students can conduct self-study analysis, which will help them formulate learning goals and research directions

Chart 1: UBD instructional design model

In recent years, the use of learning analysis to develop educational products and guide teaching practice has attracted more attention in the field of education. For example, Janice Gerbert (Shum / Ferguson 2012) and her team at Worcester Polytechnic Institute in the United States use the concepts and techniques of learning analysis to promote students' inquiry-based learning in physics, biology, earth sciences and other fields.

There are more examples to show the use of learning analysis. Phil Winne of Simon Fraser University in Canada and his research team developed NStudy, which is an online tool for tracking and supporting online autonomous learning (Azevedo / Aleven 2013). Nstudy can automatically collect the information of learners' online learning activities, integrate and analyze them in a timely manner. At the same time, it gives the results to learners in a targeted way, to help them adjust their autonomous learning process in a timely and effective manner. Other popular learning analysis and visualization tools used to improve online teaching include Readerbench (Dascalu et al. 2013), Miat which is a multi-dimensional interactive analysis tool (Kim / Lee 2012) and Personal Learning Environments (Govaerts et al. 2010). Learning analysis techniques and tools have been increasingly used in teaching to improve the teaching process and learning results.

The Application of Learning Process and Learning Analysis

Understanding Unit Instructional Design

Grant Wiggins (Shumei Zhang 2021), an American curriculum expert, proposed the Understanding First Instruction Design Model (UBD), as shown in the chart below, According to Wiggins' understanding, unit instructional design is carried out on the basis of UBD (ibid.)

The chart showed that the UBD instructional design model consists of three steps: "determine the desired outcome", "design evaluation method" and "Arrangements for learning and activities".

The first step, "determine the desired outcome", is setting goals (short for U). According to Marzano's (Shumei Zhang 2021) learning objective dimension, it is based on the understanding of students' existing level of knowledge and the teaching objective of one unit is determined. In addition, in order to make students have the willingness to learn consciously and actively, they can use meta-cognitive strategies to carry out cognitive activities. To complete cognitive tasks, master methods and understand the content of teaching the key points and difficulties of this unit are determined. The second step, "design evaluation method", is assessment distribution (Short for B). The assessment method is designed according to Sternberg's gauge classification, and the mode of "test exercise + open-ended question and answer + practical work on a project in a real situation" was adopted for the assessment to detect the learning effect (Shumei Zhang 2021). The types of test exercises include single choice, multiple choice and judgment questions. Practical tasks are divided into basic application items and comprehensive application items. The comprehensive applied project tests the ability of students to solve practical problems by using the knowledge they have gained. The third step, "Arrangements for learning and activities", is how to get the desired result (Short for D). Meriel's primary teaching principle divides the teaching process into five stages. They focus on the problem stage with integration, activation, application and demonstration. Teaching will be also based on Meriel's primary teaching principles.

Development of Learning Resources Based on Unit Design

First, teachers should design and make PPT teaching demonstration courseware based on the course outline and individual modules. At the same time, the teacher should also record instructional videos; design discussion questions; create interactive links in the classroom; develop short tests; do the practical projects, etc. Specifically, PPT should enrich the course content by combining pictures and charts. Important concepts and principles should be expressed in visual graphics whenever possible. In addition, the font should be moderate and the key words should stand out. When recording instructional videos, teachers should speak clearly and at a moderate speed. Moreover, teachers should design test questions and exercises according to the students' existing knowledge and ensure that the difficulty is moderate. These teaching processes directly affect the learning process of students.

Use "Pomodoro Technique" to Organize Learning Activities

The Pomodoro Technique is a time-management method developed by Francesco Cirillo (1992) based on the structure and working principles of the brain. This time management method become more and more popular around the world.

The Pomodoro Technique advocates break important work or study into small chunks 25 minutes long, then focus on high-quality work or study for 25 minutes, followed by a 5-minute break. The Pomodoro Technique emphasizes that piecemeal work is more efficient than continuous work. Teachers should carefully arrange learning activities of each unit according to "Pomodoro Technique", such as learning time of each unit of "Web Development Technology". It grows into two tomato bells. At the end of each tomato bell (25 minutes), students will be provided with the corresponding test exercises. Students can use the feedback results to test their learning effect.

Practice has proved that in MOOCs, learners watch instructional videos, complete test exercises, and conduct discussions of specific topics. In this process, learners actively think and fully communicate, which is conducive to the completion of knowledge transfer. The construction of MOOCs is a systematic project, and the quality of course resources depends on teachers' teaching design ability, the level of PPT teaching demonstration courseware and teaching level. Finally, teaching ability can record high-quality teaching process only when teachers have excellent teaching design level.

Conclusion

In conclusion, from the perspective of learning science, this paper explores the teaching practice scheme of talent cultivation in higher education. Based on the teaching process of teachers and the learning process of students, it studies the learning process. At the same time, this paper conducts learning analysis, combines the current educational learning methods and takes online courses such as MOOCs and cloud teaching. It took examples to design a learning method suitable for the teaching mode of higher education, which can be applied to different teaching units and online classes. As a result, it is necessary to integrate all kinds of learning resources, using the research method of learning analysis from learning process, promote the learning science, and deepen the teaching practice.

Literature

Azevedo, Roger / Aleven, Vincent: *International Handbook of Metacognition and Learning Technologies*. Springer: New York 2013.

China State Council: *Notice on Printing and Distributing the Implementation Plan of National Vocational Education Reform*. Guofa, 2019.

Cirillo, Francesco: *The Pomodoro Technique*. Lulu.com: Morrisville, 1992.

Dascalu, Mihai / Trausan-Matu, Stefan / Dessus, Philippe. "Cohesion-Based Analysis of CSCL Conversations: Holistic and Individual Perspectives". *10th International Conference of Computer Supported Collaborative Learning* (CSCL 2013), 2013, pp. 145–152.

Gobert, J. D.: "From Log Files to Assessment Metrics: Measuring Students Science Inquiry Skills Using Educational Data Mining". *Journal of the Learning Sciences*, 22(4), 2013, pp. 521–563.

Govaerts, S. et al.: *Visualizing Activities for Self-Reflection and Awareness. The International Conference on Web Based Learning*. Springer: Berlin / Heidelberg, 2010.

Guoan Zhao / Li Yanfei / Wang Xiaofei: "Research on Learning Process Recognition Framework". *China Electronic Education*, 10, 2015, pp. 75–81.

Junjie Shang / Shaoyong Zhuang / Gaowei Chen: "Learning Science: Promoting the Deep Reform of Education". *China Electronic Education*, 1, 2015, pp. 6–13.

Khousa, E. A. / Atif, Y. / Masud, M. M.: "A Social Learning Analytics Approach to Cognitive Apprenticeship". *Smart Learning Environments*, 2(1), 2015, pp. 1–23.

Kim, M. / Lee, E.: "A Multi-Dimensional Analysis Tool for Visualizing Online Interactions". *Educational Technology & Society*, 15(3), 2012, pp. 89–102.

Lindgren, Henry Clay. *Educational Psychology in the Classroom*. Wiley: Hoboken, 1971 (4th edition).

Linglun, T. *Classroom Education Psychology*.: Yunnan People's Publishing House: Kunming, 1983, pp. 303–337.

Ministry of Education of the People's Republic of China: "Modern Vocational Education System Construction Plan (2014–2020)". *Education Development*, 6, 2014.

Nianjing Ding: "Learning and Learning: Development History, Times and Prospects". *China Education Science*, 2, 2013, pp. 115–131.

Qingyou Hu: "Focus on Comprehension Learning: Implications from Learning Science for Learning Process Research". *Educational Science*, 2, 2008, pp. 5–7.

Shum, Simon B. / Ferguson, Rebecca: "Social Learning Analytics". *Educational Technology & Society*, 15(3), 2012, pp. 3–26.

Shumei Zhang: "Construction of MOOC Teaching Mode in Higher Vocational Colleges from the Perspective of Learning Science". *Journal of Jiangsu College of Economics and Trade*, 153, 2021.

Shusheng She: "Design Time Line: Enhancing Learning Process". *Research on Audio-Visual Education*, 10, 2016, pp. 104–108.

Xiaoyan Cao: "Research and Practice on Cultivating Applied Undergraduate Talents with International Vision Based on International Cooperative Education". *Journal of Heilongjiang Institute of Technology*, 1, 2015 (Natural Science Edition), pp. 73–76.

Yongfeng Wang / He Kekang / Wang Yining: "From 'Constructive Learning' to 'Effective Participation of Students': On the Legitimate Business of Classroom Educational Technology". *Open Education Research*, 8, 2007, pp. 50–58.

Zongkui Zhou: *Adolescent Psychological Development and Learning.* Higher Education Press: Beijing, 2007.

Tang Xueming

Effective Ways of Integrating Moral Education into College English Teaching

Abstract: At present, colleges and universities in China are actively responding to and implementing the moral education requirements of the curriculum, but how to effectively integrate moral education into teaching is a difficult problem for front-line teachers. In fact, college English is probably the most suitable course for moral education. This paper will explore the effective ways of integrating moral education into college English teaching.

Keywords: College English teaching, moral education, grammar teaching, vocabulary teaching

What Happened to Chinese Students?

Education has always advocated respect for teachers, because teachers continue the culture, spread knowledge and enlightenment. Therefore, since ancient times, showing no respect for teachers is shameful! In response to the outbreak of covid-19 pandemic, the schools were closed and face-to-face classes suspended. Thus, our students had to study online at home with new teaching model, which was introduced, but also caused a lot of problems.

On March 12, 2020, a video of a student arguing with a teacher during an online class drew attention. In the dialogue shown in the video, the student thought that the teacher deliberately humiliated him in class and his self-esteem was undermined, so he ends up verbally abusing the teacher for several minutes in an emotional state. The student was often late for classes and did not hand in his homework. The teacher called on him by name and criticized him. The student felt insulted by the teacher's remark and said: "Who doesn't copy the homework? Who can study well by the Internet?"

1.1 The Present Situation of College Students 'Moral Quality'.

The results of 'A questionnaire on college students 'moral quality show that the majority of students fully affirm the important position and function of moral quality in the society. A total of 231 questionnaires were collected, including 49.78 % for male students and 50.22 % for female students, among which 30.3 % for students majoring in literature and history, 61.9 % for students majoring in science and technology, and 7.79 % for students majoring in other majors.

The data given were obtained strictly on the base of samples, and the data were authentic and reliable (Zhang Lulu, 55). According to this study, 76.62 % of students think that moral quality is very important, only 0.43 % of the students think it is dispensable. 40.26 % of the students think personal moral quality is very good, and 47.62 % of the students think personal moral quality is good. 58.44 % of the students think that the overall moral quality of college students is in good condition, and the moral quality is generally improved. 41.56 % of the students say that they will politely remind or give advice to the other party in the face of the phenomenon of moral misconduct, only 2.16 % of the students had a negative attitude. On the whole, moral orientation is positive, moral consciousness is strengthened, moral requirements and moral value orientation are increasingly stable and mature; students are generally able to analyze objectively and dispassionately, and can see the linkage among individuals, families, schools and society, the attitude tends to be rational, peaceful, dialectical, and exceptional.

However, there is a difference between knowing and doing. The overall moral level of college students is at a high level, but at the same time, there are some problems that cannot be ignored in college students' moral concept and moral behavior. 40.26 % of the students chose "very good" and 47.62 % of the students chose "good" when they answered, "how do you think your moral quality is", 50.65 % of the students chose "not to negotiate, although they feel uncomfortable", and 41.56 % chose "politely remind the other person or give advice". This shows that the enthusiasm to correct moral misconduct is not high, the initiative is not strong, students do not want to take too much of the corresponding social responsibility, the sense of responsibility has an obvious trend of weakening, neutral attitude is becoming the mainstream of contemporary college students.

Some students have cognitive deviation. Some students do not pay enough attention to moral quality. Still 5.63 % of students think that moral quality is only of average importance, even some people think it is dispensable; 54.11 % of the respondents were not very satisfied with the ideological and moral courses offered, and 5.19 % felt that "such courses are not very useful" or "completely unnecessary". About 5.2 % of the students chose "unclear" in the aspect of improving their moral level in the ideological and moral courses. They had cognitive biases towards them and did not have high expectations for the moral education environment provided. Having doubts and perplexities about the essence and functions of moral courses, they failed to consciously link the promotion of moral quality with the individual's future and the overall development of society, which affects the correct establishment of moral outlook.

Analysis of the Causes of the Problems

The overall situation of college students' moral quality is good, and the mainstream is positive and upward. However, with the continuous advancement of China's reform and opening up, students' moral level is undergoing obvious changes; the impact of foreign culture on the moral quality of contemporary college students is quite significant. Contemporary college students show unsteadiness in their moral concept and moral behavior. The main reason for the phenomenon that college students ignore moral problems is that students' own moral self-esteem is low and they have no common values or good moral norms. They lack clear understanding of moral quality and have a weak concept of moral responsibility, highlighting the "self" and ignoring the promotion of moral awareness. They are often indifferent to moral misconduct, resulting in "knowledge and action" out of touch.

The lack of moral quality in child discipline is the beginning of the formation of moral quality in life. Many parents pay too much attention to their children's intellectual development and neglect the cultivation of their children's moral quality, the educational value of the daily life activities of the family to the children is neglected. Some family moral education methods are very simple; some of them pursue just doting and obedience; thus, some students' moral orientation is "self-interest", self-centered, not bound by moral norms, and some students have "stick education". Lack of equal communication does not form a good model. The aesthetic taste, values and behavior habits formed in a particular family environment will have a profound impact on children, while the lack of moral education is not conducive to the healthy development of children's character and value orientation.

The negative influence of the social environment is a dynamic and complicated process, and college students' understanding of things is still in the stage of incompleteness, instability and contradiction. It is not difficult to see that this kind of moral concept formed spontaneously by college students is unstable. We are in the period of economic and social transformation, people's production and life are undergoing great changes, moral standards and moral evaluation systems tend to be diversified, and there are failures in moral supervision and regulation. Moral values of a special social group like college students will inevitably be affected by the resurgence of hedonism and money worship, the weakness of social public opinion and traditional moral restraint.

Any knowledge of moral theory can only play its role if it is transformed into the internal moral law of the actual social behavior of human beings. In the traditional school moral education in our country, the educators mainly take the teaching material as the carrier, rely on the teaching classroom, unilaterally teach the moral knowledge and the theory to the students, but do not care whether the students understand theoretical knowledge and raise the practical ability. Students should become real "moral people", even if they do not just agree with the excellent moral theory, but also consciously abide by moral norms and achieve better results in moral practice.

It is necessary to change the traditional mode of persuasion education, enhance the appeal of moral education courses, pay attention to the guidance of students' moral practice behavior in practical teaching, and strengthen the training and cultivation of students' moral capacity, improve the moral cultivation of students, to achieve "knowledge and practice of the same".

College English Teaching Has a Natural Connection with Moral Education

Foreign language teaching has a natural connection with moral education, culture points are contained in vocabulary, ideological connotation is transmitted in discourse, and different languages come from different cultural backgrounds and even represent different political standpoints. College English as a vocational basic course for students in higher vocational colleges. During the course delivery ideological and political elements, based on the needs of students' development, are introduced. The course organically integrates instrumentality and humanity, takes root in the native land and looks abroad, and conveys the content in accordance with the core values and the main theme through the English language.

Students' critical thinking, patriotism, cultural confidence and system confidence are cultivated during the class. In College English classes, the choice of input (audio-visual, reading) materials should be related to Chinese fine traditional culture, history, economy, politics, philosophy, etc. In terms of homework exercises, we should update the exercise forms, provide topics for discussion or debate, which are built on the contrast between Chinese and Western cultures, and improve the quality and level of results (speaking, writing, translation) with questions specially designed for discussions. In the college English courses taught by the author, each unit revolves around a central theme, such as greetings, trips, hotels, meals, shopping and so on, some scenes in the unit dialogue are taken as the starting point, which is extended to the related ideological, political and moral topics, and students are encouraged to participate in the discussion. Based on the perspective of "ideological and political course", we optimize the compilation of teaching content and endow it with the function of moral education. Especially for cross-cultural content, we guide students to look at issues dialectically, build up cultural self-confidence, and practice core values of the society. During class, in order to nurture good life habit and perfect personality the students do not only complete the study of English language knowledge, but are also exposed to the study of ideological and moral cultivation by infiltrating the moral content into the teaching content.

Integrating Moral Education into the Curriculum, in the Silent Place of Self-Cultivation of Personality

Foreign Language Teachers should refine, integrate, process and further develop the moral elements into the curriculum, connect the emotional needs of students, solve puzzles and relate to life experience.

The teaching contents of foreign language courses are usually selected strictly, which reflect the rich cultural factors, the common human values, the feelings of home and country, and so on. For example, an article called 'Why Study Humanities?'(Liu Zhengguang 2018, pp. 29–30). In describing the significance of studying the humanities, the author, in designing his teaching plan, took into account the fact that some students lack the ability to think independently and strive for certainty, while others, in order to show their individuality, think that they are independent-minded as long as they are different from the mainstream view. Therefore, the author first distills the author's view "The humanities give you uncertainty, doubt and skepticism", then leads to Marxisms famous dictum "doubt everything", and further points out that to doubt everything is not to deny everything, and not to follow blindly, but to judge to listen to everything and to understand. That's how you really think for yourself. "From teachers to classmates, no one will tell you what the standard answer is. We are all looking for our own answer," students say in their reflection on learning.

While realizing the knowledge goal of foreign language curriculum, teachers should transform the implicit value idea into the behavior of teaching and learning. Teachers can start from the subtle, innovative discourse system, to avoid preaching, and arouse students' knowledge resonance, emotional resonance, and value resonance. 'My First Week at Harvard' (Liu Zhengguang, pp. 4–5) gives a vivid description of the beautiful scenery of the Harvard campus, giving students a strong aesthetic experience, but if that is all, the curriculum is still too narrow. We can conduct a deep functional analysis of the text content, leading students to think why the author's view of the campus is so delighted. The step-by-step analysis guides the students to the feelings of the characters who come to their favorite university eager for a new university life. At this point, students become active aesthetic judges, and then consider the importance of education, cherish and appreciate the opportunity for education, have concern and care about the environment and home.

After all, moral courses are not ideological or political courses. Professional course teachers cannot analyze or explain important and complex ideological and political concepts or theoretical issues as thoroughly, clearly and systematically as ideological and political teachers. Teachers of professional courses should take the initiative to set up a bridge, connect moral courses, guide students to seek answers in the courses, and form a synergistic effect. The article called "Inspiration, Jobs" (Jia Guodong 2018, 114–115) says: "Innovation distinguishes between a leader and a follower." In class, the students asked: "Does being a follower mean you are a failure in life?" The author first affirmed the students' independent thinking, then arranged for students to discuss, and finally summarized: "To be a leader is very good, but to find a suitable position is more important". It is the people who make history, and that is an important point of the historical materialism. The students can further discuss this problem with the teacher of the moral course. The students do not only have their own thinking, positive cognition, but also take the initiative to moral lessons to deeply understand the power of truth of Marxism. Some students wrote in the reflection after this lesson: "to find a suitable position, assume responsibility, show ability, whether a leader or a follower, is an important force for social progress and development". And, finally, it's not as far-fetched as it used to be.

Effective Ways of Integrating Moral Education into College English Teaching

Moral education in college English curriculum does not mean that ideological and political education should be brought into English classroom, the key lies in how to guide the students to look at the world in positive way through the English language teaching itself, and inspire the students to know themselves, to understand themselves, to integrate into the society, to care about the society, to realize self-esteem. Therefore, when we do the teaching design, we should consider how to put the idea of moral education naturally into the language materials in our teaching. Moral education requires teachers, as the actors of teaching reform, to innovate teaching methods, to design high-quality interactive teaching activities based on teaching contents, and to arouse students' recognition of cognition, emotion and behavior while imparting knowledge. Based on the actual teaching practice, the author would like to discuss how to effectively integrate moral education into college English teaching.

Deep Processing of Language Knowledge

There are many moral elements in the English teaching materials, such as some articles with the theme of struggle, self-reliance, etc., which can well let students understand and feel the importance of struggle and self-reliance, cultivate their self-reliance and self-improvement character, but for the basic knowledge of language, such as the three elements of language. As a matter of fact, English teachers can achieve this goal if they truly understand and master the basic features and rules of foreign language teaching, constantly improve their professional quality, adopt appropriate teaching methods, and deal with knowledge in depth.

Phonetics Training: To Cultivate Perseverance and Self-Confidence

Phonetics is the basis and foundation of improving students' language ability. Phonetics teaching also contains rich educational value. First of all, pronunciation is a series of pronunciation habits, which need repeated training and correction. In this long-lasting process, teachers can consciously cultivate students' perseverance character. In addition, with the internationalization and localization of English, teachers should pay attention to the explanation of the features of English varieties in the world, such as Chinese English, instead of requiring students' pronunciation and intonation to be close to the pronunciation of their native language, rather, it emphasizes the intelligibility of pronunciation and its overall impact on oral communication , which can effectively eliminate the tension and anxiety caused by students' incorrect pronunciation due to the influence of their mother tongue or dialect. In order to pay more attention to the effectiveness of communication, the use of English communication confidence should be enhanced.

Grammar Teaching: Expanding the Way of Thinking

At present, there is a popular view among both teachers and students, including some policy makers, that teaching grammar is the root cause of the inefficiency of foreign language teaching, so that the role and status of grammar teaching are seriously degraded and teachers are unwilling to teach, students don't want to learn. The reason for this situation is that people generally believe that grammar teaching is to achieve the accuracy of language forms, for examinations, the result is high scores and low ability. However, in fact the following two points about grammar learning are very important: first, grammar is the most essential part of the language, we must learn it well; second, the basic purpose of studying grammar is to develop the ability of thinking, that is, the ability to observe, discover and solve problems. Grammar learning is full of the charm of methodology and logic. Our problem now is that we forget the second point and overemphasize the function of appearances. If we can make students fully aware of the interaction between the subjective initiative of human cognition and the rules (contradictory movement) in grammar teaching, we can train students' dynamic thinking mode of concrete analysis of concrete problems, to help students better understand the relationship between "generality and individuality" (the internal relationship between grammatical rules and "special usage") in philosophy class. This is the inspiration of methodology, the process of cultivating students' creativity, the process of stimulating students' learning motivation and interest, and the process of feeling professional charm.

In fact, grammar is the method, structure, and rules that language and writing use in their presentation. Grammar embodies the logic of thinking, grammar of the word and logic of the concept of the link, grammar of the sentence and logic of the judgment, reasoning link. Therefore, the process of learning grammar is first of all language rules and methods, and then logical thinking mode of learning. In fact, teaching grammar is to help students improve their logical thinking ability and expand the way of thinking. The teacher should point out that Westerners often adopt an objective way of thinking and pay attention to the effect and influence of things on people, when expressing their views and feelings, they often use the words "It occurs to me…" or "it's my hope that…". This can effectively reduce students' misuse of subjective expressions such as "I think…" or "I believe that…"

Vocabulary Teaching: Promoting Cross-Cultural Cognitive

Vocabulary as the cornerstone of the language learning is the minimum carrier of culture. The meaning of words includes culture, Encyclopedias, and ways of looking at the world. For words with rich cultural meanings, teachers should expand their usage naturally, guide students to explore the national cultural connotation embodied in the words, pay attention to the cultural differences between the two languages, and enrich the cultural accumulation, cultivate sensitivity and tolerance to the cultural differences. For example, when we taught an article called "My First Week at Harvard" (Liu Zhengguang 2018, pp. 4–5) it says, "Where we eat is remarkably remarkable. Our dining hall is more like a church or a museum than a cafeteria." When students read this, they are puzzled: How can it be a good dining environment to eat in a place like a church? At this time, it is necessary for teachers to introduce the importance of church in

Anglo-American society and its internal structure and decorating order to solve the students' confusion caused by cultural differences.

Teachers should also teach vocabulary in a real language learning environment to enhance learners' ability of self-exploration and cognition. For example, when we taught an article called "Why Study Humanities?" (Liu Zhengguang 2018, 29–30), the teacher can point out that the image of "ass" in English and Chinese is an equivalent of "Donkey", which both can refer to stupid people. The students should be asked to think about the author's real intention in using the word in the text. After the analysis and discussion of the text is finished, the students can conclude that this is the "positive use of the opposite word".

Skillful Use of Rhetoric to Master the Way of International Discourse

Rhetoric plays an important role in language learning. If we want to grasp the purpose, means and methods of each other's discourse in international communication, we need to teach our students to use various rhetoric strategies flexibly. For example, Martin Luther King's "I Have a Dream" speech demonstrates that the use of parallelism increases the power of the language, deepening the thoughts and feelings, and has a strong appeal. After that, the students are asked to pay attention to the extensive use of parallelism in speeches by westerners, especially politicians. Finally, the students are asked to make use of the vocabulary and knowledge of advertising in the text to create sentences containing parallelism, for instance with the phrase "It has been argued, that advertising may…". One student wrote the following sentences in class: "It has been argued that advertising may increase the prices of products, advertising may mislead the public by advertising titles, advertising may cause monopoly by some big companies, advertising may bring relentless assault on the viewers, and advertising may be abused by unscrupulous people." This exercise helps students master the figure of speech, like parallelism, in order to improve the level of international discourse communication. We should train students to think critically and dialectically about the application of advertisement in daily life and its influence on people. This shows that deep understanding of the language, knowledge and ability to achieve the goal, but also at any time to carry out just the right value integration.

Teachers can integrate language knowledge with ideological and political elements to ensure the consistency of foreign language teaching and ideological and political education and the scientific nature of educational content. We should also be ensured that the ideological and political elements involved in the course gradually form a relatively complete system. The author of this article

Table 1: 3CQ discussion patterns

Steps of discussion	Contents of discussion	Moral goals
Compliment	Praise the other students' speech	Kind, Tolerant
Comment	Present your ideas and insights, and give reasons	Speculative
Connect	Make new additions to the other students' ideas	Seeking Novelty
Question	What questions do you have on the subject	Studious

has assigned a sentence for the students to translate: 'Justice has long arms.' This exercise integrates language learning and political thinking and achieves four effects: first, learning metaphor as a rhetorical device and a linguistic phenomenon; second, learning the differences between English and Chinese expressions; and third, it points out the common value orientation of Human Beings, and that evil will eventually be punished. For example, when I teach abstract writing, I remind students to explain the content of the original text instead of copying the original text, and then emphasize the observance of academic norms, to prevent plagiarism and other academic misconduct, and cultivate students' integrity.

To Improve Thinking Quality with In-Depth Discussion

The English curriculum standards for senior high schools (2017 edition; Ministry of Education of the People's Republic of China, 2018) lists thinking quality as one of the core competencies of the English language subject, allowing students to have in-depth discussion to improve their thinking quality. The key factor is the level of discussion: the higher the levels, the deeper understanding of the topic by the students. The core idea is to help students make the right value judgment. For example, "What is the most challenging part of this article?" "How does this article contribute to the understanding of a social phenomenon?" We can refer to the Bryant University discussion thread format to provide some discussion patterns for students (Table 1), to help students organize an effective discussion step by step. Let us look at the feedback from the students: "Group discussions can sometimes lead to conflict, but at the end of the day we can always find a balance. It's easier for me to listen to other people's opinions and form my own judgment by using interaction instead of one-sided output."

Question Driven: To Cultivate the Spirit of Truth-Seeking

Question is the engine of thinking, and carrying out the problem-inquiry teaching is helpful to train the students' knowledge and ability of truth-seeking. Teachers should design the problem carefully, and use the question to outline the topic, which will stimulate the students to explore the truth. The teacher uses the question to activate the teaching process and guide the student to master the subject and investigate the essence of things. If teachers encourage students to ask questions, they, thus, explore the potential of students to comprehend the truth. Teachers raise questions through the stratification inducing student's thinking ability, cognitive skills and their self-evaluation system step by step.

The core is the quality of the question. Therefore, when we are designing questions, we have to think carefully. These questions should range from the superficial to the profound, finally leading to the great goal of "realizing the Chinese Dream" in our country at present, guiding students to establish a sense of social responsibility, cherish time, pursue truth, and become a fresh force to realize Chinese dream, to shoulder the hopes of the country and nation.

Project Research: To Promote the Integration of Knowledge and Practice

Designing projects that are challenging and require teamwork in accordance with the course content make students consolidate, enrich and improve their knowledge and use it in practice, thus promoting the idea of learning by doing. The key factor is the feasibility of the project and the degree of challenge; the core idea is to cultivate students' practical spirit. For example, Cantonese opera is an excellent moral material by itself. It helps students understand the traditional culture of Cantonese opera and build up their cultural confidence when studying the content of the course However, teachers don't have to stop there. After completing the routine teaching, we assign a research project, asking students to split into groups and distribute tasks among them, in order to do research on the past, present and future of the Cantonese opera. Two weeks later, the students present a research report on the history of the Cantonese opera, analyze the results of the questionnaire, and design a cup and t-shirt with the theme of the Cantonese opera elements. Other students write a feasibility study on the modernization of the Cantonese opera.

During the research process, the students are not just involved in practical activities, but also feel the charm of the Cantonese opera, understand the connotation of the Cantonese opera and the development of the sense of urgency. The students' national cultural identity is gradually established, and they have their own understanding and thinking on how to stimulate the vitality of traditional culture. There is a reason to believe that in the future, they will be able to face reality, assume the responsibility of inheriting and developing traditional culture, and be able to tell Chinese stories to the world in English. "Through this research project, I really feel the beauty of the Cantonese opera and have a strong interest in traditional culture. Perhaps, I can do something for traditional culture", one student wrote in his research report.

Bring in Hot Issues and form a Big Picture View

English teachers should keep close to life at all times, pay close attention to the current affairs and politics, properly introduce hot issues and events of current affairs into the teaching process. The key issue is to enhance students' sense of citizenship and improve their ability to distinguish right from wrong, cultivate students in the campus, help students broaden their horizons, observe and analyze the world, form a big picture view. Teachers should adhere to the core values, which are to guide students to cultivate great sentiments and charming personality. For example, in the current global response to the epidemic of new pneumonia, teachers can deepen students' understanding of the "community of human destiny", and the role of China as a great power, through exercises, class discussions, etc. They can cultivate students' sense of home and country, sense of responsibility, as well as inspire students to think independently and overcome difficulties with strong confidence.

Conclusion

The moral education of college English teaching should be integrated with the teaching of language knowledge and skills. Teachers should help students develop critical thinking through the teaching design, implement the shaping of values in the process of analyzing and solving problems systematically, and guide students to consciously practice the correct values in the new context. In-depth teaching helps enhance the moral nature of foreign language teaching, deepen the connotation of teaching and improve teaching efficiency.

We should concentrate on effective teaching of the actual action to return to duty, affecting students to return to common sense getting them really busy, guiding them in truth-seeking knowledge, practicing real ability, and achieving connotation development. With the love for our motherland, the love for education, the love for the subject and the specialty, and the love for the students, we should show that our teachers are returning to their dreams, to better inspire students to pursue their dreams, consciously and diligently become the builders and successors of the cause of socialism. It is enlightening and instructive for foreign language teachers to pay attention to every link in the teaching process and to feel the change of students' demands.

In addition, college English teachers should improve their comprehensive qualities, pay attention to strengthening the details of Chinese traditional culture, and disseminate to students the excellent Chinese traditional national history and culture, so that they have a sense of world culture, have a strong sense of national cultural self-confidence, have a correct process of thinking about the Western culture of English-speaking countries, and form a correct outlook on life and the world.

Literature

Liu, Zhengguang: *Basic Objectives of College Experience English Comprehensive Course, Vol. 1*. Higher Education Press: Beijing, 2018.

Jia, Guodong: *Basic Objectives of College Experience English Comprehensive Course, Vol. 2*. Higher Education Press: Beijing, 2018

Liu, Zhengguang: *Basic Objectives of College Experience English Comprehensive Course, (Volume Vol. 1)*. Higher Education Press: Beijing, 2018Ministry of Education of the People's Republic of China: *GSS English Curriculum Standards* (2017 edition). People's Education Press: Beijing, 2018.

Further Reading

Chow, Yiu-Tung: "Western Rhetoric and Foreign Language Education in China: An Interview with Prof. Liu ya-meng." *Foreign Language and Literature*, 1, 2004, p. 4.

Halliday, Michael A. K. / Hasan, Ruqayia: *Language, Context and Text: Aspects of Language in a Social-Semiotic Perspective*. Deakin University Press: Victoria (AU), 1985.

Jinping, Xi: "Speech at United Nations Educational, Scientific and Cultural Organization Headquarters." *People's Daily*, March 28, 2014.

Liu, Na / Shitai, Yang: "The Historical Origin and Connotation of the Idea of Establishing Morality and Fostering People." *Education Review*, 5, 2014, pp. 141–143.

Martin, J. R. (ed.): *Interviews with M. A. K. Halliday: Language Turned Back on Himself*. Bloomsbury: London et al. 2013.

Stern, Hans H.: *Fundamental Concepts of Language Teaching*. Oxford University Press: Oxford et al. 1983.

Walsh, Steve: *Investigating Classroom Discourse*. Routledge: London, 2006.

Zhang, Lulu: "Current Situation and Countermeasures of College Students' Moral Quality. Taking Xi'an University of Posts and Telecommunications as an Example". *New West China*, 502(03), 2020, pp. 55–56.

Qin Yuan, Yigang Peng

The Present Situation, Dilemma and Path of Internationalization of Higher Education in Central Region of China – Taking S University as an Example

Abstract: Since China's reform and opening up, the internationalization of higher education has gradually resumed. China's higher education has made remarkable achievements in terms of internationalization. However, the internationalization of higher education in China has also presented a serious development imbalance between different regions: the central region of China has become "the swamp area" in the internationalization of higher education. Therefore, this paper suggests that the governments and universities in central China need to promote the internationalization of higher education in their regions and implies certain measures.

Keywords: Central China, Internationalization of higher education, path and dilemma of internationalization of higher education

The Internationalization of Higher Education in China

Definitions of Key Concepts

Jiang Kai and Zhang Junfeng (2017) state: "Internationalization is an important development trend of world higher education." What is the Internationalization of higher education? To give an accurate definition of the concept is not easy. It is a very controversial concept. At present, the representative viewpoints for the Chinese scholars include "system theory, standard theory and process theory."(Shao 2016) According to the system theory, "the internationalization of higher education refers to a system, and the internationalization of universities should include the international system of international courses, transnational studies, and cross-border mobility of teachers and students."(Zeng et al. 2008) The standard theory holds that "internationalization of higher education is a kind of standard, including the acceptability of foreign cultures, the intercommunication of different countries and cultural information, the openness of organizations and so on." (Xiduocunhezhi 2016, p. 254). The process theory considers that "internationalization of higher education is a process in which the international and transnational dimensions are integrated into the purpose, function or transmission of higher education." (Knight 2001, pp. 25–26) Among them, the process theory has a high degree of recognition, and the International Union of Universities under UNESCO has generally adopted this theory, according to which "the internationalization of higher education refers to the process of integrating cross-border and cross-cultural perspectives and atmospheres with the main functions of universities, such as teaching, research and social services; and this process is inclusive, both internal and external changes, both top-down and bottom-up, as well as the policy direction of the school itself." (Xi 2002) The concept of internationalization of higher education is not agreed by Chinese researchers. For example, Zhiding Shu considers that "internationalization of higher education means that university education faces the world, takes specific and diversified higher education activities as the carrier, absorbs and draws lessons from the idea of running a school of world-class universities, and aims to improve the higher education system of China, so as to construct and transform the management mode of higher education." (Shu 1998) According to Yanxun Wu, "the internationalization of higher education is a development process of pursuing excellence based on the country, facing the world and the future, and putting the higher education work of the country in the trans-national and trans-cultural context." (Wu 2000) Liaoyuan Xia has different opinions. In his opinion "the internationalization of higher education refers to the process of integrating domestic higher education into the world education track on the premise of meeting the needs of economic and political development." (Xia 2006) On the whole Chinese scholars are greatly influenced by the "process theory".

This paper tends to agree with the "process theory", which holds that internationalization of higher education refers to the higher education, which is a process and development trend facing the world based on the national conditions. These developments in higher education proceed on the background of broader developments of cross-border, cross-cultural and cross-ethnic relations. Through extensive international exchanges, cooperation and competition, the internationalization of higher education is reformed and disseminated while absorbing advanced experience. The manifestations of internationalization of higher education include cross-border flow of students, cross-border flow of teachers, academic and ideological content flow of scholars, sino-foreign cooperation in running schools and so on.

The Functional Status of International Exchange and Cooperation in Higher Education

Opening the door to the outside world is increasingly important in today's higher education, and its manifestation is the international exchange and cooperation with foreign universities. International exchange and cooperation itself is also an inherent requirement of universities when they develop to a certain stage. In 2017, The CPC Central Committee and the State Council issued the "Opinions on Strengthening and Improving ideological and Political Work in Colleges and Universities under the New Situation" which states that "international exchange and cooperation" and "talent training", "scientific research", "social service", "cultural inheritance and innovation" are listed as the important mission of the university. The international exchange and cooperation becomes the fifth function of higher education. As an important function of universities, international exchange and cooperation reflect the internal international activity of universities, and is also a response to the globalization trend and the reform of university governance structure in the new stage of development of higher education The international exchange and cooperation of universities stimulate a new vitality of the innovation and development of higher education and also become an important symbol to measure the degree of education modernization. In today's increasingly fierce international competition environment, it is more and more important to cultivate high-quality international talents for the development of the country, and international exchanges and cooperation among universities is an important way to cultivate such professionals. Therefore, it is very important to list international exchange and cooperation as the fifth function of universities.

In addition, international exchange and cooperation, as one of the functions of universities, also conforms to the law of higher education development. Universities are characterized by the production and dissemination of knowledge, but knowledge itself has no national boundaries and is shared. Therefore, international exchange and cooperation of universities, as an endogenous mechanism, is constantly strengthened along with the changes of the whole society's demand for the development of universities. When defining the connotation of internationalization of higher education, a series of contents listed can be used as the main contents of international exchanges and cooperation of universities, such as academic mobility of teachers and students, new international academic programs and research plans, new cooperation agreements, etc. Therefore, we can also take internationalization as the evaluation indicator of university development, and international exchange and cooperation is one of the forms of university internationalization. (Zhao / Chen 2017)

Literature Review and Prospect of Internationalization of Higher Education in China

A Review of Internationalization of Higher Education in China

In 1978, the historical third Plenary Session of the 11th Central Committee was successfully held. Since then, China has embarked on the great journey of reform and opening up. At the same time, China's higher education international exchange activities are also increasing, and the degree of opening to the outside world is deepening. In the past 40 years of reform and opening up, the history of internationalization of Chinese higher education can be roughly divided into three stages: exploration period, development period and maturity period[6].

The exploratory period refers to the period from 1978 to 2001, when China was still in the early stage of reform and opening up. The country's door was just opened, and China's higher education began to gradually open to the outside world under the guidance of the concept of "crossing the river by feeling the stones". However, in general, the degree of opening up to the outside world was relatively low during this period, and the number of students studying abroad or in China was relatively small, among whom the students studying abroad were mainly students from public universities. In May 1986, The State Council issued the Notice on Several Issues concerning the Improvement and Strengthening of the Work for Students Studying Abroad, which clearly pointed out that sending students to study abroad in various forms fully conforms to China's long-term policy of opening up to the outside world. In December of the same year, The State Council approved and transferred the State Education Commission's "Interim Provisions on The Work of Students Studying Abroad". In 1996, The China Scholarship Council was formally established. At the same time, the State Education Commission decided to try out the selection method of state-funded study abroad in a comprehensive way, namely, "individual application, expert review, fair competition, selective admission, signing a contract and compensation for the breach of a contract." China's government-sponsored study abroad system has been gradually improved. In addition, the main characteristic of the internationalization of higher education in China during this period is to serve the economic development. (Xu 2019) For example, in 1985, Deng Xiaoping made a famous speech at the National Education Work Conference entitled

---

6   . Institute of International Education of Beijing Foreign Studies University: *70 years of China's education opening to the outside world: China's international education development report.* East China Normal University Press: Shanghai, 2019, pp. 16–23.

"We should Earnestly Grasp the Education Work", which clearly pointed out the importance of promoting education and giving full play to the huge advantages of human resources for China's economic development. This conference is of profound significance in the history of Chinese education. It has directly affected the establishment and development of the later government-sponsored study abroad system in China, and the purpose of higher education opening to the outside world. In general, during this period, China's education system had just been restored, and the opening of higher education to the outside world was still in the exploratory stage. By sending students overseas to study various subjects, China opened the door of higher education to the outside world.

The development period refers to the period from 2001 to 2012, during which the internationalization of China's higher education reached the stage of rapid development. In 2001, China joined the World Trade Organization, which provided many opportunities for the internationalization of higher education in China. The Chinese government has issued a series of documents related to international education, vigorously promoting the exchange and cooperation in education with border countries, and increasingly paying attention to the role of market factors in promoting the internationalization of China's higher education. During this period, the internationalization of higher education in China has undergone a series of significant changes. First, the majority of overseas students who studied abroad moved from the government support to the self-funded one; The Chinese government has lifted many of the previous restrictions on university students studying abroad, encouraging citizens to study abroad on their own, and the number of self-funded Chinese students studying abroad has considerably increased, far surpassing the number of government-funded students. Secondly, China's higher education took on various forms of opening to the outside world. In the past China's higher education opening to the world was just limited by the students studying abroad, but in this period, China's higher education opening to the world took on other forms. In addition to the larger number of students studying abroad, the number of foreign students studying in China increased. At the height of the Chinese-foreign cooperation, joint academic and research activities became more frequent. Finally, the purpose of China's higher education opening to the outside world is no longer limited to acquiring advanced knowledge and experience from abroad to promote the development of China, but it begins to pay attention to improving the international competitiveness of its culture. For example, in 2004, The State Council of the Ministry of Education approved the Action Plan for Education Revitalization 2003–2007, which proposed to "vigorously promote teaching Chinese as a foreign language and actively explore the international education market". In the same year, the

Confucius Institute Program was launched and the first Confucius Institute in the world was established in Seoul, South Korea.

The maturity period refers to the period from 2012 to the present, during which the internationalization of China's higher education has gradually developed, various institutions have been improved, and various forms of international exchanges have appeared. In 2012, the 18th National Congress of the Communist Party of China (CPC) was held, and the CPC Central Committee headed by Comrade Xi Jinping emphasized the importance of higher education opening to the world, thus starting a new stage in China's higher education development. By 2018, China had signed agreements on mutual recognition of academic degrees with 46 countries and regions, and 2,385 Chinese-foreign jointly-run schools and programs had been established. (Chen 2018, p. 6) High-level Sino-foreign cultural and people-to-people exchanges mechanisms had been successfully established between China and Russia, China and the United States, China and France, China and Britain, China and Germany, China and the European Union, China and India and Indonesia.

Internationalization of Higher Education in China

Internationalization of higher education in China is now at the highest stage in history. Many policies and decisions made by the Chinese government have promoted the opening-up of higher education in China to a new level, especially bringing more opportunities for the internationalization of higher education in central China.

In 2010, the CPC Central Committee and The State Council introduced and implemented the Outline of the National Medium – and Long-term Plan for Education Reform and Development (2010–2020), which proposed to "optimize the regional layout structure, set up special funds to support local higher education, and implement the revitalization plan for higher education in central and western China". The implementation of the "Central and Western Higher Education Revitalization Plan" provides opportunities for the opening up of universities in central China. In the past, due to the unbalanced regional economic development in China, colleges and universities in rich coastal provinces in Eastern China developed rapidly, with a large number of key universities and more convenient access to resources, and the level of internationalization of higher education in these provinces was significantly higher than that in Central China. The implementation of the "Central and Western Higher Education Revitalization Plan" is aimed at reducing the unbalanced development of higher education, bringing more high-quality resources to the universities in Central

China, and thus promoting the internationalization of higher education in this region.

In 2013, General Secretary Xi Jinping proposed the "One Belt, One Road" strategy with great foresight. "One Belt and One Road" strategy is a major strategic concept, which is designed not only to further improve the level of China's opening to the outside world, but also to further promote the internationalization of higher education in China, deepen the comprehensive reform in the field of higher education and improve the quality of education, providing a major strategic opportunity. (Li 2017) In 2016, the General Office of the CPC Central Committee and The General Office of the State Council issued several Opinions on The Opening up of Education in the New Era and the Ministry of Education's Act on Promoting the Construction of Education along the Belt and Road, and other policies, urging countries along the Belt and Road to take joint efforts to achieve the win-win cooperation. The strategy of "One Belt and One Road" has given priority to the development of higher education in the Central China, paying special attention to local colleges and universities which currently have a unique geographical advantage, being located in Central China and playing a positive role in promoting international exchanges and cooperation. (Wang 2015, p. 13)

On August 18, 2015, the Central Leading Group for Comprehensively Deepening Reform considered and approved the National Plan for Promoting the Construction of World-class Universities and First-class Disciplines in a coordinated way (hereinafter referred to as "Double First-class"). The introduction of "double first-class" program has broken the original "985 project", "211 Project" university list fixed practice, so that more central universities have the opportunity to participate in the evaluation of "double first-class" university, so as to obtain more resources to promote the opening of higher education in our university. (Wu 2017) At the same time, the "double first-class" plan requires to actively explore the construction of world-class universities and first-class disciplines with Chinese characteristics, which itself has the requirement of facing the world, and it is its due meaning to promote the opening of higher education to the outside world.

At the same time, the rapid development of globalization also puts forward more requirements for the internationalization of higher education. Along with the economic globalization, the internationalization of higher education is more and more driven by economic interests and has entered the stage of global competition. (Huang 2003) In order to compete for international students, countries constantly reform their higher education systems, improve the quality of their higher education, and enhance the competitiveness of their higher education to meet the needs of international competition in higher education. In addition, globalization has also led to increasingly fierce competition in the comprehensive national strength of various countries, and the high demand for talents in various countries has prompted countries to strive to improve the internationalization of their higher education and train more international talents. For example, in order to attract overseas talents, Chinese Human Resources and Social Security Ministry issued the development of human resources and social security undertakings in 2017 emphasizing "much starker choices-and graver consequences-in planning outline", which offered to implement a more open policy of talent development with greater efforts to implement high-level study abroad talent scheme. We will organize and implement plans for introducing high-level talents, such as the support plan for overseas students returning to China to start their own businesses, the Action Plan for Overseas Red Children serving the country, and the work of returning experts. We will further strengthen the work of pioneering parks jointly built by provinces and ministries for overseas students. We will promote exchanges in science and technology projects involving talents at home and abroad, expand the international talent market and cultivate international talent intermediary service agencies.

The Prospect of Internationalization of China's Higher Education – Building an International Community with a Shared Future for Mankind

Since the 18th National Congress of the Communist Party of China (CPC), General Secretary Xi Jinping, in the light of the progress of human history, has thought deeply about such major issues as "what kind of world should we build and how to build it", and creatively put forward the important idea of building a community with a shared future for mankind. Its essence is to accommodate the legitimate concerns of other countries while pursuing its own interests and promote the common development of all countries while pursuing its own development. The concept of building a "community with a shared future for mankind" is particularly important in responding to the global pandemic.

The opening up of Chinese higher education to the outside world helps to promote the construction of an international community with a shared future for mankind (Zhou 2019), because as a new international social form, the community with a shared future for mankind needs to adapt to the people and culture. A community with a shared future for mankind can be truly established only when it has the consciousness, values and capacity to act that are compatible with it, but such culture and people with such qualities cannot be created in a vacuum; education is needed to make a difference. Among them, educational activities, especially international education, have indispensable special value, which is a basic and fundamental work in the process of building a community with a shared future for mankind. Internationalization of higher education has an important mission of building a community with a shared future for mankind. China has proposed, advocated, practiced and promoted the building of a community with a shared future for mankind. Actively promoting the opening up of China's higher education can enhance the penetration and influence of Chinese culture, spread the sense of a community with a shared future for mankind and high level of consensus among people of all countries. At the same time, it will show the world China's responsibility, set an example for other countries and encourage them to join China in building a community with a shared future for mankind. (Zhang 2020)

As a provincial normal university in Central China, S University sends graduates of different disciplines to schools of different levels in Jiangxi province and even all over the country every year. They teach and educate students in different teaching positions. Teachers, whether they have global consciousness and whether they have the consciousness, values and behavior ability that are compatible with the community of human destiny will directly affect the values of the majority of young Chinese students as adults. Therefore, as a normal university, S University, compared with non-normal universities, has more responsibilities in cultivating talents with international vision and practicing the concept of a community with a shared future for mankind.

Status Quo, Problems and Causes of Internationalization of Higher Education in Central China – Taking S University as an Example

The Importance of Development of Higher Education Internationalization in Central China

The National Medium and Long Term Education Reform and Development Plan (2010–2020) has made a significant contribution to improving the quality of comprehensive higher education, which has increased the international competitiveness of China's higher education, as well as demonstrated the advantages of Chinese higher education over the world. International organizations for academic cooperation have been created to support high-level international education, as well as research institutes to create a joint research and development base for jointly developed scientific plans. Higher education in central China is an important part of the national higher education in China. The internationalization of higher education in this region is a part of China's mid – and long-term education reform and development plan implementation. The level of internationalization development directly affects the level of international competitiveness of China's higher education and the improvement of the overall quality of China's higher education.

In 2015, The State Council issued an official document on the Overall Plan for promoting the construction of world-class universities and first-class disciplines, clearly proposing the reform task of promoting international cooperation and exchanges in China's higher education. For example, we should strengthen substantive cooperation with the world-class universities and academic institutions, effectively integrate high-quality foreign educational resources into the process of teaching and research, and carry out joint training of high-level talents and joint scientific research. The internationalization of higher education in central China is conducive to promoting the construction of the world-class universities and first-class disciplines in China, better serving the needs of economic and social development in central China, and providing intellectual support for the development of the central region in various and multi-level aspects.

The State, Difficulties and Reasons for the Internationalization of S University in Central China

The State of Internationalization Development of S University

S University, founded in 1940, is a university jointly built by the Ministry of Education and the People's Government of Jiangxi Province and a university of basic Capacity construction project in central and Western China. Schools of philosophy, economics, law, education, literature, history, natural science, engineering, management, art and others became part of the university, which is located in Nanchang, the capital of Jiangxi province. The university has a rich history and culture and a good reputation. It affects the political, economic, cultural and social development of Jiangxi Province. The Jiangxi Provincial People's Government has designated it as the province's key (normal) University. After reform and opening up to the world, the stages of development of S-University internationalization can be roughly divided into infancy, exploration stage, and development stage. Compared to the general level of internationalization of higher education in China, which tends to be more mature, S-University is still in the development stage.

Initial Stage (1978–2000)

After the reform and opening up, the international exchange work of S University began to develop. However, the depth and breadth of Chinese universities' international exchanges are closely related to their geographical location and national development strategies. Due to its location in central China and its failure to be selected for "Project 211" and "Project 985" successfully, the university was in the initial stage of reform and opening up with a low degree of international exchanges, and the number of students studying abroad or in China was relatively small.

Exploratory Phase (2001–2016)

After entering the 21st century, S University's international exchange activities have become more extensive. In order to adapt to the new educational situation, further expand the scale of higher education, improve the level of teaching, study and use the experience of foreign universities, strengthen cooperation with foreign universities and student exchanges S University in 2001 created a foreign college within the framework of the Institute of International Education. Its main task is to recruit and train students, recruit foreign students, and establish contacts and implement of Chinese-foreign cooperative education and overseas education. In 2005, the name of the International Exchange Office of S University was officially changed to International Cooperation and Exchange Office, which is separate from the School of International Education. It is the administrative department of the university to centrally manage foreign affairs, and its main functions have been stipulated. For example, to be responsible for the friendly inter-school exchanges abroad, to carry out inter-school cooperation in running schools, to be responsible for the introduction of overseas intelligence, the recruitment and management of foreign experts and teachers, and the dispatch of overseas students, etc[7]. Nowadays, with the vigorous development of international cooperation and exchange in education, the functions of the International Cooperation and Exchange Office are more complete and the responsibilities are more detailed. In order to better implement international cooperation and exchange and integrate internationalization into the mainstream of university education, the Office of International Cooperation and Exchange has also set up the Office of International Education Cooperation and Study abroad, the

---

7   Document of S University, the University issued nel [2005] 119 "Notice on The Name Change and Function Adjustment of The International Exchange Office".

Hong Kong, Macao and Taiwan Studio and the Chinese Language International Promotion Office, which are in charge of the related affairs.

S University complies with the general trend of internationalization of higher education. With the strong support of school leaders and the international Cooperation and exchange Department, S University actively carries out international cooperation and exchange activities and has made certain achievements. This is mainly reflected in the internationalization of teaching and teachers. In terms of teaching internationalization, S University has established friendly cooperative relations with more than 50 universities and institutions in more than 20 countries and regions. We have implemented credit recognition and teacher-student exchange programs with more than 20 overseas universities, and recruited students from more than 10 countries and regions. A master's degree program in computer Science has been established in cooperation with the University of Leicester. It has hosted two Confucius Institutes, namely the Confucius Institute at the University of Antananarivo in Madagascar and the Confucius Institute at the University of Illinois at Urbana-Champaign in the United States. Among them, the Confucius Institute at the University of Antananarivo has won the title of "Advanced Confucius Institute" twice and the title of "Model Confucius Institute" in 2015. In terms of the internationalization of teachers, more than 40 teachers have obtained overseas degrees, and more than 10 teachers work in international organizations and academic journals. The university has hired a number of overseas honorary professors or visiting professors; foreign experts are invited to deliver lectures and more than 20 foreign teachers are hired to teach language and professional courses. Among them, foreign teacher Constance Gibson won the national "Friendship Award"[8].

Development Stage (2016–Present)

In order to further enhance international cooperation and exchange in higher education, S University has issued a notice to the Plan for Enhancing International Cooperation and Exchange in Education at S University in 2018[9]. The notice to the plan proposes the following activities to promote international cooperation

---

8   Document of CPC Committee of S University, the university party issued in the 2016 with the no.10, "S University Special Plan for International Cooperation and Exchange during the 13th Five-Year Plan Period".

9   Document of S University, the university issued in the 2018 with the no.135, on the issuance of the "S University Education International Cooperation and Exchange Level Improvement Plan" notice.

and exchanges within the guiding ideology, namely: adhere to the philosophy of "open development and mutually beneficial cooperation", follow the teaching rules, update the idea of open education, adopt successful foreign experience in school or university management, study how education corresponds to the real situation of school development in the framework of international cooperation and exchange, constantly improve the quality of school education, international cooperation, and communication. Based on the guiding ideas, S University has set a five-year development goal, according to which the main indicators of international cooperation and exchange in schools will reach the top level of provincial universities and the advanced level of local teachers in China by 2020. In addition, six specific goals were set. For example, the awareness of international cooperation and exchange at schools has been significantly enhanced, the level of international cooperation and exchange of teachers has been significantly improved, the proportion of international students and overseas students has been significantly increased, and the international academic and scientific research exchanges have become more frequent. In order to ensure the achievement of the goal, S University has put forward incentive and safeguard measures from multiple levels. For example, increase the investment of funds, no less than 10 million yuan per year to support international cooperation and exchange at schools; Building a talent training system for international cooperation and exchange, implementing a plan for students' international experience, encouraging undergraduate and graduate students to go abroad for elective credits or a degree, rewarding colleges with high numbers of students studying abroad, and improving the performance of students studying abroad we will build faculty for international cooperation and exchange, intensify efforts to introduce outstanding and innovative talents from overseas, and give strong support to young teachers and administrators to study abroad. Finally, JIANGXI Normal University also formulated the "Rules for Evaluation of International Education Cooperation and Exchange Index System Assessment Rules" to urge the school to actively promote international education cooperation and exchange. In the same year, in order to comprehensively improve the level of international cooperation and exchange, and give full play to the principal role of the School in international cooperation and exchange, S University formulated the Construction Standards for International Cooperation and Exchange in Education of S University College[10]. It aims to promote the international cooperation and exchange level

---

10 Document of S University, the university issued in the 2018 with the no.136, "Construction Standards for International Cooperation and Exchange of Education of S University".

of the colleges in terms of educational objectives, discipline construction, talent training and scientific research. The construction standard has made detailed provisions in seven aspects: concept and strategic objectives, organization and management, teaching and curriculum, overseas background of teachers, international research cooperation, international exchange of teachers and students, supporting measures and financial guarantee, thus providing a basis for each school to promote international cooperation and exchange.

The formulation of relevant policies undoubtedly provides the guarantee and support from the policy level for the international cooperation and exchange in school education and makes the international cooperation and exchange work in education more orderly. S University and the University of Hull, Lincoln University, Avila University, Ashland University in the United States, Moscow State University in Russia, Sweden Linnaeus University, Hungarian University signed dozens of contracts with foreign universities on the topics, such as undergraduate and graduate (master's, doctorate) level of student exchange programs mutual recognition of credits and double degree programs. Among them, two cooperation projects with South Korea's National Jeju University and National Chonnam University were approved by China Scholarship Council "Outstanding Undergraduate Program" in 2018. In addition, the school also organises overseas study Tours to the United States, The United Kingdom, Australia, Japan, South Korea, Thailand and other countries during summer and winter vacations. The school also provides a certain amount of funding for overseas study Tours. At present, more than 1,800 students have participated in the above cooperation projects and have gone to study at foreign partner universities. In 2019, S University joined the "Sino-Russian Education University Alliance", becoming the eighth university in China. In the 2019 Evaluation of the internationalization level of undergraduate Education in Jiangxi Province, the overall internationalization level of S University ranked the fourth place in Jiangxi Province[11].

However, the outbreak of COVID-19 in late 2019 has affected international cooperation and exchanges in education among universities in different regions of the world. Moreover, China is also subject to political repression from some Western countries. As Zhang Yingqiang and Jiang Yuanmou pointed out:

---

11 Jiangxi Provincial Department of Education: *Authority issued! Ranking of international level of undergraduate education in Jiangxi province (2019)*, retrieved 1.6.2021, from http://m.ncu.edu.cn/mtnd/7111ec46935d4caa9f97d075c6c51432.htm.

In the process of responding to the epidemic, some Western countries, especially the United States, have pursued the unilateral policy of 'putting their own countries first' and taken anti-globalization actions, which have also brought severe challenges to the internationalization of higher education. (Zhang / Jiang 2017)

S university is no exception, universities in other countries also moved teachers to part-time or distant mode and delayed overseas visit plan, many colleges and universities also stopped international development projects because of the outbreak of the pandemic, held some international scientific conferences using online mode, significantly reduced the number of international students, and the development of international cooperation and communication has almost stopped.

The Gap in the Internationalization Process of S University

As an ordinary institution of higher learning in central China, S University is highly representative in its source of students, mode of running schools and organizational structure. The internationalization of its higher education also reflects the internationalization process of central China. Like many other local universities in central China, S University has made many achievements in internationalization since the reform and opening up, but there are also many problems. Based on the recommendations of the Chinese Communist Party Committee, S University in 2016 published a much harsher choice and more serious implications for international cooperation and exchanges at S University during the special planning period, highlighting the gap between internationalization within the school education and education in Jiangxi province colleges and universities within the undergraduate education. Jiangxi Provincial Education Department published the internationalization level list (2019) and relevant sections of information were published on the official website of S University, which summarized the problems and gaps in the internationalization process at S University.

The Consciousness of Running a School Internationally Is Still Weak

Although S University has formulated a plan to improve the level of international cooperation and exchange from the school level, and also formulated the assessment rules from the school level to urge the school to actively carry out international cooperation and exchange, the implementation of the plan still requires active efforts and cooperation of all institutions in the school. First, at the level of schools and colleges, although S University has established friendly cooperative relations with more than 50 overseas universities, less than 20 overseas universities have carried out substantive cooperation with the university[12]. Second, most colleges have not yet incorporated internationalization into their development planning and daily agenda, and the sense of running an international school is not strong. Third, at the level of functional departments, the website of the International Cooperation and Exchange Office of S University releases very little relevant information every year, which does not provide rich information sources for students to study abroad. The Office of International Cooperation and Exchange of S University has failed to play its due role in assisting teachers to carry out international cooperation and exchange programs, and mainly focuses on helping teachers to go through the procedures for overseas exchange. In addition, the administrative staff of the International Cooperation and exchange Office have bureaucratic style in their work, which, to some extent, hinds teachers from carrying out international exchange and cooperation. Finally, the teachers of S University need to apply to the school to attend the international conference, but the approval process is cumbersome and complicated, and the possibility of successful application for approval is usually needed at least 2 months in advance, which frustrates the enthusiasm of the teachers to participate in international conferences.

The International Level of Teachers Is Still Lagging Behind

At present, less than 3 % of the school's full-time teachers have overseas degrees, and even fewer have overseas PhDs. The proportion of teachers with overseas study experience or working in international organizations and academic journals is also low. The foreign teachers employed by the school are mainly language teachers, and the proportion of foreign teachers in science and engineering is relatively low, only accounting for 14.3 % of the total number of foreign teachers. The university has not fully realized the goal of promoting the leapfrog development of its teaching and research through the introduction of international high-end talents (ibid.).

According to the ranking of The International Level of Undergraduate Education in Jiangxi Province in 2019, S University was not ranked in the top

---

12 . Document of CPC Committee of S University, the university party issued in the 2016 with the no.10 "S University Special Plan for International Cooperation and Exchange during the 13th Five-Year Plan Period".

10 in Jiangxi Province for such important indicators as "percentage of teachers with foreign degrees from the total number of teachers" and "percentage of teachers who have studied abroad for 3 months or more from the total number of teachers". In the index of "the percentage of teachers who went abroad to conduct collaborative research for more than a week out of the total number of teachers", it ranked only fifth in Jiangxi Province[13].

The Construction of International Curriculum System Urgently Needs Strengthening

The foreign language program is limited to English, Japanese, Korean, Russian, German and French, and the foreign language program is only English, Japanese and Korean, before French was added in 2018. As of 2016, the university has not set up any courses taught in foreign languages (excluding foreign language courses), let alone any subjects taught in foreign languages (excluding foreign language courses), and the effect of semi-English courses is not obvious. In the 2019 Ranking of The International Level of Undergraduate Education in Jiangxi Province, S University still was not ranked among the top 10 in the index of "percentage of courses in non-foreign language majors using foreign languages or bilingual teaching in the total number of courses in the university" (ibid.).

The Proportion of International Students in China and Those Going Abroad Needs to Be Increased

The number of international students in 2015 was 170, accounting for only 0.55 % of the total number of students in 2015, which is far from the national average of 1.8 %. In 2015, 160 students went to study abroad, accounting for only 0.52 % of the total number of students in the university. This proportion has slightly increased in 2019, but only accounts for 0.53 %, ranking 307th in mainland China[14]. The number of undergraduates studying overseas was 231, accounting for 3.45 % of the total number.

---

13 Jiangxi Provincial Department of Education: *Authority issued! Ranking of international level of undergraduate education in Jiangxi province (2019)*, web.

14 Xiaoli: In *2019, S University ranked 307th in the international student rankings with 0.53 % of international students*, retrieved 5.6.2021, from https://mip.zjut.cc/article-39364-10414.html.

International Academic and Research Exchanges Are Not Active

There are few high-level international academic conferences organized by S University. By 2016, only 5 international research cooperation projects have been implemented with the participation of teachers and students, and only 3.7 million yuan of research funds have been funded by overseas or international organizations. The number of high-level papers published by teachers and students in overseas academic journals and conferences, the number of papers included into SCI, SSCI, CSSCI, EI and ISTP, and the number of international science and technology patents and international competition awards won by teachers and students are few. It has been observed that most of S University schools do not organize students to go abroad for exchange throughout the year, except for a few schools such as the School of International Education that organizes students to go abroad for a short period of time every year. Few foreign scholars are invited to give lectures at the university.

The Number of International Cooperation in Running Schools Is Small

The number of sino-foreign cooperative undergraduate programs in S University is very few. At present, only one major of visual communication design is jointly held by S University and Highport University in the United States[15].

Factors Influencing the Internationalization of S University

The serious obstacles faced by S University in internationalization actually reflect the various unfavorable factors in promoting internationalization of most universities in central China. In this paper, by consulting relevant materials, combined with daily practice and observation, summed up three aspects of the influencing factors.

---

15 The Ministry of Education of the People's Republic of China (MOE): *Notice of the Ministry of Education on the approval of Sino-foreign cooperative education projects in the first half of 2018*, retrieved 5.6.2021, from http://www.moe.gov.cn/srcsite/A20/moe_862/201809/t20180903_347081.html.

S University Was Not Selected for the National Major University and Discipline Construction Project, and the Financial Support from the Local Government Was Limited

Since the reform and opening up, the Chinese government has launched three major projects to build universities and disciplines. They are the construction project of "Facing the 21st century, key construction of about 100 institutions of higher education and a group of key disciplines" (also known as Project 211), "Construction Project of World First-class University" (also known as Project 985), "Construction of World First-class University and first-class disciplines" (also known as double first-class). These three projects have a great impact on the development of Chinese universities, as well as the international development of universities. Nowadays, China's "985 universities", "211 universities" and "double first-class universities" are significantly higher than other general universities in terms of internationalization. Inclusion in these three projects enables Chinese universities to become outstanding and meet a high standard, giving them the opportunity to receive more funding, acquire higher social recognition, recruit more high-quality students, and outstanding professors. Such advantages are factors that directly affect the degree of development of the university's internationalization, but S University has never been included in one of these projects. To promote the internationalization of colleges and universities, it is inevitable that they need corresponding human, material and financial support. However, the colleges and universities in central China are mainly local ones, few of which are directly under the central ministries and commissions, and the development funds of colleges and universities are heavily dependent on local governments. However, the central region is a relatively backward region in China's economic development, and the local government's resource investment in higher education in this region is far from that in the eastern region. According to the information released by the Finance Office of S University, the Jiangxi Provincial government allocated only about 600 million yuan to S University in 2019. Zhejiang Normal University, which is at the same level as S University, received more than 1.2 billion yuan in 2019[16], twice as much as S University, because it is located in the economically developed Province of Zhejiang. Therefore, universities in the central region invest relatively little resources in internationalization, which directly leads to two consequences. First, college students in the region who go abroad

---

16 Document of Zhejiang Normal University: *Notice of Zhejiang Normal University on the financial and final accounts of 2019*, retrieved 10.6.2021, from http://xxgk.zjnu.edu.cn/2020/0916/c3388a332718/page.htm.

to study or participate in brief exchange activities can get very little school subsidies, and students often have to go abroad at their own expense. However, the main source of college students in central China is still from the provinces where the colleges and universities are located. These provinces are relatively backward in economic development in China. Most students' families are not rich, and they cannot afford the high cost of studying abroad, so they have low enthusiasm for studying abroad. Second, the main channel for teachers of S University to apply for study abroad is the government-funded study abroad program provided by the China Scholarship Council. Provincial government departments hardly provide special funds for college teachers to study abroad, and the limited quota of government-funded study abroad also limits teachers' study abroad to some extent. Third, due to the restrictions of material conditions, S University can only provide on-campus accommodation for several international students. Most international students need to rent houses off campus through local agents, which directly increases the cost of studying abroad for international students, and they tend to choose other universities.

The Orientation of Professional Title Evaluation of Chinese University Teachers

According to the method of calculating teaching workload and research workload for assessing professional qualification introduced by the School of Education of S University in 2020, the classroom teaching, particle publication, monographer publication and the number of subjects declared by teachers at different levels are the main reference indices and calculation points to assess professional qualification. In addition, papers published in journals other than NATURE, SCIENCE, CELL, SCI and SSCI will not be counted. The international exchange and cooperation work carried out by teachers has not been quantified and directly included in the calculation scope of workload, such as the international academic lectures organized by teachers for schools and international academic conferences attended by teachers every year. This means that even if teachers spend a lot of time to organize an international academic conference, or spend at least 2 months to apply for an international seminar abroad, there is no direct benefit for teachers' professional qualification assessment.

The professional qualification assessment method of the School of Education of S University is based on the relevant requirements of the school. This kind of professional qualification assessment is not conducive to the international cooperation and exchange between the leadership and teachers of the college. At the leadership level of the college, teachers with overseas study background are not valued, and the information and channels they have about international communication are not fully explored and utilized. Some college leaders even ignore the relevant plans proposed by teachers who are capable of international cooperation and exchange, and do not support the willingness of teachers to invite foreign professors to deliver lectures. These practices seriously hinder the internationalization process of the school. At the level of teachers, although international cooperation and exchange are conducive to the improvement of teachers' research ability, the amount of time and energy paid by teachers is not proportional to their gains because the professional qualification assessment does not directly include them in the calculation scope. In addition, the relevant administrative departments do not provide assistance to teachers for international exchanges and cooperation, and many teachers with international cooperation and exchange enthusiasm when they first entered the office are ruthlessly extinguished. In addition, SCI and SSCI are mostly journals hosted by English-speaking countries, while core journals hosted by non-English-speaking countries, such as South Korea, Japan, France, Russia, etc., are considered as D journals published in China (A journal has the highest rank) and included in the workload calculation scope during the professional qualification assessment. Under this professional qualification assessment system, the enthusiasm of teachers to carry out international academic exchanges is greatly diminished, because the efforts are not in proportion to the gains.

The Overall Foreign Language Level of Teachers and Students in S University Is Not High, and the Motivation of Studying Abroad Is Poor

The overall English level of teachers in S University is not high, and the number of students who know a second foreign language is even less, which directly affects the development of the international curriculum system of S University and the international academic and cultural exchanges of the University. It is embodied in the following aspects: 1) The teachers' level of English is not high, and there are only few teachers who can teach international students in English, which hinders the development of the international curriculum system; 2) Most teachers tend to choose Chinese professors from foreign universities as their tutors in order to facilitate language and cultural communication when they apply for overseas study places sponsored by the China Scholarship Council; 3) Without foreign language proficiency as the basis, many teachers can neither integrate into the local culture, nor can they make the best use of geographical advantages to study the advanced subjects at foreign universities, let alone the establishment of new academic exchanges and cooperation with foreign universities; 4) The low level of foreign language also creates obstacles for teachers to publish high-quality SCI, SSCI, CSSCI, EI and ISTP. In addition, many teachers apply for participation in international studies not for the purpose of understanding the disciplines associated with foreign universities advanced concepts and practical experience, and dissemination of their excellent cultural ideas and practice experience, but for the purpose of assessing the professional qualifications, prescribed by the school. Therefore, schools and individuals do not formulate clear visiting plans and tasks for many teachers during their overseas study visits. Even if there are plans, there are no rigorous performance metrics for assessing the visiting plans and tasks after the visit. Motivating university teachers to visit and study abroad also slows down the development of international exchanges and university cooperation.

In terms of students, the level of English of non-English majors in S University is generally not high. For example, the English taught Courses offered by the School of Education are chosen just by a few students and have never been opened. Many graduates of bachelor programs in their thesis, due to the low level of the English language, refer only to Chinese literature; The level of English among many graduate students is low, it is difficult for them to use foreign literature, not to mention direct communication in English. Without a guarantee of a high level of foreign language knowledge, students' enthusiasm for studying abroad is greatly reduced, which directly affects the share of foreign students at the university.

In addition, the school also has many disadvantages regarding student intercultural communication, although there are many foreign students in the school, but these students and Chinese students communicate very little with each other in all kinds of school daily activities, which directly leads to the fact that Chinese students do not find a way of communicating with international students and do not improve their international vision. The inability to understand foreign culture also makes foreign students in China unable to truly understand the local culture in order to better promote S university and attract excellent students.

Countermeasures and Suggestions for Higher Education in Central China Going to the World

Compared to the developed provinces and cities of the east coast, universities in central China are at a disadvantage in terms of geographical location. They have encountered many obstacles in the of development of internationalization of education. For example, many excellent overseas students tend to choose universities in developed regions for admission; excellent domestic returnees prefer universities in the eastern regions with sufficient funds and abundant resources as a platform for development after returning to China; more parents of students in the eastern regions have conditions for paying their children's education abroad at their own expense. In the face of objectively unfavorable conditions, how should higher education in the central region out into the world? Taking into account the problems and reasons suggested in the previous article, based on the actual situation in the central region, this article puts forward four suggestions and countermeasures.

Deepening the Understanding of International Cooperation and Exchange, and Carrying Out International Cooperation and Exchange Work Efficiently through the Internal Reform of Colleges and Universities

Consciousness guides practice, and the change of practice depends on the change of consciousness. Compared with universities in eastern China, universities in central China are not sensitive to new foreign ideas and experiences due to their geographical location and the relatively backward economic development of their provinces, and their awareness of international cooperation and exchange is not strong. In order to change this situation, provincial governments and universities in central China need to deepen their understanding of the internationalization of universities, which is the key for higher education in central China to go out into the world. First, the essence of internationalization of higher education is the internationalization of knowledge and academic environment, which is mainly reflected in the international flow of knowledge, scholars and students. (Clark / Weng 2001, pp. 15–16) Without international movement of knowledge, scholars and students, it cannot be called internationalization of education. Secondly, the logic of the internationalization of higher education has undergone a fundamental change: from the "epistemological" logic of the development of knowledge and academic logic to the "political theory" serving the development of national competition. (Zhang / Jiang 2017, p. 2) This transformation makes universities not only develop and disseminate knowledge, but also apply knowledge to promote social development – universities become the "power station" of human social development. Finally, the global pandemic of COVID-19 makes Xi Jinping's concept of building a community with a shared future for mankind even more valuable. The internationalization of higher education aims to cultivate talents with a sense of responsibility for the future of mankind. Therefore, the international development of colleges and universities is not only about the interests of a certain university and a certain region, but also about the well-being of the whole country and the whole mankind. Provincial governments and university leaders in central China should understand the role and significance of university internationalization from a new height and depth, change traditional ideas, and support university internationalization activities with a more open and broad vision.

Most universities in central China, like S University, have formulated relevant policies at the policy level in the process of promoting internationalization. However, from the formulation of policies to the implementation of policies, cooperation between multiple departments is required. The internationalization of colleges and universities is not the business of a certain international exchange and cooperation office, nor is it the business of a certain school leader. It is necessary to establish close cooperation and division of labor among the school leaders in charge of international exchange and cooperation, the international traffic and cooperation Office, the student affairs Office, the foreign affairs management team of the school, the Student affairs Office of the school and other departments. In order to achieve this goal, colleges and universities should deepen internal reform, clarify the responsibilities and functions of each department, rectify the bureaucratic style, gather various forces, and carry out international cooperation and exchange activities efficiently. On the one hand, the leadership of the college should change the backward concept and break through selfish interests. Starting from the overall situation of the development of the college and the university, it should vigorously assist the university teachers to carry out international exchange and cooperation projects, and fully tap and utilize the resources of the returned teachers who have studied abroad. On the other hand, the Office of International Cooperation and Exchange should increase the publicity of studying abroad among students, and provide students with a variety of information about studying abroad, especially the information about universities that can provide scholarships for Chinese students, so that more students can understand and participate in studying abroad activities. Finally, the university and other departments of the college should cooperate with each other to create a good environment for international students to acquire knowledge and integrate into the local culture, thus attracting more international students.

Avoid the Disadvantages of Geographical Location and Economic Development Level, and Actively Promote "Internationalization at Home"

The COVID-19 pandemic has greatly restricted physical movement of teachers and students, but the essence of internationalization of higher education is international academic exchange and cooperation. Zhang Yingqiang and Jiang Yuanmou proposed that in the post-epidemic era, universities should make use of the stock of international resources and actively promote "internationalization at home". (Zhang / Jiang 2017, p. 4) According to B. Nilsson, "internationalization at home" refers to "any activities related to international except the cross-border mobility of students". Its purpose is to enable all students to receive international concepts and culture during their study to improve their quality and respond to the demands of globalization. (ibid.)

"Internationalization at home" means that students can be influenced by diverse cultures at our school, to form an international vision and international pattern. Due to the economic constraints of their families, college students in central China cannot afford to study abroad. However, "internationalization at home" enables all students, no matter their families are rich or poor, to receive international education without leaving their home countries. This is an effective way for universities in central China to go out into the world. In order to realize "internationalization at home", we can start from the construction of university curriculum, that is, "introducing international and cross-cultural factors into courses" through curriculum internationalization. (ibid.) Gao Yurong proposed: "The so-called internationalization of curriculum means that under the background of economic globalization and internationalization of higher education, from the strategic perspective of the future, with the purpose of cultivating talents to solve the obstacles, barriers and differences encountered in the process of communication, cooperation and development between different cultural groups, through comparison, analysis, identification and screening, The process of integrating cultural, social, technological and managerial knowledge and experience from other countries into the curricula of our own universities." (Gao 2010, p. 37)

What is emphasized here is the explicit curriculum of colleges and universities, which means that colleges and universities consciously let students understand and learn the advanced ideas and experience of different countries and ethnic regions through professional setting and course teaching. Or if in the course teaching, the teacher edits the course and consciously introduces into it other countries' education idea, education mode and teaching method, comparison and analysis, some reference materials of foreign content, or the newest research results, etc. In order to achieve this goal, university teachers, regardless of whether they have overseas study background, should have an international vision and actively add international content into their courses, so that students can receive the most advanced knowledge and ideas at home and abroad without leaving their Alma mater.

University curriculum is divided into recessive curriculum and explicit curriculum. The internationalization of hidden curriculum in colleges and universities refers to "the whole campus learning environment with international and multi-cultural atmosphere, namely international campus culture". Regarding the internationalization of hidden courses in colleges and universities, S University also proposes to strengthen the construction of basic conditions for internationalization, such as: "the signboards in the campus, the slogans in the main teaching, scientific research and management sites should be in Chinese and English, and the dormitories for international students should be built as soon as possible to improve the accommodation conditions for international students"[17].

However, this is only the internationalization of the hidden curriculum pursued in the material space level, but also needs to build the internationalization of the hidden curriculum in the organizational system and cultural and psychological level. At the organizational system level, colleges and universities can consciously guide domestic students to establish contacts with international students and strengthen cultural communication and exchange at the regulation level. For example, they celebrate major traditional festivals for international students every year and require domestic students to participate in the organization and planning. In addition, there can be sports competitions between domestic and international students, such as badminton, basketball and football. At the cultural and psychological level, teachers can guide students to participate in international conferences, actively learn about relevant foreign subjects and read foreign literature and works based on their expectations and attitudes towards students, so that students can broaden their horizons, open their minds and become international talents with the mission of the mankind.

---

17 Document of the Communist Party of China S University Committee, the University Party issued in the 2016 with the no. 10 "Special Plan for International Cooperation and Exchange of S University during the 13th Five-Year Plan Period".

Improve and Refine the Internationalization Evaluation Mechanism to Improve the Internationalization Promotion Mechanism

As mentioned above, in the process of promoting internationalization, S University has not formed an ideal top-down mechanism, and most of the content on internationalization of colleges and universities formulated at the university level remain on paper and have never been implemented. For example, although S University proposed in its 2016 plan that the signs on campus should be in Chinese and English in five years, half of 2021 passed but this plan has not been realized. A foreign affairs working group set up in the college only plays the role of uploading and issuing documents, but does not effectively promote the internationalization of education in the college, which shows that the promotion mechanism of internationalization needs to be improved. Colleges and universities can improve the internationalization promotion mechanism by perfecting and refining the internationalization evaluation mechanism, which is the institutional guarantee for the internationalization of colleges and universities in central China. Just as S University put forward in the special Plan of International Cooperation and Exchange during the 13th Five-Year Plan period: "Integrate internationalization indicators into the university's talent evaluation system, give different weights to the faculty and staff who actively carry out internationalization work in personnel assessment, professional evaluation and workload calculation, and implement necessary rewards." (ibid.)

Moreover, such incline and reward should also be detailed and quantifiable, so that the university personnel department and the college can calculate the workload according to the data. For example, how should the workload of teachers participating in international conferences be calculated? How can an international academic conference organized by teachers be reflected in professional qualification assessment? How should the workload of a teacher publishing papers in non-English journals be calculated instead of putting them all in category D. Is there a weight bias in the professional qualification assessment of teachers who are leading an international project? What are the rewards offered by the faculty? Only when each internationalization index is detailed, can the college and staff attach importance to internationalization work and form and improve the top-down, cooperative internationalization promotion mechanism. On the contrary, the internationalization work will always remain on paper, and the school staff lack motivation to promote the internationalization work.

Improving the Level of Oral English, with a More Open Attitude to Actively Integrate into the Culture of Other Countries

To some extent, the level of English of teachers and students in S university represents the level of English of teachers and students in central China universities. To carry out international work, English level is a stepping stone, which is just like two legs for people. People can't move forward smoothly without legs. How to improve your English? As a matter of fact, many college students have passed CET-4 and CET-6. They have little problem in English reading comprehension, but the key is English speaking, listening and writing. Universities in central China generally lack a foreign language environment, and teachers and students do not have a chance to speak English daily. Therefore, colleges and universities should provide a linguistic environment for students to listen and speak English on a daily basis. Colleges and universities can make full use of the resources of international students and let domestic students establish "language and culture mutual assistance". On the one hand, it can promote the improvement of the spoken English level of domestic students and the spoken Chinese level of international students. On the other hand, it can enhance their understanding of the culture of each other.

As for teachers, visiting teachers before leaving, in addition to enhancing language training, should also learn in advance the culture of the country they are going to visit, leaving behind the idea that visiting an overseas university for a year for more aims than just to facilitate their promotion back home. Instead, they need to involve themselves in the day-to-day and academic activities of local communities. Without fear of leaving their "comfort zone" in an the academic sense, they should go out to communicate with foreign teachers, and not with the Chinese researchers with whom they are familiar. Only in this way can visiting teachers create more opportunities for establishing academic exchanges and cooperation with foreign universities, in order to contribute to the development of the internationalization of universities.

Conclusion

To conclude, compared with universities in eastern China, universities in central China have many inherent deficiencies in internationalization, including geographical location, regional economic development imbalance and different ideologies. Deepening the internationalization of universities in central China lies in the concept of change. The provincial government and the universities should fully understand the connotation of university internationalization, its nature, role and significance, by advancing "the internationalization" concept, to avoid flaws generated from the geographical location and slower economic development. Teachers and students can receive international education at their home universities. This international education has laid a solid foundation for the cross-border mobility of teachers and students and the cooperation in running schools.

Literature

Clark, Kerr/Wang, Chengxu (translator): *Higher Education Cannot Avoid History–The Problem of 21st Century.* Zhejiang Education Press: Hangzhou, 2001, pp. 15–16.

Chen, Baosheng: "Education: A Forerunner, Beneficiary and Booster of Reform and Opening-Up". *Guangming Daily*, (06),12.12. 2018, p. 6.

Document of CPC Committee of S University, the university party issued nel 2016 with the no.10, "S University Special Plan for International Cooperation and Exchange During the 13th Five-Year Plan Period".

Document of S University, the University issued in the 2005 with the no.119 "Notice on The Name Change and Function Adjustment of The International Exchange Office".

Document of S University, the university issued in the 2018 with the no.135, "Plan for Upgrading the Level of International Cooperation and Exchange in Education of S University".

Document of S University, the university issued in the 2018 with the no.136, "Construction Standards for International Cooperation and Exchange of Education of S University".

Document of Zhejiang Normal University: *Notice of Zhejiang Normal University on the Financial and Final Accounts of 2019,* retrieved 10.6.2021, from http:// xxgk.zjnu.edu.cn/2020/0916/c3388a332718/page.htm.

Gao, Yurong: "Reflections on the Internationalization of Chinese University Curriculum". *Education Exploration*, 11, 2010, p. 37.

Huang, Futao: "Internationalization of Higher Education in a Globalization Era: A Historic and Comparative Perspective". *Peking University Education Review*, 02, 2003, pp. 93–98.

Institute of International Education of Beijing Foreign Studies University: *70 Years of China's Education Opening to the Outside World: China's International Education Development Report.* East China Normal University Press: Shanghai, 2019, pp. 16–23.

Jean, Knight / Liu, Dongfeng (translator) / Che Qiaoyun (translator): *Higher Education in the Current: International Change and Development*. Peking University Press: Beijing, 2001, pp. 25–26.

Jiang, Kai / Zhang Junfeng: "Basic Characteristics of Opening-Up of Higher Education in China". *Tsinghua Journal of Education*, 38(06), 2017, pp. 7–15.

Jiangxi Provincial Department of Education: *Authority issued! Ranking of international level of undergraduate education in Jiangxi province (2019)*, Retrieved 1.6.2021, from http://m.ncu.edu.cn/mtnd/7111ec46935d4caa9f97d075c6c51 432.htm

Li, Junhong: "The Strategic Thinking of International Education Development of Local Colleges and Universities in the Background of 'the Belt and Road' Initiative". *Journal of National Academy of Education Administration*, 06, 2017, pp. 66–71.

Shu, Ziding: "The Connotation, Characteristics and Enlightenment of Internationalization of Higher Education". *Foreign Education Materials*, 03, 1998, pp. 55–59.

Shao, Guanghua: *Research on Regional Higher Education Internationalization*. Zhejiang University Press: Hangzhou, 2016, pp. 5–9.

The Ministry of Education of the People's Republic of China (MOE): *Notice of the Ministry of Education on the approval of Sino-foreign cooperative education projects in the first half of 2018*, retrieved 5.6.2021, from http://www.moe.gov. cn/srcsite/A20/moe_862/201809/t20180903_347081.html.

Wang, Yanxin: " 'One Belt and One Road' Strategy Leads the Internationalization of Higher Education". *Guangming Daily*, (13), 26.6. 2015, p. 13.

Wu, Chen: " 'Education Opening to the Outside World' and 'Internationalization of Higher Education' – Review of the First Annual Conference of International Education Professional Committee of China Education Development Strategy Association". *Research in Educational Development*, 37(03), 2017, pp. 81–84.

Wu, Yanquan: "Internationalization of Higher Education and Its Thinking". *Journal of Chongqing University (Social Sciences Edition)*, 01, 2000, pp. 73–76.

Xi, Ming: "On the Internationalization of Higher Education". *Social Science Exploration*, 04, 2002, pp. 84–93.

Xia, Liaoyuan: *Research on Internationalization of Higher Education in China*. (Northeast Normal University). (master's thesis), 2006.

Xiaoli: *In 2019, S University ranked 307th in the international student rankings with 0.53% of international students*, retrieved 5.6.2021, from https://mip.zjut. cc/article-39364-10414.html.

Xiduocunhezhi: *The Internationalization of University Education*. Yuchuan University Publishing Department: Tokyo, 1984. In: Shao, Guanghua / Shi,

Chunyang / Zhou, Guoping: *Research on Internationalization of Regional Higher Education.* Zhejiang University Press, 2016, p. 254.

Xu, Xiaozhou: "Achievements, Opportunities, and Strategic Concept of Higher Education Opening-up in China". *Journal of Higher Education,* 40(05), 2019, pp. 1–9.

Zeng, Manchao / Yu, Zhan / Li, Shupei: "Research of Internationalized Higher Education in China and Japan". *Research in Educational Development,* 21, 2008, pp. 42–51.

Zhang, Junzong: "Educational Internationalization: The Crucial Force in Building the Community of Common Destiny for Mankind". *Journal of Higher Education Management,* 14(02), 2020, pp. 21–28.

Zhang, Yingqiang / Jiang Yuanmou: "The Direction of China's Higher Education Internationalization in the Post-Epidemic Era". *Journal of Higher Education,* 12, 2020, pp. 2–4.

Zhao, Min / Chen, Haiyan: "Research on the Function Orientation of International Exchange and Cooperation in Universities", *China Higher Education,* 17, 2017, pp. 19–22.

Zhou, Guangli: "A Community of Shared Future for Mankind and Global Governance of Higher Education". *Exploration and Debate,* 09, 2019, pp. 22–25.

Hildesheimer Schriften zur Interkulturellen Kommunikation
Hildesheim Studies in Intercultural Communication
Herausgegeben von
Edited by
Friedrich Lenz, Stephan Schlickau, Beatrix Kreß

Band   1   Stephan Schlickau: Neue Medien in der Sprach- und Kulturvermittlung. 2009.

Band   2   Sonja Klinker: Maghrebiner in Frankreich, Türken in Deutschland. Eine vergleichende Untersuchung zu Identität und Integration muslimischer Einwanderergruppen in europäische Mehrheitsgesellschaften. 2010.

Band   3   Elke Bosse / Beatrix Kreß / Stephan Schlickau (Hrsg.): Methodische Vielfalt in der Erforschung interkultureller Kommunikation an deutschen Hochschulen. 2011.

Band   4   Friedrich Lenz / Stephan Schlickau (Hrsg.): Interkulturalität in Bildung, Ästhetik, Kommunikation. 2012.

Volume   5   Beatrix Kreß (ed.): Totalitarian Political Discourse? Tolerance and Intolerance in Eastern and East Central European Countries. Diachronic and Synchronic Aspects. In collaboration with Karsten Senkbeil. 2013.

Band   6   Vasco da Silva: Narrative des Erasmus-Auslandsaufenthaltes: Freizeit, Liebe, Institution. Linguistische Studien zum sprachlichen Handeln in deutschen und spanischen Interviews. 2016.

Band   7   Yassir El Jamouhi: Nonverbale Interaktion deutscher und marokkanischer Studierender. Fallstudien zur interkulturellen Kinesik. 2017.

Band   8   Kristin Bührig / Stephan Schlickau (Hrsg.): Argumentieren und Diskutieren. 2017.

Band   9   Beatrix Kreß / Vasco da Silva / Ioulia Grigorieva (Hrsg.): Mehrsprachigkeit, Sprachkontakt und Bildungsbiografie. 2018.

Band   10   Beatrix Kreß / Katsiaryna Roeder / Kathrin Schweiger / Ksenija Vossmiller (Hrsg.): Mehrsprachigkeit, Interkulturelle Kommunikation, Sprachvermittlung: Internationale Perspektiven auf DaF und Herkunftssprachen. 2021.

Volume   11   Beatrix Kress / Holger Kusse (eds.): Enhancing Teaching Practice in Higher Education. International Perspectives on Academic Teaching and Learning. 2023.

www.peterlang.com

Printed by
CPI books GmbH, Leck